UNDER A TIE DYE SKY

Mary Lou—
Keep the legacy
alive in people's
hearts. Thank you!
I. LOVE. YOU.

SUZEE CARSON BRANCH

Suze Carson Branch

4/13/14

ISBN 13: 9781491214145
ISBN 10: 1491214147

"Mankind was my business."
Charles Dickens, A Christmas Carol

Dedicated to Steve Branch, my husband,
the most unselfish person I know.

And to the Children of the Dream, far and wide.

TABLE OF CONTENTS

PROLOGUE

"IF THERE'S ANYTHING that you want, if there's anything I can do, just call on me and I'll send it along, with love from me to you."
The Beatles

Here we go! The start of my odyssey. I hope you're ready for a crazy story. It's got a little something for everyone, and there's a payoff for all your time and attention, I promise.

The Dream began it all. And I was a child of The Dream.

Many characters peopled The Dream—human highlighters drawing attention to a treasure trove of relationships. Larger than life, I knew the characters' stories would help reveal The Dream. I've gift-wrapped it with their tales. Several characters became my teachers. But mostly, the hodgepodge of fantastical fellow travelers formed a centerpiece that showed off the Love at the heart of my life.

Two life dramas helped me understand The Dream. First, the Haight-Ashbury phenomena in San Francisco in the 1960s. During this period I had sensational (if questionable) adventures, answered Siren calls, pursued hilarity, shouldered guilt and knew desperation. I went astray, lost plenty, felt alone and ridiculously scared. I was knocked down and bounced back.

But see, I was like a lot of people: uncertain and troubled, searching for meaning and that all-embracing Love. I'd felt the world slipping. Something had gone wrong, out of whack. A number in my generation, a happy throng of misfits, felt it too. Our Search-For-Something-More wasn't an aberration but a divine desire to go for something more than a status quo existence. It became an uncompromising quest to find and wear this Love, so all the world could see.

Love simply made sense when nothing else did.

I learned that love works best with trust, but love is so primal, so atomic, so over-the-top, it works anyway.

It also took a certain amount of growing up, and a horse named Delay, for me to get it. And that's the second part: a horse who showed me unfailing love through forgiveness by repeatedly offering me his back. No matter what I'd done. The truth is, that animal taught me how to forgive myself.

Forgiveness is the hot magma core of Love. When it happens, it's an unstoppable flow, spreading over mankind inch by inch, engulfing and healing hurting hearts. One at a time. Then, presto change-o...life is transformed.

It's the one thing you need to know — Love and forgiveness saved my life.

And now my special wish-upon-a-star is that you'll find the same relief I did from guilt, loss, shame and dread. Because maybe you, too, wonder what is truly going on in this world. Somewhere along the way, down a path I didn't even know I was on, I learned it's all okay and that being human requires relief, and lots of it.

Still Love and forgiveness mend it all.

Peace found me as surely as I found I wasn't the only needy one out there.

And in the end, I don't think you and I are that different. In fact, if you really want to know what I'm talking about, I'll tell you. Three brazen words. Ready or not, here they come.

I. Love. You.

That's it. And you don't have to believe me. But I chased my maverick Dream along some pretty loco trails to track down the headwaters of Love, and it was a wild ride.

And now I can't wait to take you there...

THE TRAIL

I SEE THE story of my life as a trail with me on my horse, Delay, one of the true heroes of this adventure. Having passed into the spiritual realm, home at last, means now he's an insider! I wish I could talk to him. From his back I could stretch my eyes to the horizon and watch my life passing by. It helped make sense that way because I was able to see the whole course of my existence up till that moment. It was only from that vantage point I could even imagine telling my story all the way to the finish line.

My biggest desire? To have you understand.

The longer I live, the more folks of all ages ask me, "What happened back then? In the 60s?" I tell them it was the Time-Of-All-Times.

They persist:

"You say 'it'. Explain 'it'."

Well, taking a peek way far ahead with my bewitched binoculars, I see 'it': San Francisco inhabited by the enchanted ones. The Summer of Love flickers madly, making the famous San Francisco fog shine.

But before I can tell you about the Time-Of-All-Times, I need to fill you in on where I came from and what set me up to experience the Love that enveloped me that incredible summer. Scores of colorful, charismatic, and often-challenging characters want to star in my story. They would. Every dang one of them.

Knowing them as I do, I suspect they want to lend a hand.

I kind of get their point though, wanting to be part of the driving force to help you understand.

To paint a true picture I'll have to start at the beginning of my life.

LET'S TAKE IT FROM THE TOP

1947: THIS IS the year I was born in Geneseo, Illinois. I came home from the hospital to live with two people who were not my parents. Not yet anyway.

Helen Imogene Down from Odebolt, Iowa married John Russell Carson (nicknamed Kit) from Dierks, Arkansas. After a few years they realized they couldn't have children and adopted me, their one and only. Because this decision would turn out to be a fierce challenge for them, I consider myself a very lucky lady and life-lottery winner of a great big family. Star-quality aunts and uncles on the Carson and Down sides provided me with seventeen lovable and loving first cousins. And the best part? We were all close.

I relished going to visit Grandma Carson on her small farm in Independence, Missouri, and my favorite place in the world was Grandma and Grandpa Down's farm in northwestern Iowa. Theirs, on a section of farmland big as a childhood dream, was the one where mine all came true. Pigs! Mud! Cows and chickens! And oh, that dangerous haymow with undetectable holes to swallow you up, impossible to resist. I still see the dust motes in the shafts of sunlight that found their way in through the cracks in the barn walls. It seemed like thousands of bales were stacked going all the way back into the dusky corners, and it smelled good in there. Just right.

Grandma's yard had a dark, mean-looking root cellar with a thick wooden door that creaked. Dank air snuck out and I could smell it. I'd stand outside when one of my aunts had to get something that had been stored.

Put to bed upstairs in what was called 'the little room', shapes other than canning jars floated from the cellar into my dreams.

Alas, no horses (the drafts, Pearl and June, who pulled plows were long gone). No amount of begging for a pony or horse worked. Still, fourteen of us first cousins from Mom's side shared perfect Christmases, summers, Easters, and Thanksgivings on the Down farm.

Without my parents and this family behind me perhaps I wouldn't have survived. Their generous acceptance and nonjudgmental support influenced the woman I was to become.

Tied with bows, two gifts were placed within me before I even got here: you know, like born. One, a helpless attachment to horses. The other, a love for the stories of life. Discovering new adventures and the best words to describe them became an endless treasure hunt. These gifts were given to stay young at heart even if I live to 110. And I'll have plenty to say about it.

My new daddy instilled a few more traits: an out-and-out love for dogs, a relentless sense of humor, curiosity to beat the band, persistence.

And most important in many ways, the gift of Character Appreciation, which turned out to be a vanguard of the maverick Dream. So, you see, my steady focus on characters is as eloquent a tribute to my daddy's memory as I can come up with.

The final gift came from my new mother. She planted it in me from the get go and nurtured it as long as we had each other. She took me to plays, and with that came the desire to be on stage, opening one more door: to always keep playing!

When you're young at heart and love plays, you love to pretend. On a stage, the child inside me never gets sent home and gets to stay and play as long as she wants. That's the whole point, to keep the magic and wonder alive.

These gifts shaped my life. I look like them.

I prance.

I inspect.

I show off.

At my age this is kinda pathetic, so if you meet me when I am showing off, remember I can't help it and please, roar with laughter.

I am trying with all my might to entertain you.

At age three I cantered everywhere, and by four had turned into a prize whiner whenever I spotted a riding stable. Seems I'd also been favored with another gift: a superhero nose that could detect the smell of a horse who needed riding.

One day there'd come a horse I'd belong to for more than twenty-seven years: Delay. We were a matched pair, joined in spirit. He, too, pranced, inspected everything, and showed off. We were the same...we were equals. Except he knew more about forgiveness and in this respect would become my teacher.

He'd be the superstar, and me, his supporting actress. I'd fulfill this role with devotion, right up till the end.

My Hometown In
The Heartland

GEEZ, MY FRIENDS and I shared ideal lives. These were influential friends. Mary Shelley, author of Frankenstein, wrote: "The friends of your childhood hold a certain power over your mind, one that is almost impossible to obtain later in life." If you knew some of those friends I had back then and still hold dear, you'd find that quote as disquieting as I do. Heh heh!

Oh well.

Compared to now, it seems like the 50s were science fiction. It's hard to imagine such a time ever existed.

But let me tell you, it was a wonderful time to be a kid. We roamed the neighborhood on our bikes and explored the outer limits of the woods lots of times until just after dark. Jan and I tobogganed at night with snow showcased under the streetlights, and in the summer stayed out late playing Kick The Can and Capture The Flag. Freedom without fear, because we were safe and our parents knew it. They'd drop us off ALONE at a public swimming pool and retrieve us at the end of the day after we'd had our swimming lessons and spent the rest of the time, without sunscreen, playing and playing hard!

We'd sneak out our windows and go adventuring. One time my friend Joanie and I walked, hiding behind billboards when car lights loomed in the distance, for miles thinking we'd make it all the way out to the riding stables

7

we lived for. It was too far and we had to turn around, but crawled back in the window as the sun came up.

After begging a long time (years!), and with enough intensity, Daddy finally bought me a horse. I named him Butterscotch and my horse crazy girl-friend's (Joanie again) parents bought her one called Sonny. For some strange reason we thought riding those many miles from the stables into town to my house was a perfect idea. When we got there an addendum to this perfect idea struck me. I'd lead Butterscotch up the front steps into the living room and open the drapes to watch people's faces who might look that way as they drove by wondering if my mom was home. Of course she was not. She was somewhere playing bridge. A few cars went up over the curb, but no head–ons. However when my mom heard about it, she told Daddy, and Butterscotch would not enter our house again. So I brought my bike in and put it in the bathtub. I'd show them.

Remember the show Your Hit Parade? In 1953 the number one song in the USA was How Much is That Doggie In The Window? Ouch. The innocence implied by that song pierces my heart.

Divorce? An unknown. A bizarre thing that no family I knew had gone through.

I hadn't even heard my parents or any of my friends' parents raise their voices at each other.

In those days girls took a class called Home Economics and boys took Shop.

We learned how to make deviled eggs and boys learned how to use ham-mers and weld something. I doubt the Jr. High kids of today have even heard of those class names.

If someone had used the word 'dysfunctional', my face would have scrunched up. If they'd explained what it meant, my face would have stayed that way. Clueless. Wow, I feel like crying.

Things start heating up in 1963, the year I enter high school. By now, I am a typical teenaged girl from a typical high school in a typical Midwest town. I am a cheerleader. I am PEPPY!

Music is beginning to influence my generation. The Beach Boys, surf music, car music, and adolescent love songs. Buddy Holly and The Big Bopper for example. Good for dancing and making out to (only kissing of course, for sure). Teenage idols have appeared on the scene with sensational hair like Elvis and Fabian.

In English class I write a paper on the dangers of marijuana. I don't know about your high school, but mine showed the entire student body the documentary Reefer Madness. Pot propaganda. We now knew that after smoking marijuana a maniacal musician would become an axe murderer. I lean forward in my seat as I watch, believing I am being shown a factual movie. When it ends, I applaud with gusto, feeling the urge to stand up and make a Girl Scout salute.

I have a 'good reputation', you see. This is most important. I know enough to know what a virgin is and I am definitely one of them. You got that?

There is one teeny weeny deviation due to the lure of challenge. You know, like a double dog dare mixed with hormones. This amounts to some cagey out-of-town excursions tracking down the Beach Boys. There are urges that can be ignored, and then there are urges that must be followed. We had two excellent reasons for following ours.

One, because we could. My talented friends and I were beyond superb at crafting ways to meet up with the 'Boys'. Of course we kept our reputations intact. You got that? Just making sure.

Two, because we (a select group of talented groupies as it turns out) knew how to plan. Planning itself became a lovely obsession. Maybe I should mention that The Planners were an offshoot of the larger group of twelve regulars (I'll tell you about them later) just because not all of those regulars were natural born groupies.

Now, as I was saying, normal female teenagers. But when we were awarded our drivers licenses, of course we pushed the envelope. Not doing so would have been un–American.

In my hometown, two long streets ran parallel, allowing one–way traffic in opposite directions. Naming them 'the one–ways' or 'the ones' for short, we'd cruise four miles until the street ended, cross a block over and roll back. Up and down we'd drive, looking for the normal male teenagers. At stoplights, we'd jump out for Chinese Fire Drills, running around the car single file, seeing if we could regain our original positions before the light changed. A popular training exercise of our day.

Picture a red Chevrolet Malibu convertible, top down, stuffed with eleven girls, arms and legs hanging over the sides. See us driving through a dark alley, making the short cut between 'the ones'. Now watch as I, the driver, fall out of the car. Form a mental image of the car continuing on, doing about five miles an hour, driverless. Can you believe no one notices my absence?

Suzee is running after her car to save her pals from imminent danger. Alas, they're oblivious, in stitches, howling too loud to notice poor Suzee.

See Suzee? See Suzee run!

Nan and one of the other passengers notice no one is driving, and after identifying their ex-driver running frantically behind the vehicle, Nan makes a swift move toward the driver's seat, executing an airborne sort of flop, landing behind the wheel. Hitting the brakes, she backs up to reclaim poor Suzee.

Amidst all this levity, a day stands out in my sophomore year: Friday, November 23 1963. The day our President, John F. Kennedy, is assassinated.

Later, I saw it for what it was: foreshadowing.

Yet, in 1963, I believe in God without question, college is a given, and joining a sorority is my top priority. Nobody I'd grown up with questioned these things yet.

We had our special group of girlfriends naturally. The ones who did everything together, the twelve regulars (you'll see their names pop up here and there). Oh, there were the questions we tortured our baby brains with at slumber parties, like, "What's on the other side of the universe?"

Sharon would shop for words. "The universe has to stop somewhere, but is it like a wall or something? 'Cause then there'd have to be something on the other side." She would say this with knitted brow, each word a couple seconds apart.

My friends and I accept what our parents have taught us and what they've planned for our futures. We do this with ease because such is life.

It's all good. Without question.

It is this 'without question' bit that will eventually become the root of unsettling events.

PROFESSIONAL PLANNERS

I SHOULD TELL you about nearly meeting The Beatles. How can I not?

My heart sinks and I bite my knuckle. And that peculiar noise you hear is the sound of me whimpering. I can't handle this story. It's that 'nearly' word; it gets me every time.

The Beatles would nurture my generation. Although still a ways off, the Time-Of-All-Times was aiming right at us.

When they came out with I Wanna Hold Your Hand, I was beside myself. Think about being so moved, you are thrown out of your body to stand beside yourself.

I spent years in Beatle Exaltationville. Part of me still lives there and will forever.

Many women my age know of what I speak.

Again, think of the innocence of those lyrics. The admirer just wants to hold her hand? Impossible!

In 1964, though, it's absolutely possible. In fact, it's perfection.

The Beatles were coming to Chicago, a mere 160 miles from my hometown of Moline, Illinois. And The Planning began. Six of us went into high gear months before the scheduled performance. Our whole group wouldn't be able to go, which was a pity, but I had an aunt in Chicago. This could not be a coincidence.

Furthermore, my aunt was a noteworthy aunt, the kind without kids of her own. This placed her in a league of enabling second-to-none when it came to her sister's daughter. Me.

First, this deluxe model of an aunt scored seats to see The Beatles. She excelled at stuff like this. Thanks to her I'd seen the best musicals, the best international horse shows, and eaten at the best table at the foot of the Marshall Field's Spectacular Christmas Tree. So close I could touch it. Which, of course, I did.

Next, I took it upon myself to call the ritziest hotels in Chicago to inquire about room availability on the date of the concert. I'd need to be stealthy to find out what I wanted to hear. On my eleventh call I heard it. Of course I could've smelled his lie had I met this man in person. My superhero nose was agreeably affecting my hearing. Yes I now also had superhero ears!

The desk person at the Conrad Hilton Hotel had been trained, but not well enough. His guarded tone gave him away. And he did not hear the thrill in mine. He'd been assigned to protect his famous guests and the hotel from maniacs like us, female Beatles fans.

"How many rooms would you require, Miss?"

"Mrs., actually. I will need one room that can accommodate six. My husband and I are bringing our family to visit the Museum of Science and Industry. We reside in Moline, Illinois."

"Moline? How far away is that?"

"It's on the Mississippi River, across the bridge from Davenport, Iowa."

"You have a youthful sounding voice."

"So I've been told. Do you have a room?"

"That depends. There is a rather big name concert happening in Chicago on the date you are interested in. Have you heard about that?"

"No, and if your hotel will be involved, I am not interested in making a reservation. We'd like to enjoy a peaceful vacation."

I could hear the man shuffling papers as he whispered to one or two others. He came back on the phone, his voice now silken. Persuasive.

"We would be pleased to have your family stay with us. Our management has advised us to use extreme caution concerning reservations for the date you've requested. I am sorry if I have seemed abrupt or discourteous. You may rest assured your stay in our hotel will meet your expectations."

We six schemers wheedled permission from our moms and dads to take the train to Chicago unchaperoned. Didn't they know better? Evidently not, because they also paid for everything: concert tickets (a bank-breaking twelve dollars and fifty cents per ticket), train, hotel, food. Astonishing! I'll never know how we finagled the whole thing.

Hold on. Were our mothers with us as secret, silent allies in our covert operation? I wonder...which Beatle would each of them have liked best? John, Paul, George? Or Ringo? That, right there, is my brand new thought of the day.

I've just succeeded in gobsmacking my own self.

Anyway, it seemed my parents would be driving to Chicago to visit my 'deluxe' aunt the very same weekend (gee, what a shock). We'd take a taxi from Union Station to our famous hotel where our room would be ready for us.

Our room...in the same hotel as The Beatles.

Sleeping in the same building.

For the whole night, which was almost as good as spending the night with The Beatles.

And nary a doubt we would be.

After all, we were professional Planners!

THE BEATLES

WE LEFT MOLINE the morning of the concert, September 10 1964. My parents took us to the train station with me on crutches.

'Accident-prone'. That's what my relatives called me, along with 'horse crazy' and 'pleasingly plump'. The last term still grates on my nerves. Not once had the Chicago aunt used it, adding yet another star to her unprecedented eighteen-star rating.

I'd broken my foot and, although the cast was gone I still had to use crutches. But hell would freeze over before I'd ever let Paul, George, John or Ringo see me on crutches. As my parents drove away, heading to Chicago, I handed the loathsome things off to Jan and took up limping which was fine because Jan liked playing with them.

Snapshots show us sitting in the train wearing scarves covering our huge rollers. I used beer cans. Our hair needed to be works of art. Way, way straight was way, way 'in' and I'd gone so far as trying to roll my frizzy curls in big empty Crisco cans. It didn't work.

We pulled into LaSalle Street Station and set off to find a cab. Like we knew how to hail a cab? I guess so since one stopped and we crammed in, giddy as all get out. I remember my stomach felt the way it did when plunging down the first steep drop on the roller coaster at Joyland in Wichita, Kansas.

When we announced our hotel to the driver, he stopped the car and turned to look at our faces. "Are you kidding me?"

"No!" we said as one. "Hurry."

"You girls don't understand, you haven't got a chance of getting any-where near that hotel. Don't you know what's going on?"

"Yes, and guess what? We have a reservation at that hotel," I said. He looked at me like my brain was 'accident-prone'.

But he took the Conrad Hilton Hotel confirmation letter and read it. He handed it back, shook his head, and shifted into drive. We were on our way! As we made loud girl-noises, I watched his skepticism turn to admiration in the rear-view mirror. By the time we were on the Congress Parkway, he was smiling.

LaSalle Street Station wasn't far from our destination. Eager puppies, we made nose prints on the windows. As we exited onto Michigan Avenue the driver warned us not to roll them down. Why not, I wondered. Hmm. I asked Jan for my crutches back.

Then we saw it and fell silent. An authentic mob. None of us had seen anything like it before, let alone one made up of thousands of teenage girls. Our admiring driver explained that they were surrounding all four sides of the hotel three blocks deep. Police on the ground. Police in the air. We were in awe. And we had something none of these people had: a reservation!

The cabbie drove at snail speed through the crowd as we showed our confirmation letter over and over to an endless stream of police officers. It took an hour to go four blocks. They had to let our cab through. Girls stared at us teary-eyed. I knew ecstasy for the first time in my young life.

We reached the entrance of The Conrad Hilton, which now resembled a posh fortress. Exiting the cab was bound to be unforgettable. The driver now looked like he pretty much wanted to ask for our autographs, but there was no time. We were not whisked so much as hurled through the front doors by a brigade of doormen and cops.

I approached the desk, leaning hard on my crutches to gain sympathy points from the long row of clerks eyeing us. Their misgiving showed, as did suspicion, doubt, wariness, and disbelief. They squinted at us, exchanged fur-tive looks, looked like trapped animals.

The six of us marched up to the long mahogany desk, exuding power. The hotel had added staff in preparation for their packed establishment and pos-sible catastrophe. This gave us the advantage. Linda and Nan stood together with our reservation letter, worth thrice its weight in gold, stretched out for the gentleman to see. He snapped it out of their hands, but it took him awhile to line up the particulars. Our check-in person was obviously a temp. His lack of confidence showed in the way he kept rearranging papers on the counter. His eyes scanned our reservation, missing anything to do with 'Mrs.' or 'family of six'. He looked at us in defeat, and we watched his posture deflate as the air of self-importance leaked out of him. He had no choice. "Welcome to The Conrad Hilton." I saw his lips moving, muttering to himself as he handed us keys and pointed to the elevator. We reinstated our power march. He stopped Sue, last in line. "You should be aware we have an extra team of hotel detectives on special duty for these next two days."

"Thank you," Sue said, batting her eyes, "That makes me feel safe, Sir." Game on!

Alone in the elevator, all talking at once, we punched the button for the nineteenth floor. When the doors opened we clammed up and made straightaway for our room. We passed a man in a dark suit. My superhero nose smelled 'Detective'.

We locked the door of our room behind us and relaxed. Marg improved the pictures hanging on the wall. Equipped with paints and pastels, her artistic hands sent her into action. Onto the glass she added a palm tree here, a monkey there. Abracadabra, the boring pictures became true art.

The rest of us began formulating ideas. The Beatles could already be here.

We'd need to spread out. I'd take the roof. We primped until we were breathtaking to behold, then left our room one at a time.

I looked around corners before turning, rerouting when I spotted more men in dark suits.

I found the service elevator and pushed the button. Stopping itself on the nineteenth floor, it picked me up like a nice elevator. I stepped on and pressed the button labeled 'roof'.

Two things bothered me. One, it was a huge, wooden, rickety thing with an uneven floor, and two, it started going down where roofs do not live.

My elevator groaned to a stop in the basement. A man with greasy hair got on pushing a big cart. Room service? He looked lecherous. He said something in a foreign language. I stretched my hand out to the control panel, eager to get moving. He ogled me some more, his eyes flitting to see what button I pressed. It was a long, long ride to the roof.

As the elevator creaked to get its ancient self going, he took a step toward me. I took a step back. His eyes gave me the once-over. His mouth twisted into a lewd smirk. I stared at the buttons and started humming Good Day Sunshine, one of my favorite Beatles songs. He came a step closer.

Spinning on my heels to face him, I hoped to intimidate the sex maniac. "You tell me where The Beatles are. Now!"

He shrugged, not able to understand a word. He hunched over and I stepped back again. He crept slow, coming at me. A voice in my head shouted, stay out of corners, keep out of the corners. That is when my new best friend, the elevator, started its shaky coming-to-a-stop-dance.

In my head I heard John Lennon blaring Twist and Shout.

Glory be, the doors opened. Waiters and waitresses had summoned the elevator and I got off as they got on.

My foot had healed enough to climb the stairway. Many steps later, having neither seen nor smelled anymore detectives (my compadres were keeping them busy), I walked out onto the blessed roof. Way up there, I could see for miles. I could see Lake Michigan. I could see journalists and cameras. I could see news reporters from television stations. Lifting my prop, a notebook with pen clipped onto it, I felt official and breathtaking.

Just in time. I turned my eyes to the sky where the others were staring in silence. The thup-thup-thup grew louder as a helicopter descended and then I saw their faces! More than that, they saw mine. The helicopter stopped in the air, hovering. Why didn't they land? Talk about perfect position.

Then the worst of the worst happened. Their helicopter spun around and flew away.

Noooooooooo!

Maybe they were going to enter the hotel through the basement. A secret passageway?

Back down the stairs to the top floor, I found the regular hotel elevator waiting and got on. It started moving before I pushed a button. A few floors down it stopped and a woman stepped in. My gorgeousness caught her eye.

"I'm sorry, ma'am," I said, "but I have to tell someone what just happened. I've been on the roof! With reporters and camera crews! And a helicopter almost landed. You won't believe this, but The Beatles almost landed in front of me! Right where I stood waiting. The Beatles!"

"Oh yes," she responded with a British accent. "They were astonished by the size of the crowd around the hotel. Their manager diverted to another hotel by the Chicago Stockyards. They'll be performing in the arena there anyway."

I was stricken by the news. I didn't want to let go. "They were supposed to stay here," I whined.

"They very much wanted to. This is a marvelous hotel compared to the one at the stockyards."

"Oh well, I got close." If my dejection level had been uranium, a Geiger counter would've blown itself to smithereens.

"What a shame for you," she said. "I am so very sorry."

"Who in the world are you? How do you know this?" I'd started to revive, my adrenalin rush huge enough to prevent embarrassment over the fact I'd begun panting.

"Honey, I am George's sister. I live in southern Illinois. You know, the lads are going to be calling me. Come to my room and you can say hello to them on the phone. I know they won't mind."

She told me her room number. Flabbergasted, I asked if I could go get my friends. She said, "Sure."

I got to the room and found everyone gone. On the case. Drat. I hurried to George's sister's room. It took some time to locate. Through the door, I heard her say, "All right, I'll see you later then. Cheers."

I knocked. Her face dropped when she saw crestfallen me standing there.

"You missed them by five seconds. They've just left to go and rehearse."

"Five seconds?" The blood from my face must've drained and left me looking like a zombie because she reached both arms out as if to catch me. But I didn't fall. Instead I wandered off muttering. "Five seconds? Five seconds?"

See what I mean about the 'nearly' word?

By the time it struck me that I should've begged her to help us meet them later, she'd left the hotel.

THE PROMISED LAND
CALIFORNIA

THE REST OF 1964 and up to June of 1965 are carefree. I have finished grades K through 12. The bond between my parents, friends and my home town is tempered into solid gold. These ties are more secure than Ft. Knox, faster than a speeding bullet, able to leap tall buildings in a single bound! All in the name of love.

I've witnessed Elvis's pelvis on Ed Sullivan, met the Beach Boys, very nearly (whimper) met The Beatles and been introduced to not only rock n' roll, but real blues by going to see The T.A.M.I. Show at the movies. A noteworthy undertaking, the show presented James Brown and The Famous Flames, Jan and Dean, The Beach Boys, The Supremes, Leslie Gore, Chuck Berry, Marvin Gaye, Gerry and The Pacemakers, and The Rolling Stones to teenage America.

Okay, the first time I watch Mick Jagger and Keith Richards I feel a strong sense of the coming chasm that will separate them from John Lennon and Paul McCartney. I made it out in the way these two bands looked at each other and the audience. One group used gentle wit and giggled, while the other band wasn't at all playful. They strutted! Later, The Rolling Stones would advise 'Let it Bleed' while The Beatles recommended, 'Let it Be'. At the time I couldn't know, but looking back, I think of this as an interesting observation that will play out much later (having to do with attitude: the two bands had two distinct attitudes).

Things begin to change the summer of 1965. I am out of high school. In July my parents drive me and fellow Planner, Linda, to southern California. We've been invited to stay with a high school friend's parents who live in the beach town of Playa Del Rey.

A dream come true.

When we get there, Linda and I fall over ourselves getting out of the car. California! The promised land! Endless sand, endless summer.

We'd heard about these beach towns, jam-packed with surfer girls.

Plus a boy or two.

Our friend grabs us and we run for the beach.

In 1965 the worst possible thing for any girl is to be cursed with natural curly hair since California girls are nationally acclaimed for straight shining locks. Halos would fight over getting to adorn one of these goddess-type heads of hair. My substandard hair rebelled at my heavy-handed straightening attempts. It stuck its tongue out at me and turned gummy, even frizzier and green. Straight, yes, but a very horrid variety of straight which I blame specifically on my last ditch effort...a straightening permanent. I wear head scarfs. Charming.

I do, at least, have a genuine itsy bitsy, teeny weeny, yellow polka dot bikini. I go surfing. I stand on my board and it slides on a wave until the ocean tries to murder me. It makes me lose my balance, drags me under the water upside down.

At least my wet hair hangs straighter.

Other Moline Planners join us. Our friend's parents are California parents. A different breed. They are cool. Laid back. Groovy. We go wild with new found freedom. California pretends to be one of the United States, but it is not like the other ones. It has a different flavor of mindset and attracts an eccentric category of human. A person can experiment here, excused for being independent. My dad, Kit, knew this. Daddy knew many things. A philosopher and psychologist in his own right, he drove thousands upon thousands of miles selling Johnson & Johnson Band-Aids while he studied human nature. Harvard would've benefited from his wisdom. Yet he still let me spend weeks there that summer, knowing I might suffer the affects of 'California-ism'. I've come to think, had he been my age, he would've joined me.

But the all-important thing in the summer of 1965 is the shift in the music when disturbing song lyrics started hitting the top forty radio stations and certain ears perk up. Two of them belong to me.

Eve of Destruction, by Barry McGuire: "If the button is pushed, there's no runnin' away, There'll be no one to save, with the world in a grave." When the song ends, so does my childhood, without even saying good-bye.

In fact, a long time passes before I realize it has deserted me.

But when I do, I know I'm not the same.

Thinking back, there'd been signs. How had I dismissed them? Childlike hope? Believing my parents when I asked what it meant and they told me, "Oh hush, that isn't going to happen. Sweet dreams," and they turned out the light? I suppose I wanted those sweet dreams so bad that I put the growing fears to sleep next to me. And then I piled the blankets on hard, to suffocate them. And it worked. For a while.

I am talking about the air raid practices in every hometown across America. I am talking about being a second grader bumping her head under her desk so a bomb wouldn't get me, couldn't find me. The children knew something was up. We weren't allowed near the TV when they aired a special program about nuclear war and some quirky word radiation. Why couldn't we watch? What did nuclear mean? Radiation? What was that?

The summer undoes me. I develop a split personality enjoying California's risky worldliness of which I'm naive as they come, but also experiencing a deadly serious side of scary stuff that comes with this world's reality. I arrive an innocent and leave with just enough new knowledge to unnerve me for years.

I need more information.

August comes too soon and it's time to leave California and go back to Moline to get ready for college. But I'm uneasy now. I know I've become atypical. From the constant blare of transistor radios, I hear the change in the music that sings to my soul. I don't know why my lifelong friends aren't on the same page. We listen to the same music, but they don't hear the words that carry warnings. I don't know why I can hear them, and am far from realizing it'll change my life forever.

MISSION POSSIBLE

WHOPPING CHANGES TARGETED us. I couldn't make my friends understand. They were still busy following the rules, for now. One day I hoped they might be inducted onto my page as my love for them was large. But it bore no resemblance to what I felt for my parents.

I had to make them understand. This was my mission.

As a child I became frantic if Daddy was late coming home. I didn't think I could breathe without him. My day revolved around my mommy. I believe this is part of the design. The world is too big to dive into. So when the design is working right (and of course, it often isn't these days), parents map out a child-sized world, a beginners' world of safety. This attachment burrowed itself far within me, a permanent devotion that will never die. I could not bear the idea of them being lost and not getting 'it'.

We'd need to be able to still recognize each other when, in a flash, our lives changed shape. The warning bells rang loud and clear. 'It' had been conceived, but was still in the incubation period. When 'it' matured, there'd be a drastic cosmic switch. Think of a switchman working the tracks for trains. One switch means a train goes in another direction altogether. And if not on the ball, the switchman can make a mistake. A life or death mistake.

My generation came of age in another time than that of my parents. Coming up would be unfamiliar choices they'd need to deal with. Choices they'd never had to make for themselves would be required. Hard choices for most, but these choices appeared to me as a single overpowering call.

The invitation resonated in my soul, soft but strong, a prodding summons I had to heed. No namby-pamby invitation, this. More like orders issued to report to boot camp.

Pointed toward being worried sick, unaccustomed anxiety distressed me.

The 'Eve of Destruction' was near. That song resounded like an apocalyptic dirge in my head, heralding the birth of an epic era. From this era would surface a generation of youngsters who knew innately something was happening. You could see it in questioning eyes, and perched minds. What? When? We wondered, not knowing how to move through our surroundings while we kept guard and waited.

This generation would live through the Time-Of-All-Times.

They would be part of 'it'.

But not all of them.

Returning home from California that August of 1965, waves of loneliness were trying to drown me like the ocean had when I'd gone surfing. At the time I would've given a lot to know I wasn't alone in this, whatever 'this' was. And I didn't know a soul who thought along the same lines. That's what first made me consider sharing my story, why I started keeping notes. I'd been born to put it down on paper, but it would take me more than forty years to pull it together.

So what?

Still, the telling would have to be my desire, that free will deal I'd always heard god was supposed to be so big on. Doing my part. Like writing the whole damn thing down.

I want you to see how The Dream played its role in bringing some of us to our place of contentment, our thirst eternally quenched. I also want you to know how others from this generation got lost, trading The Dream for the commonplace. Little by little they shaved off parts of their uniqueness till it passed away. And maybe I even want to help some of the others who are still wondering whether there really was/is a Dream out there to be found at all.

To them I say, keep on keeping on. When it finds you, you'll know.

So many remain intrigued. I get the same questions over and over. And there's a ton of misinformation out there.

All these years later, people want to know what they know they missed. I recognize the anxiety and I hear the echo of that call I experienced in 1965. As in the 60s, this mysterious beckoning remains concealed from the majority. Don't you wonder why?

Time for a disclaimer. Say no to drugs. And hitchhiking, which used to come along with The Dream as a benign benny. These things have become significantly corrupt. Probably you know this, but I'm just saying.

To those who hear and see that the world is making a bee line toward something like what they call in movie language a 'wrap', my story will have significance.

COLLEGE?

MY FIRST SOJOURN at the U. of I. in Iowa City begins in the autumn of 1965. Alarming questions had started forming, hatching like eggs and making a lot of noise in my head. Too much noise to concentrate on things like text books.

My questions won't stop pecking away.

Why do the girls in my dorm all dress alike? Why do they think alike? When we started smoking, why did we all smoke the same brand? (Larks? No, Tareytons). Worse, why are the doors of the dorm locked after eleven o'clock at night?

Then, inevitably, why in the world am I here? Not here in college, but here. Period.

Questions turn into analyzing, which become frosting on my cupcake of meaninglessness.

More questions. Were the eggs of change laid on that day when Oswald murdered John Kennedy? Or did it happen in grade school when we practiced our first school drill for the 'unlikely event' of an atomic bomb falling on our then eggless heads?

Neither I nor the hallowed halls of higher education were ready for each other.

But birds of a feather did flock together so when I found other kids like me, it was like Yes! Plop plop, fizz fizz. Oh what a relief it is. Others with newly-hatched bird brains, uncontrollable, flighty, and acting out just like me. Their once-tame minds tuned into constant, crazy cheeping sounds, just like mine!

A month at college reassembled me into a distinct ex-cheerleader and a dedicated atheist. I could hardly remember my home nest of eighteen years. And what was up with the virgin thing anyway? Come on, let's get that over with. I liked the word, 'deflowered'. So dramatic! As would be 'de-feathered' in keeping with my new favorite metaphor of the day.

I migrated fast in the direction of the flock, pulled by an energy I welcomed with open wings. Compared to the college's total enrollment of 30,000, the flock was tiny but I didn't care. My soul soared when led to the other birds. Nocturnal like owls, we kept awake with unending questions.

You could make these folks out easy, didn't take eagle eyes, that's for sure. Atypical Gary became the first 'freak' (as they were labeled back then), to swoop near enough for me to smell his nonconformity with my super hero nose. Out of those 30,000 students, no one had outrageous hair. Long, frizzy, and, his natural color, bright orange. It was splendid plumage — shocking, clock-stopping hair.

The image of Gary reminded me of a photograph I'd just seen. It'd been a picture of some new singer with hair like Gary's, but dark brown instead. Searching for clues, I went straight to the record store and bought his album. After listening with my ears pressed against the speakers, I found myself flapping in turbulent air, trying to stay upright as unheard of questions bounced me around.

Bob Dylan affected most of us that way. She Belongs To Me hinted at the mystery: "She can take the dark out of the nighttime, and paint the daytime black." In the song Like A Rolling Stone the message was even more tantalizing.

The chorus spoke for me, haunted me, baptized me into a wound-up family, looking around with a sense of full-on desperation for something unnameable.

On a visit home, my one impelling purpose being to enlighten my parents, I pleaded with them to sit stock still in our living room while I put Bob Dylan's Like A Rolling Stone on the hi-fi. Gentle but firm, I asked them to concentrate hard on the words, certain it would blow open the gates for communication between us. They'd hear the words and 'get it'. 'Get' me. Their changeling would bring them along into her new world.

Leaving them behind was unthinkable. I refused because to me it would mean losing my dearest loves. The three of us made a mosaic of our hearts. They'd given me their all. I didn't want their approval; I wanted them. As my brother and sister, we'd belong to the same new family of Love. They'd be part of fitting our world to The Dream. I couldn't do anything about other people's parents, but mine were mine and they would understand when Dylan sang: "You've gone to the finest school all right, Miss Lonely, but you know you only used to get juiced in it, and nobody has ever taught you how to live on the street, and now you find out you're gonna have to get used to it."

They listened. They tried. Their faces told me they were lost in the dark.

I was doing an about-face in spiked heels on the morals and values they'd taught me. Their selfless, heartfelt dreams for me were not coming true. When I discovered they weren't coming with me, I was shattered.

As I waited for a chance to meet Gary of the orange hair, I looked closer to home for a fellow misfit, someone to be in league with, to wade deeper into the muddied waters of this different kind of a life. I auditioned my best friend, Nancy. We'd grown up together in Moline and planned for years to go to the same college. I could count on her being a cuckoo. However, Nan's lukewarm interest couldn't compare with my steaming hot need. She'd be due to arrive in my life again about two years later. Right on time. We've stayed stitched together ever since.

Dylan sang: "And you know something is happening here, but you don't know what it is." I became consumed with that 'it'. I knew identifying 'it' meant I would find Truth and Love and Answers.

TORN IN TWO

I TRIED ONE more time to bring my mom and dad along. I'd heard a Dylan song called The Times They Are A Changing and toted it home back to the same setting: living room with green shag carpet, hi–fi, curtains open as usual. Mom had her Halloween decorations out.

I felt sentimental and anxious. They had to be taught.

But in my imagination I heard an ominous sound of fabric being ripped in two. Me on one half with them on the other. I wanted to prevent the jagged tearing.

"I have another song I think will make you understand what's going on. I don't see how you can miss it in this one. It's really important. Just listen." I was excited. The message was so big, missing it would be like standing in front of Niagara Falls and not seeing water. Even then, the crushing sound and the spray should be plenty obvious. I put the forty–five rpm record on the turn-table, sat down and shut my eyes.

I crossed my fingers and listened along. "Come mothers and fathers throughout the land, and don't criticize what you can't understand. Your sons and your daughters are beyond your command. Your old road is rapidly agin'. Please get out of the new one if you can't lend your hand, for the times they are a–changin'."

But we came to the end and still no dice.

I loved them, and I felt their fear. I didn't know what to do, how to lend them my antennae so they could tune in. I'd have to go on without them.

Ralph Waldo Emerson said, "Do not go where the path may lead. Go instead where there is no path and leave a trail." Maybe Mom and Daddy could follow my trail?

Okay, what I can tell you is this. Listening to Bob Dylan with ears to hear and eyes to see was a supernatural event. To the thirsty of my generation, Bob Dylan's song lyrics quenched our parched souls with springs of fresh hope. Offbeat models wearing his groundbreaking word-ensembles sashayed down the runway of our minds, flaunting a new Dream to believe in. The rest of the population went, "Huh?"

The Stones, The Zombies, The Who, The Moody Blues, Donovan. These English bands made music that, as their albums, kept me spinning and seeking out whoever I could find who got 'it'. We were lone planets looking for our one-of-a-kind sun, eager to do the orbit dance with more planets who gravitated to the same star.

A girl in my dorm, Maggie, kept showing up on my radar. Tracking her became easy. Her blip led to certain hangouts I already frequented. I took this as an omen. She and I connected, and like bats, hung out in those dark caves on campus, pondering the Great Mystery. Together, using our nifty bat sonar, we detected the presence of the others. Others. This is beginning to sound like aliens here, which I guess is what we were. Myself and some new friends including Hawk and Dunc. We knew that we knew; we just didn't know what we knew.

What I did know was that me and academia were mismatched. There were signs the size of billboards announcing our failed relationship.

It was obvious in my choices: go to class or take part in a game we called 'Spies' with the others? We formed two spy rings.

Dunc consumed vodka, lots of vodka, sort of a fresh approach to your basic science project, so he was too busy to play. And my friend from the dorm experimented with studying. I tried to leave her alone.

What consumed me was not Zoology 101, but field research in spying, attacks and counter attacks.

It came more naturally to me. Designing spy strategies reminded me of The Planners from the good old days.

Our base of operation was up a flight of stairs above a store called Paris Cleaners. We converted the third apartment on the left into our Headquarters and a door straight past the flat at the end of the hall opened onto a maze of rooftops. So accessible. These were beauteous to behold when viewed with spy eyes. Stairways, alleys, hidden boxed canyons made of bricks awaited the spy with the most imagination.

Much later, after I'd left the University of Iowa, I realized Kurt Vonnegut had been teaching creative writing right there, right then, at my school. To think my imagination could've been sitting in his class! The 'nearly' word comes to mind again.

Pardon me while I stifle another whimper.

Instead, I excelled as a spy and learned sleuthy moves, able to squeeze inside those box canyons of the alleys. I roosted on rooftop pinnacles crowning Main Street. Balance was critical. I could throw an egg grenade with each hand at the same time.

Telephone calls to my dorm room were coded. Think of my dorm room as a 'safe house'. This had to be worth a healthy percentage of the thousands of dollars my parents were dishing out to get me educated.

Picking up instructions in person required supreme stealth. It had to be real, ya know? We're talking method acting. I still refuse to check into who taught acting right there, right then at my school. Enamored with acting, I shudder to think whose tutelage I may have missed. Like the blunder I made not taking Kurt Vonnegut's class.

If discovered by someone on the other team, I was an escape artist. Let's just say, I had my 'vays'. When it came to vanishing without a trace, I was the real thing. I could tell you how I accomplished this, but well, you know, then I'd have to kill you.

I received a message informing me of a high level mission in Iowa City's sewer system to commence after Thanksgiving break. When offered a part in this op, I pounced.

Looking back, I wonder why we did this? Were we creating imaginary distractions to draw a veil over the fears creeping up on us? To mask the real dangers threatening to take us out?

SPY VS. SPY

A COLLEGE BREAK meant taking your dirty laundry home. My pile started to breathe, having acquired a life of its own after a three-month incubation. As I tackled the massive mess, I wished I could launder my midterm grades as well.

Scholastic probation. I could see the letter in my mind, honing in on my parent's mailbox stamped with an evil grin for postage.

My parents had visited that fall of 1965, making the most of having a kid in a college their favorite football team, The Iowa Hawkeyes, hailed from. They knew I held a frivolous attitude, but turned their heads. Daddy told me to have a ball, that these days would be the best of my life. Proud to assign me my first checkbook, Daddy didn't even get too upset with my constant overdrafts. God knows, I couldn't handle a checkbook.

They out-and-out ignored that I'd changed and become a stranger to their system and the lessons they'd taught me. I'd been thrust out of their world like a rocket, powered by stardust. Thanksgiving came and went with no inroads made, so I stopped campaigning to make them understand though leaving them behind made me feel rotten.

I met with old school friends also back for turkey and pumpkin pie, and I bombed out there, too, in the communication arena. I remained incognito, meeting to drink beer in familiar bars, feeling surreal. It already felt like my hometown days were a million light years ago. I still loved my friends dearly and they loved me. A few asked why I tried running away from my problems, warning me they'd turn up wherever I ran. It'd be hopeless to try to explain that my one problem happened to be reality. Not a big attraction in my book, avoiding reality caused me no shame. That worried them more, so I slid into pretend mode. I made it a point to shut up, fit in, and they stopped worrying. I wouldn't be seeing much of them anyway.

Installed back in the dorm after Thanksgiving, I prepared for my spy mission with vigor. When the time came to sneak out of my building into the night, I was invisible in black tights, turtleneck, boots, gloves, and hood. I slunk toward the predetermined manhole cover to meet my team and we lifted the lid into the bowels of the treacherous sewer hours before the clock would strike eleven.

Our mission? Something to do with eluding the other team, a big kid interpretation of hide and seek.

It took a long, long time to pass under the river through the tunnel. We were enraptured by success, cackling madly with the rats. They acted like they were in on the fun, popping their heads up and down in a syncopated manner, although the cheap wine we were swigging (Boone's Farm Strawberry Hill rings a bell) may have had something to do with our take on that.

Ascending from the depths was an ethereal event, like the mist rising off the river.

A miracle! I wondered if it was a little like Lazarus had felt.

Proud and unflappable, I stepped out of the sewer. And then I saw it: the sun. Its optimistic little self gleaming away. Oh no. The night had slipped by like Elvis's hand might have slid, turbocharged by the grease in his hair. My serene sense of accomplishment evaporated like the mist.

The Dean of Women. I'd be found out for sure when the dorm Nazi saw I hadn't signed back in. I was in big, no, make that mega, trouble.

A girl returning to the girl's dormitory one skinny minute after 11:00 would have to appear before a review board that would've made Cinderella's wicked stepmother seem kind.

I'd returned from playing in the sewer w-a-a-a-y past eleven o'clock. My coach had been w-a-a-a-y past pumpkin.

The Dean of Women made sure I felt like an abomination.

Now that I'd be on disciplinary probation in tandem with scholastic probation, I would qualify as a 'two title holder', which is only favorable if you're a boxer or a wrestler.

I'd been dormitorily deflowered.

ROAD TRIP

I RELAXED WHEN my dorm friend, Maggie, threw in the towel on the studying experiment. I needed her. The call of the wild continued wooing my soul, like Nelson Eddy luring Jeanette McDonald with his singing.

The song calling me? The Sound of Silence by Simon and Garfunkel: "Hello darkness, my old friend, I've come to talk with you again."

To this day there is a bar in Iowa City named The Airliner. Its best friends shortened its name to The Liner and my kindred spirit and I spent hours in a booth there, our ears glued to the mini chrome jukebox on the wall. We played The Sound of Silence like a worship song leading up to the service comprised of every Dylan song inside that shiny box.

Midwestern to the core, we knew nada about the major league music happening out there in the wide world. Not until later.

Sitting in The Liner early December, fake I.D.s in hand, we enjoyed our beers as we watched the first snow flakes of the year having some fun in the air. And this made us want to have some fun, too.

Then we got an idea. Road trip!

We chugged the beers and hurried to the dorm, grabbing the phones in our respective rooms when we walked in the door. Maggie told her mom she needed a sign out pass to go to my parents' for the weekend. I told mine the opposite story.

Piece of cake. Now, where to go? How to get there?

My ex-boyfriend might be of use. He had become my ex when he ridiculed Bob Dylan. I didn't blame him, he just didn't get it.

Road trips, however, made sense to him. As did beer.

I tried to convince ex-boyfriend to lend me his car.

He didn't. So, Saturday morning we took off hitchhiking.

We headed for the Windy City on Interstate 80, the first interstate in the United States, thanks to Eisenhower. We planned to surprise Hawk who had gone home to Chicago. Seemed like a daring prospect, a scrumptious adventure. We'd be having fun just like those snowflakes!

A car stopped when we stuck out our thumbs, a car going straight through to downtown Chicago. I watched Iowa cornfields line out as we whizzed by. When we neared Davenport, I noticed the junction for Highway 61, the one Dylan had written a song about and I was struck that Ike's 80 intersected it. The irony of that junction and what it symbolized has stayed with me. The junction symbolized a huge intersection of change in the world. Having been born not far from that junction could explain a lot.

We were dropped off in Chicago on State Street at dusk. It was cold, but not windy or snowing.

We worked our way by thumb to the part of the city where Hawk's parents lived. Finding the address was easy. We rang the doorbell and waited for Hawk, intent on blowing his mind. Instead we perplexed his parents. Hawk wasn't there. The parents were leery. My superhero nose smelled their leer. When we admitted to being students at Iowa, they cross-examined us. Obviously, they wondered if we were related to any of the causes ruining their son.

If I do say so myself, I played an outstanding Eddie Haskel to the Mom's Mrs. Cleaver. So convincing was I that she offered to call a friend of Hawk's who produced an address where we might find him.

"Why thank you very much Mrs. Cleaver. And by the way, may I say your hair looks especially nice today." I'm sure she believed us to be a fine influence on her child.

Stars shone in the dark sky. Thumbs out. A car stopped with two young men in the front seat. The kid on the passenger side reached behind to open the back door for us. We climbed in and told them where we wanted to go. They knew the address and asked us who we were looking for.

"Hawk," we said at the same time.

"Hawk? You gotta be kidding. We know Hawk!"

They didn't seem abnormal enough to know Hawk, but we tried to believe them.

"Hawk is at this party a few minutes from here. Should we drop you off there?"

"Why not?" I said as my friend elbowed me in the ribs. It was hard to swallow, but hey, they even knew the apartment number.

Gullible? Don't forget now, it hadn't been that long since I'd been a blonde cheerleader, come on.

Third floor, apartment B.

Knocked on the door.

Door opened.

The place was on fire!

But the place wasn't on fire, just filled with so much smoke I couldn't see the person's face who opened the door. Then it hit me. I knew what this was. I'd seen Reefer Madness!

The fumes smelled sweet, the crowd smelled stoned. They smelled sweet, too. The room had a cheery atmosphere and everyone acted casual in a chummy sort of way.

Not an axe murderer in sight. This was fascinating.

We asked for Hawk.

No one had ever heard of Hawk, but, boy, were they glad we had come to the party!

Before I could orient myself, we heard a deafening crash behind us. The door we'd just entered and closed burst open, shooting splinters of wood across the room since the police hadn't bothered using the doorknob. In rushed cop after (notorious Chicago) cop.

I grabbed my friend and yanked her toward another doorway in the back. The smoke in the air became our ally. We made it to the door and shut it fast. It was a bathroom.

Aha, an open window. Escape hatch.

We were out in a twinkling, standing on a rusty wrought iron ladder attached to the brick on the building. We lowered ourselves, arm over arm as fast as we could go. Dropping the last few yards onto the pavement, we landed on our feet and took off down the alley.

Running until we were out of breath was a no-brainer. That's what you do in dreams like this. Except this was no dream.

Were we having fun yet? Not quite. The real fun was coming up.

We stopped, bent over on some street, panting and laughing. The laughter had a deranged edge, and we had to pee. Now what? A carload of drunk fraternity boys Johnny-on-the-spot. Harmless enough these college boys who thought they flirted us into the car. Had they noticed how inclined we were to hurry in, they wouldn't have felt like such studs.

Wanting out of there immediately-if-not-sooner, we didn't much care where we went. Their frat house was nearby and after turning off the car, the crew rolled out. We pitter pattered along behind them.

The night had sent the stars away and turned Tarbaby-black, but we kept up by following the belches one of them emitted every few feet. It reminded me of tracking bread crumbs thrown by Hansel and Gretel except our course led through a maze of halls, not a path through the forest. When our sloshed saviors started making words out of their burps, it motivated us to untangle our destinies from theirs quick like a bunny.

With as much pluck as I could manufacture, I decreed that one of them was to chauffeur us away. This plan had no future until the disembodied voice of their house mother reached the ears on their small pointed heads. Out on the prowl, doing her job, she had clout. Bless her!

Heatedly disappointed at the failed prospect of two loose women, one of the merry men (but not honorable in motivation as was Robin Hood with his merry band), pushed us into the night and into his jalopy.

He hadn't driven far when he stopped by a lane, dark with tall pine trees on each side. No streetlights. "Walk down this drive. At the end there's a safe place to wait until morning." Faker.

"What do you mean by a safe place?" I didn't like the creepy smile on his face.

"No, no, really, it's a community hall that stays open all night, like a hostel. There's an excellent lobby," he said.

Humph.

We got out, tromped down the lane and up some steps. Opening the front door, we let ourselves into a well lit foyer.

The promised sanctuary.

Could it be?

Did he tell the truth after all?

What do you think?

Looking around, we saw a woman sitting behind a counter. The scene reminded me of a hotel reception area. Groovy. We marched over to her, feeling less tired, and she asked us our names. After we told her, she asked more questions. Where had we come from? Why so late? Did we have family in the vicinity?

She appealed to our sense of trust with her soft doe eyes and an expression that said, "Go on now, you can tell me all about it."

So we did. We were featherbrained to begin with and it didn't take long to lose it completely. Giggling like mad-hatters fresh out of Wonderland, we attempted to tell her the whole story, for the most part. Saying words out loud made us crazier, we couldn't believe how outrageous our adventure sounded to our own ears.

The woman was quiet, so understanding.

After we finished sputtering, she ushered us into a cozy pastel room. We were exhausted again.

Something my super hero ears heard in her brisk walk back to the desk made my stomach turn over. About then my friend and I clutched, staring into each others matching bug eyes. I leapt to my feet and snuck to the corner of the doorway where I could listen. My spy experience was paying off.

She summoned a doctor 'so and so' on a low frequency intercom. I turned around. My playmate had become animated, doing something like jumping jacks. Now was not the time for exercising. I looked closer. Using both hands, she gestured at a sign. I read the sign through the semi-barred window.

North Shore Mental Institution.

Perfect. Just perfect.

It was absurd. Our lives were absurd. The evening was absurd. We were absurd people.

A fragment of my fatigued brain recalled seeing a wall phone outside the room by the door. The woman had left her post so I tiptoed around the corner, dialed zero, and asked the operator to call a cab for an emergency pick up at 2200 North Shore Drive.

As I fell into the plush sofa, the woman showed up to ask a few more questions, checking to make sure we hadn't left. I could tell she thought we were looney tunes, drugs likely involved. She assured us everything would be all right and left the room. I knew she went to meet the doctor en route.

We watched our cab pull up outside the big window and knew there was but one choice. Throwing open the window, we squeezed between the bars like Gumby and Pokey.

We charged the taxi.

The ancient cab driver (though he was probably all of 50), had the back door open, his eyes trained on the front entrance. By the time he saw us, we'd planted ourselves on his backseat. Slamming the door, we screeched at him to, "Punch it, go, go, go!" Which he did. The old geezer was scared and figured we were escaping. We were hysterical, lack of sleep and all.

I still had the address Hawk's parents had given me and managed between fits to recite it over and over. After driving a few blocks, the cabbie squealed the taxi to a stop and yelled, "Get out of my cab. Now." His eyes, wiggling around in their sockets, said he meant it. We rushed out, and watched the back door swing open and shut as the yellow car sped away.

From there we decided to call it quits. My partner and I traveled by thumb system two hundred miles back to Iowa City. Interstate highway 88 passed beneath the huge Chicago Postal building through a tunnel that descended on one side, ascending on the other. As we rose from under the structure we watched the Sunday morning sun rising along with us.

We didn't have to sweat being late to the Dreadful Dorm.

PEYOTE

CHRISTMAS BREAK HAD been something to look forward to, but it ended, landing me back in my college cage the middle of January 1966.

I stopped studying, in favor of devoting my attention to a detailed investigation of the peyote cactus (maybe if I'd switched from zoology to biology? Naaah).

Peyote buttons (disc-shaped dried tops of the cactus) cause hallucinations when eaten. For centuries Native Americans in Mexico have used the little cactus for spiritual questing.

I was no longer an atheist. The order in our Milky Way Galaxy had tipped me off. Whatever I had become eluded me completely, but I aimed to find out. With fervor.

My associates and I had moved in the direction of the unseen world. Drugs had the reputation of increasing a person's sensitivities. Most would start out trying marijuana. Not me. I flat out passed 'go' and went directly not to jail, thank god, but to 'full tilt boogie' psychedelics. I'd been guaranteed peyote would give me much more than the giggles. I'd become enlightened instead of ending up with nothing except a case of the munchies.

A guy knew how to prepare it and warned us that no matter how you took it, you could count on throwing up before you 'got off'. I'm not into barfing, but I was born curious. Climbing to the top of a twenty-thousand foot mountain might make you sick, but hey, if the view was worth it...

'Getting off' means your consciousness expands in every direction. Inward, outward, down and up. So heightened, the reward is seeing like you've never seen before. Crisp. Dazzling.

I don't want to sound like I'm encouraging anything with this mini-lecture, but this is data you might need if you haven't had peyote before.

My inner writer just reminded me to show not tell.

Anyone unfamiliar with the mescal adventure would want to know more.

Wanna take some peyote? See what I'm talking about? You won't even have to throw up.

Okay. First, shut your eyes.

It's night. You and I are walking back to the dorm two hours after eating the buttons. The air feels like no air you've felt. It is alive, soft and comfortable against your cheek, buzzing with sheen. You may touch it, pet it.

Look at the sky. The stars are spelling, "Hi!"

We're here, walking through the door into the lobby so bright. The florescence greets us with a happy tinkling noise. Slow-motion to the elevator.

No, the stairs, tons more entertaining. Like climbing a tower. Visualize being inside a picture storybook, inside the world of the story. Rapunzel?

It'll take awhile to get to my dorm room on the twelfth floor, lots to investigate on the way. For instance, the shiny metal strip on the front of each step reflects an image of you and me as holograms. We're following ourselves up the stairs. Whoever invented these strips deserves a Nobel Prize!

You can understand why I said it'd take awhile to make it to the twelfth floor, but now we're here, opening the door to my room. The doorknob is a clown nose. Peyote is a prankster. Here's a note taped to the mirror. Birthday Party in Room 1134. Oh boy!

Okay, let's go. The hall looks like a rabbit warren, open doors peeking into rooms that go on forever. No end in sight. Mesmerizing, but we're expected at the party.

Uh-oh, forgot you and me will be the only ones at this party seeing the world through Alice-in-Wonderland-eyes.

"Hey you guys, we made it. Happy Birthday!" Notice the balloons for instance. They are everywhere. "Say, Terry, I've never seen so many balloons. Take you days to blow them all up?"

"How many beers have you had, Suzee? There's four, count them, one each of the true colors."

"Right, ha ha, but you went all out on the crepe paper. Wonderful job, Ter."

"What crepe paper?"

"Just kidding, Ter, ha ha." The non-balloons are performing everywhere at once, exuberant dancers multiplying themselves in the mirrors. The girl's faces have balloons passing back and forth across them, changing the color of their complexions. We should go.

Back in my room again, still nobody here but you and me.

Look at the movie screen that used to be a window. The film has trees for actors. A big oak has the leading role.

A fire engine speeds by, and we see the faces of the firemen in detail. It must be a practice run since they are smiling and chuckling. Oh, and waving.

Wave back!

They have families waiting for them at home. The family members pass across the 'screen' in a line introducing themselves. No, they don't. This is ridiculous and our cheeks are aching from overuse of mirth muscles.

We are there until past midnight when my roommate returns from the homework lounge. "Nighty night, Nan." I am feeling Nan is not ready. Not yet, anyhow.

I've got an idea. Lets explore the tunnel connecting these dorms.

Not a girl to be seen. We've got the whole tunnel to ourselves. It's never looked the color of molten gold before. It's never breathed before either.

Peyote brings out the life in everything. It's encouraging because you can have a relationship with anything that's alive. In some unofficial way, isn't everything alive in an elementary sense?

What about that genius, Sherlock Holmes? When he solved preposterous riddles, he'd tell his doctor partner the reason it'd been so easy, "Elementary, my dear Watson." He knew how to get to the simple pieces. The basic elements. Uh-oh, my lightweight brain wants to wrestle with a heavyweight idea. I could hurt myself. If I had to describe peyote in one word, it would be "elemental." The periodic table of the elements is an attempt to break down the building blocks of all matter. Different mixtures of these ingredients make air, water, solid materials, living creatures. Somebody made these elements. I tend to think of this somebody as a spendthrift mad scientist slinging out butterflies! Seahorses! Rainbows! Turtles! Singular snowflakes! Pink sand! Tropical fish! Galaxies! Redheads!

Catching my drift? That in the making of everything, alive or not, the same invisible building blocks are used. Peyote opens the door so you can see in far enough to glimpse those unseen blocks.

Still there? Back to our peyote journey, then.

What do you think about the length of this tunnel? How about the mellow wind blowing through? Go on ahead of me. Now look back. What do I look like? A bird? I should've known. Well, you look like a bird, too. With a narrow beak and stately, straight legs.

We've been in this pleasant tunnel for months, although the clocks say just fifteen minutes. Can we make it to the lobby of the other dorm at the end of the tunnel? If the entertainment will let up long enough, we can.

The tunnel is nothing compared to this enormous lobby filled with over-stuffed chairs. The chairs are for containing boy's bottoms that come to visit or pick up their dates. Wait. Bottoms can't date. It has to include the whole boy to qualify him as a contender. We are cracking ourselves up. We are a riot!

A subdued glow from the streetlights make the furniture visible. This lobby is a continent of its own. The chairs combine to make the prettiest landscape of BIG mushrooms and perfect round bushes. We thought we understood round, until now.

Tables are hedges shaped into animal forms. No, they are animals. Many, many kinds of animals. Sleeping peacefully.

We could wander around in this place for who knows how long.

Hey, wait a sec. 'Who' DOES know. 'Who' alone does and where is 'Who' when you need him?

The heavenliness of the lobby is excruciating. Let's live here!

And now you have tried peyote.

DENVER, ROUND ONE

I HADN'T STARTED dodging bullets yet; I looked for them. Why? Because if I could catch a bullet between my teeth, I'd have a story to tell.

I wanted to run away with the circus or make love while free falling (on purpose) in a single engine small plane or hop a freight. These would be fodder for grand adventure stories. I was on bullet patrol.

Life moved, cut corners, demanded celebration. Surges of joy, gut level and vast, floored me. Emotions I couldn't identify stalked me. I wanted more, wanted to jump into life's mystifying current without a life jacket.

I craved an address change.

There was one coming. I'd hear and follow the first of the Siren calls that would steer my young life. I'd describe my 1966 Siren as a cross between mother hen and pistol packing mama.

The call came through The Moonrakers, a Denver band. They did a show for one evening in our student union building. Maggie and I went to hear them. They played music of the time. A five-piece band, including twelve-string guitar, they sang songs by The Byrds, Bob Dylan, The Turtles, The Beatles, The Rolling Stones, The Zombies, The Kinks, The Who...these bands had things to talk about. And this was the scoop: there were strands of hope.

After the show, we hung around, talking to the guys in the group and they invited us to drive back to Colorado with them. In their van. In the middle of the night.

Yes, Siren, I'm coming.

51

Brooding, bewildered, excited fledglings, we took our chances and flew the coop.

Endings happen. For good or bad, richer or poorer, they just do. For me that March of 1966, an ending meant a lighthearted 'Ta-Ta' to whatever. Young and selfish, my spirit on fire, endings brought no melancholy. They didn't yet drag a sodden sack behind them, heavy with poignant and agonizing memories.

But this ending brought nothing other than pain, confusion and fear to my parents. I'd left everything in my dorm room where they went to gather the remains of the plans they'd had for me, their child and the love of their lives.

The mile high city had no smog back then, allowing the air to electrify the edges of the Rocky Mountain's front range. They jumped out distinct in your face, like cutouts made with razor sharp scissors. Although miles in the distance, they appeared up close. Happy jingle jangle mountains, these. Like me. Free at last.

Spellbinding, too. Because not a single thing didn't seem like magic to two girls in high adventure mode. Everything was brand spanking new, as if the world had just come fresh out of the oven and been set in front of us.

We rented a one room apartment in a building where Alan, who drove us in the van to Denver, lived. Parents, exhilarated we were alive, pitched in on the money end. Mom and Daddy were reeling in disbelief and confusion. Too selfish and involved with that sassy Siren of mine to grasp their heartache, I guzzled all the experience I could get my hands on.

Veeder Van Dorn of The Moonrakers wrote:

"The world is ending.

Things are ending fast, sliding.

Life is a fine wine, it always has potential,

but it must be seasoned and aged just perfectly,

before it is truly ready for the connoisseur's palate.

Be a connoisseur, make the wine a tasty delicacy,

one you'll never regret tasting."

His words fit the escapade I found myself in the middle of. Life was heady wine, aged with potential. I wanted to grab the bottle and chug it, while being a connoisseur at the same time. No regrets. Because the world was ending, sliding downhill, wasn't it?

Speaking of chugging, we weren't doing any drugs. No more peyote and still hadn't tried marijuana. We were drinking pitchers of beer at Shakey's Pizza Parlor. Wait, we did fiddle with white pills that had cross marks on them. They were called 'bennies' and the equivalent of a souped-up diet pill. We enjoyed the beer more.

I got a job. J.C. Penny's Department Store. For some reason they hired me as a lunch counter waitress. I worked one whole day!

The job made my feet hurt. How could I live life to the full with sore feet? I may have been a little spoiled.

I tried working again at Luby's Cafeteria. This job also made my feet hurt. It's possible I could've toughed it out, but for the fried chicken. This chicken, weighted down with seductive batter, forced me to quit my position at once. We're talking a bad boy batter causing fat to accrue within twenty-four hours. Add to that, an installation of cellulite that would remain forever! My personal private horror movie. And so obvious that it was the chicken's fault, not mine.

My friend had an actual work ethic, thank god.

We lasted in Denver until mid-April when I broke my leg the first time I went downhill skiing and learned my first lesson about trust. Not on purpose, but it was about time I gave trust some thought. It hadn't occurred to me how relationships can live or they can croak depending on trust. The way I grew up I assumed trust was some sort of birthright. I told you I started out vulnerable and gullible. I trusted everyone.

TRUST FOR DUMMIES

THIS IS HOW I broke my leg.

An acquaintance, Brian, took me to Arapahoe Basin to 'teach' me how to ski. This would be my first time, a new adventure. He was a real humdinger of a friend. After that day not ever again did I think of him in the same way.

Humdinger? Yes.

Friend? No.

Fiend? More like it.

I'd never seen such a tall mountain. I wasn't able to see all of it, since what appeared to be clouds obscured the top.

He permitted roughly thirteen minutes on the bunny hill, showing me how to snowplow. Which I did not master. I developed my own form of stopping. I tipped over like that little teapot in the nursery song. "That's good enough, perfect actually. Let's catch a chair lift. You are doing great!" said Brian.

We boarded a chair lift. Sort of. He had grabbed hold of the nape of my neck like a mother cat picks up a kitten, using his hands instead of his mouth to load me on the lift. Great.

We de-boarded at the sunny mid-mountain station. My first winter tan coming right up. Fun. So far. I saw hearty-looking people with these cool leather wine containers strapped over their shoulders.

The fact that we'd been on the chair lift for a long time and were far from the top of the mountain scared me.

Brian bought me lukewarm wine in a paper cup. Big spender. He watched me as I sipped it in a ladylike manner. I smelled his impatience with my super-hero nose. Nervous, afraid he'd noticed my stalling, I looked at him over the edge of my cup, fluttering my eyelashes. I prayed he find me puppy-cute, and feel protective. Offer me another one of those paper cups half full of cheap wine.

No way. He was there to ski.

Did we take time to make our way down from there? Did my soon to be ex-friend, with patience and in the fashion that goes with a gentleman pick me up as I failed to learn the important art of turning in an instant? Nope.

He hoisted me into a gondola, which did its best to carry us upward, huffing along and swinging from side to side like a possessed thing in the increasing storm. He spouted out compliments like a fountain in a frenzy. "Suzee, I can't believe what a natural you are. I've never seen anyone ski their very first time like you can. You are nothing short of a miracle. I've taken a ton of people for their first time and you are the best."

"Oh yeah, where did you end up burying them?"

"That's a good one, Suz, ha ha ha." Our little-gondola-that-could stopped at the summit of the mountain. Well above timberline, we fought our way out its door into a blinding snowstorm. What I'd assumed were clouds from far, far below was a blizzard. Having left the smiley face sun back in the tropics, we entered the Arctic circle. Fighting the wind, I tried to wrench the door open so I could get back in. No way. Brian clasped both my hands and pulled me over the ice (what happened to the fluffy snow?) as the gondola floated away like a ghost, disappearing into the white-out.

My teacher slid me to an edge of the peak. Did I have goggles? Are you kidding? I was way too outstanding to need goggles. I was a bloomin' miracle on skis! Brian had goggles, but as I grabbed to rip them off his face or maybe just go for his whole face instead, he slipped over the edge with a smile and a wave. I saw his mouth move, but the deafening noise of the storm obliterated his words.

As far as I could tell by feel, the way down was straight down. I sat on my bottom, hoping I'd poke along like Brer Tortoise. However, the texture of snow pants lend themselves to go faster than even Brer Rabbit. The air so thin I needed oxygen, I shut my eyes and went for it.

A big bare rock stopped my descent, a good thing. I made a plan to go from rock to rock. It didn't hurt that bad. At one point I flipped onto my belly, facing up the slope, to see if the clawing approach might slow me down. Not. "Thank you thank you thank you," I proclaimed to the trees while reentering tropical air. The adorable sun smiled on my frozen face as I crept along on my rock to rock route.

When I reached the mid-mountain warming hut, it had closed. I'd been gone a long time.

From there, where trees existed, I felt encouraged to go faster on my bottom. I was inventing a new sport!

At last, when I could see the rental shop, the terrain flattened. I stood up. If I pointed my toes straight, I'd glide to the bottom where the buildings were. No turns needed. Then I met the moguls. These are bumps in the snow made from other skiers who lived for making turns. Sick.

My arms went into the air, my poles like helicopter blades around my head as I fought to stay upright. I made it through those bumps, I did.

Now here's the sad part. Just when the snow became flat as a pancake, and I saw Brian up ahead, I fell. Broke my leg. On even ground in the waning light.

The medics gave me pain killers and my ex-friend drove me back over Loveland Pass to the E.R. in Denver. Crumpled in my seat, in my mind I dared him to say one word. He didn't.

My parents, who would always love me more than themselves, sent my broken leg and me a plane ticket. The hip-high cast and I were tickled pink to fly home.

Maggie went back to Iowa.

The spring skiing accident was nothing compared to other accidents that might've ambushed me during my first stay in Denver. I was a risk-taker.

The issue of trust had been broached, though, and in time I'd be better for the initiation. In fact trust becomes an integral part of my story, and I would thank Brian for the experience if I had any idea where he is now.

GUILT LIKE AN OUTHOUSE

I LOVED THE yellow brick road ever since I can remember. I think it's because it made me hopeful.

Those guys, the tin man, the lion, the scarecrow, and even Dorothy, all traipsing down that road wanted to be more, even though they were already their own dream come true. They just didn't know it. Down the yellow bricks they sang and danced, on a mission. And they changed, were transformed along the way. The best part? Each of them lived happily ever after. My kind of story. It's just that transformation can be grueling and harsh.

After my broken leg healed, I made an emergency trip from my parent's house in Moline to Oklahoma City that June of 1966. I had an abortion there in an office belonging to a shady M.D. He had a widespread reputation I guess, since the person who gave me his name lived in Illinois.

I asked a loyal friend if she'd loan me money for airfare, taxi and procedure. One night she left cash in an envelope on the ledge outside her bedroom window. Somehow she'd managed to get it out of her savings account without her parents knowing. Crawling through thick bushes in the dark, I snatched the envelope off her window sill and stuffed it in my pocket.

The entire trip to Oklahoma City took fifteen hours. When I flew home, the resulting infection and blood loss required telling my parents. They held me.

I healed.

So to speak.

It took a long time, much much longer than fifteen hours to get rid of the images in my head.

Countless women have experienced what I did. We find our way through however we can. When I came through to the other side of the experience, peace and hope were waiting to tuck me into the bed of relief they'd made up.

Whoever said, "Time is a great healer," sure knew something about how our bodies and souls do heal with the passage of time.

But the rest of that summer I spent a lot of time sitting on the floor in my bedroom with a giant heap of guilt sitting on my head. It looked and felt like an outhouse shaped hat, making me feel shitty and shittier.

I felt stupid for walking into that office where there was a butcher instead of a doctor. I could tell by the look of the waiting room. Its drab green paint was peeling. Stuffing stuck out from rips in chair cushions. Sometimes pieces of sausage poke out from their casings, ya know?

What kind of doctor would provide such a seedy place for patients to wait their turn? There wasn't even a receptionist. The butcher opened a door and called the name of his next piece of meat himself. My instincts teamed up with my imagination, registering and prodding, gangrene...gangrene. The room smelled wrong. Of course my nose knew. Its super hero powers detected too much fresh blood in the air.

The floor was covered with threadbare carpet. The people waiting stared at it. I knew I should've turned around and gone back to the airport. But I did not.

I remember lying on a table, and I remember long tongs in the butcher's hands. I remember him telling me I would not get anything for pain. I remember him hissing, "Don't you dare make a sound." I remember clapping both hands over my mouth where the screams fought to break out. I remember him taking me to the back door and giving me a small shove toward the waiting cab. I remember walking funny due to the padding between my legs already saturated with blood.

I felt bad for wounding my parents, bad for getting pregnant, bad for having an abortion, bad for lying, bad, bad, bad. So much so I decided I should try going to college again. I guess the word 'again' doesn't apply since I didn't try the other time.

I knew this decision would make my mom and dad happy, and in secret I wondered if education meant I could learn anything at all about myself.

Now and then there were flickers of forgiveness on the rim of my consciousness. I didn't know where they were coming from. I chased those moments, trying to get close enough to find the source. Forgiveness spread a balm over my bad. Was it, like, god maybe? Could it be possible I was forgivable?

The truth is, if I could go back, yes there are things I would do differently, but guess what, a 'choice makeover' isn't an option. Without living through each occurrence, honorable or dishonorable, I wouldn't be the me I am, the me I have learned to love. Wouldn't trade this me for anything.

To regret or not to regret, that is the question. Whoops. No worries. I will not bog down here, get stuck worse in guilt that sucks me into quicksand sorrow. I can climb to higher ground.

Suppose my creator makes even my funky choices work out? That'd be peachy. In other words, when I get to heaven and try to bring any guilt along I'll be advised, "Put that away, your guilt's no good here!" Being human, I'm always forgetting that possibility.

To own regret without guilt is the trick, staying put in that place it brings me to. It means braving the reality of all kinds of possible pain and facing it head on, eyeball to eyeball while staying on my feet. Otherwise the wallowing pit is inviting me in. Better to let the consequences have their way with me, to learn from them, grow, and in that process share with others. We are in this life together.

Balloon Love and Go-Go Boots

When fall came I entered a junior college in Moline, lived at home, and fell in love with someone I met at school. I auditioned for a melodrama, got cast as the female lead, and my new love got the male lead. I thought this would improve my staying power in a college.

They drafted him. He went to the army and our love went MIA. It's still there somehow, that love.

See, not for a moment have I stopped loving anyone I've fallen in love with, but the love undergoes a change. The transformation removes the life-breath out of the love, leaving a memorial in my heart. When air is let out of a balloon or it pops unexpectedly, it no longer soars, yet what's left of the once magnificent balloon is still there. Fragments can be kept. A reminder that once upon a time it was precious.

I managed to finish the fall quarter with acceptable grades and behaved myself...kinda. Theater took up spare time, as did learning how to be a go-go girl for college dances. I felt frisky up there on my round box, performing choreographed moves with my go-go sister across the stage on her box. Another stellar qualification for my resumé? Go-go boots, oh yeah.

During this stretch I collected a significant gaggle of new friends. I called them 'The Moline Connection'. We smoked pot. Little tiny joints skinny as toothpicks made little tiny stars twinkle in our eyes, cracked us up and gave us the blind munchies. Think about being ravenous, famished for something amounting to seven desserts for starters, then square it. Now you got yourself the blind munchies which score about a 7.5 on the Richter scale of hunger, and are accompanied by a perma–smile.

Marijuana linked us, created a fully–loaded camaraderie. Surging inspiration came with the package, having to do with freedom, hope, and belief in the power of Love. We felt like a stepping stone on the road to creating a divine new world.

I didn't want to grow up in the world such as it was, waiting for the horrific damage from radioactive fallout the coming nuclear war would deliver.

I didn't really ever want to grow up. I'd known others who couldn't wait, wanted to become adults in the worst way. Not I.

a poem by me -- 1966
peter pan, of thee i write,
here beneath this starlit night.
from grown up world i try to feel,
just how it was when you were real.
it's i who left, i don't know why.
if i came back could i still fly?

Growing up meant, if the world lasted long enough, chances were I'd outlive my parents and that wouldn't do. This was an irrefutable fact I couldn't cope with.

I had a Planner friend who went to an all–girls college in Denver. Pleased with my grades for once, my parents bought me a ticket on Ozark Airlines so I could visit her for the Thanksgiving holiday.

Oh dear.

DENVER, ROUND TWO

IF YOU WERE able to look me up in the dictionary, the word 'bystander' would not be included in my description. I'll show you what I mean.

My pal, Val, picked me up at the airport and we drove back to her dorm at Temple Buell Women's College in Denver. It'd been renamed in 1967, but reverted to Colorado Women's College in 1973. I have a sneaking suspicion the girls I met there had something to do with that. They may have scared the new name away.

I had known Val ever since she lived in her mother's womb. I'd already been out for a year so I should've ended up knowing more than she did. It turned out I didn't. She knew how babies were made. When she was seven and I was eight, she filled me in...with details. A horrifying thing to hear while my innocence and I frolicked on her neighbor's swing set. I became UPSET. That's all I remember.

Upsetting me has become a ritual part of our long term friendship. I look forward it! She tends to be excessive in her excitement and to this day infects me with this 'noteworthy' part of her personality. I can't seem to prepare well enough. Forewarned does not guarantee being forearmed.

After spending even a short amount of time in her presence, I walk away displaying drama queen characteristics. My arms begin gesticulating without my permission. At the same time my dialogue, having stopped to fill up at the Val pump, accelerates onto the Indy 500 track of exaggeration.

My voice takes on her timbre. Even phone conversations have been known to complete the transformation. My husband has walked into the room after

I've just said goodbye to Val on the phone. All I have to do is begin speaking and his eyes narrow. "You've been talking to Val, right?"

It's weird.

It's okay.

She has one of the best senses of humor ever.

Anyway, we pulled up to the dorm, went in. Val introduced me to her roomies along with some other girls on her floor. The beauties, Candy and Annie-Fanny became and have remained my favorites.

There were plans to go to Aspen for Thanksgiving break 1966. A house big enough for the seven of us had been rented. One of the girls had met a boy who offered to drive us to Aspen in his 1957 white Chevy with red interior. He brought a friend nicknamed Jiminy Cricket. We squeezed into the car, six ravishing straight-haired babes, me, and the two boys. Our stuff went on top. We'd rent ski equipment.

Now, these boys had just returned from San Francisco. They brought back some 'keepsakes'. Unable to explain what was happening in San Francisco, they recommended we partake in these 'souvenirs'. They would be self explanatory. Not a bystander among us, we were eager to delve.

The souvenirs were 'hits' of 99.9% pure LSD dubbed White Lightning. Each tablet contained 270 micrograms of lysergic acid diethyl-amide, a substance discovered in Switzerland in 1938 at Sandoz Laboratories. Stanley Owsley made ours at his house in Point Richmond, California.

All nine of us dropped acid at the same time, just about sunset. 'Dropping' means swallowing the tablets.

LSD was in a different league than the peyote cactus. Dropping acid is not described as 'taking a trip' for no reason. You might as well pack your bag, although you'd either forget you had one or spend hours investigating it, maybe just the handle. Or the zipper.

The trip/vacation is more like a 'staycation' since our bodies stayed put, but how far our minds traveled!

For me, the venture changed my life. How? In every way.

I saw objects, nature, people, you name it, with new eyes. Things around me, when scrutinized, started out one size and when studied further, showed off! All right, for instance, a mote of dust in the air caught my attention. I looked at it and then into it, deeper and closer and deeper yet. At first I saw a glint, then a speck, then a rounded shape, then a world. Inside that world I found a village with waterfalls, lanterns, carts moving down paths, and people moving to and fro. Such a busy place. Who knew?

Time didn't pass. In fact, it became nonexistent. Part of the vocabulary that grew out of tripping is the term 'getting hung up'. There were just about endless layers to whatever I looked at, or heard.

Music! Music was something I entered, as in walking straight into. Like into a note where the sound is born. Gorgeous, tangible, colorful, pulsating, caressing. Putting a record on, I could meld with the flavor of music. I joined the truth of music, not standing outside a watered down form of the real thing.

There was no lack of control going on, but fascination took over on a whole new level. I could go along with anything that caught my attention for as long as I liked, and then move on to something equally as phenomenal. Like Prell shampoo.

One of the girls found a tube of Prell and she shared. We amused our-selves as every one of our sense organs vibrated to the magic of its green gel-ness. We ended up finger painting the walls. But, somehow, not each other.

Jiminy Cricket and Spike sat in chairs all night, smiling. Cheshire cat smiles vanishing, then reappearing around the room. They were on their own journeys.

At some point, the seven of us girls sat on a bed and realized we were part of everything, including each other. To this day, when I speak to one of these old friends, we refer to each other as 'Parts'.

The word 'cosmic' fits. By that I mean life showed up in all things, alive or not. I called it enlightening because LSD showed me we are related to what-ever turns up in front of us. The natural outcome of that idea is to love it all. I now had more facts to support my belief in a creator.

I never had a 'bad trip'. After I 'came down' or 'returned home', the doors that opened to 'seeing' and 'knowing' closed. However, I remembered everything.

LSD rewired my consciousness permanently. I count this alteration as a blessing. It taught me there is more out there, more than what we come across in this dimension. There is an unseen world much realer than this one. In fact, it's the REAL, real thing!

Shakespeare said, "There are more things in heaven and earth, Horatio, than are dreamt of in your philosophy."

William Blake said, "To see a world in a grain of sand, and a heaven in a wild flower, hold infinity in the palm of your hand, and eternity in an hour."

Shakespeare and Blake. Did they have LSD back then? Maybe god spilled the beans? Whatever, they were endowed with mind-boggling perception.

A few years later I would stop tripping. One reason being I was happy with what I'd learned. This satisfaction combined with dwindling curiosity took away my urge. The truth was that the purity and power of the drug would become diluted, tampered with, a method to make money in this weary world rather than more Love.

After Thanksgiving break, I finished the fall quarter in good stead. I'd presented a request to my long-suffering parents. I petitioned to resume college at Colorado State University in Ft. Collins. Instate tuition fees were, of course, much less than out of state. Part of my petition pointed out I should move to Denver to facilitate residency.

I couldn't wait to get back to Coors Beer, LSD, and freedom. Those I'd met over Thanksgiving would be joined by more new acquaintances with ears that heard what mine did, becoming what I would later think of as the 'Denver Connection'.

Denver, Round Three - The Man

With predictable love and support, my parents sent me back to Denver in January 1967. While staying with the beauties, my other Parts at Temple Buell College, I looked for an apartment. Instead of crashing on the floor, I slept in a guest room provided for visitors. A mature step, plus a legal one so I didn't have to sneak around. Truth be known, college rules still scared me. Now I could take my time, searching for an apartment from the lap of luxury.

As usual, Mom and Daddy cheered me on, ready to hand out more tuition money in March. They footed the bills as I bided my time, waiting for Colorado State University's spring quarter to begin.

The girls and I kept meeting more 'kinfolk', friends of the boys that drove us to Aspen. We bonded with these new companions since they were also of the 'Parts' persuasion. We bounced back and forth between fraternity parties where we acted like lunatics, to hanging with serious mind–expanders, with whom we behaved like explorers. Intrigued by the phrase Turn on, tune in, drop out, we discovered Timothy Leary. He offered plenty of new information to study. He even wrote guide books resembling travel logs. 'How to' books for getting the most out of your trip. Handy!

I found my apartment in a high rise on Pearl Street. A truly insane human being rented it to me. More about him coming up.

The two and a half months I spent in Denver, revving up for my next go at college, was like riding out a cyclone. There were unending revelations spinning around, catching and messing with me before chucking me back into the turbulence. I found it stimulating, sometimes scary, but thrilling. Like a roller coaster.

Still about the music, we listened to songs that described us, instructed us, befriended us. Music created the backdrop of daily life. We were shepherded by the music.

The Exodus, a dark cubby hole of a club tugged like a magnet, pulling my kind in.

The place also acted like a magnet for the Denver police force. A Lieutenant Bosco and Detective Bozo (not their real names, but you know and they know who they are), crime fighters to the marrow, were an infamous duo obsessed by the new youth culture and the drugs we experimented with. These fellas headlined the newspapers, local news and talk shows.

The measure of commitment and attention the two poured out on us might've made me feel exceptional, except for one thing. Making a 'bust' was much more than a job to them. In the movies of their minds it was the main feature, playing nonstop. No doubt they saw themselves, hand in hand, accepting the Oscar for the world's most staggering bust of all time.

We entered the age of the 'narc'. Becoming part of our language, if anyone narc-ed on you, i.e. tattled on you, it was bad news. They deserved to be shamed for acting like an undercover cop.

There are an eye-opening number of words introduced in the 60s that found their way into Webster's Dictionary. Between 1963-1968 new slang words were introduced. You'll recognize lots of these throughout my story.

If not a narc, we knew our enemy as The Heat or The Man. Ever present, like god, he cruised Denver's city streets and made routine visits to La Petite Cafe, The Exodus and The Family Dog. Even Dunkin Donuts and MacDonald's hosted The Man who perpetually showed up without an invitation. Tacky.

On farm land beyond the city limits of Boulder, Colorado, news came of a party barn in an obscure location. You needed inside information, such as a detailed map. Lastly, you used the secret knock followed by, "Joe sent me." Get the picture?

Gary, Candy's boyfriend, had driven to Denver from Florida. Candy was excited and so were we, the rest of the Parts. Gary had a reputation for being an endearing madman. He proved it the night he and I zoomed to the barn party in his Triumph sports car. With Candy's blessings of course, since she couldn't join us.

Inside were three bands and a sizable barrel of punch containing LSD. Still first class stuff, straight from San Francisco. Upstairs in the loft, talented artists created a pulsating light show. Strobe lights did their thing while living colors with paisley amoeba shapes performed cartwheels around the walls and ceiling. It was all good.

Until.

I couldn't believe my eyes. And my LSD eyes were such that the entrance of Lieutenant Bosco and Detective Bozo brought to mind something reminiscent of a nuclear explosion. You can imagine.

HOW DID THEY FIND US???

LSD hadn't been made illegal. Bummer for them. However, possession of pot was a felony. The place cleared out like ants leaving a picnic after being sprayed with Raid. Because that is what it was, a raid. Me and Gary peeled out of there, his sports car fishtailing and reaching a hundred miles per hour in a jiffy.

The Man.

The group, Buffalo Springfield, wrote an anthem about him. They named it For What it's Worth: "What a field day for the heat. A thousand people in the street."

Like the song said, we lived in perpetual fear of stepping out of line, and having The Man come and take us away.

SAME TIME, SAME STATION - HEBREW

BACK TO THE landlord of my apartment building as promised. He may have been the model for describing a person as 'a piece of work'. I don't know, but he could have been the archetype.

Although I lived by myself, regular visitors, quiet and mellow...smiling and stoned, dreaming of Love, dropped by. One evening I sat home alone. Someone knocked on my door. The manager, landlord, whatever, stood in front of me with a furtive look on his face. I gotta say, he reminded me of a nervous ferret as he glanced to the right and left before asking to come in. He moved his head in quick jerks. I hadn't talked to him since I'd signed the month-to-month lease. He acted odd.

Sliding his lips over to one side so he could talk out of the corner of his mouth, he said, "Better tell your friend to call off his boys."

I thought, Hmmm, my goodness, something like that. I stared at this weird person standing in front of me, beady-eyed like said ferret. My head followed his head as it switched back and forth. It reminded me of a squirrel's tail. A two part animal! I got into it, like watching tennis. Too twitchy, though, not smooth enough. I had smoked a doobie which helped me find this kook amusing.

Shortly, I got the gist. My six-foot-five buddy, Spike, stopped by daily. This landlord lived in some made up La La Land, imagining that Spike was the Don of some underworld mob scene. There's more. This fancied gang of mobsters was hot on the ferret's trail. I listened, mouth open, nodding along to his paranoia-inspired story. He took this as confirmation I understood his problem, because he started nodding, too. We stood there nodding at each other in unison. I kept right on doing the nod dance, afraid to stop, afraid to break the spell. Nodding felt safe and comfortable. What might he do instead?

He stopped first and winked at me like a confidant, a new best friend. It appalled me, but what could I do? He backed away, winking one eye and then the other in time with each step. He executed a spasmodic turn to leave, then looked back over his shoulder with important intel.

"Hebrew. Hebrew...that's me."

Now, I knew from signing the rent papers the idiot's name was Ted. Plain Ted. Not Hebrew. Gawwd!

"Mention my name anytime, to anyone, and they'll take care of you. Now please, just tell your friend to call off his boys."

Huh? His boys? Give me a break.

Then, after giving me a knowing look, he left.

I still didn't know how really 'special' Ted was.

Until next time, when he knocked on the door, inviting me to his apartment for dinner.

"No, I have plans. Had 'em for ages, sorry."

"You don't understand!" He jumped up and down clapping his little paws. "It's salad! Salad on my wife. We eat the salad off my wife. It's a wonderful thing. She lays on the floor, see, and..."

Ooooooh boy, I pretty much slammed the door, careful to squeeze in a, "No, thank you." Hebrew: one person I did not want mad at me.

More outings...an attractive plan. I began spending less time at home. The guest room at Temple Buell suited me fine.

I mentioned attending fraternity parties with the beauties, the Parts. We crashed those functions when in a group mood to get drunk. No moderation for us. Not one of us had yet learned the art of enjoying a cocktail or glass of wine as an aperitif. I wondered why anyone in their right mind would want to ruin a promising alcohol buzz with food? That seemed counterproductive.

Did I say 'crashing' a fraternity party? Oops. Wrong word. Sounds as though we weren't wanted. No, no, not the case. Tailing the beauties into a room guaranteed me the best view of the crowd. Heads turned. Boys drooled; I was embarrassed for them. One night, we swigged booze like thirsty fishies who'd been beached and dried up. Leaving the party I fell down flagstone steps. Being young, I wouldn't have had a problem except I refused to let go of the two bottles of Seagram's 7 in each hand so I could break my fall. My bottom hit a corner step hard enough I heard my tailbone crack. By the time we got to the apartment, I couldn't walk. There was no elevator, except for the one in Ted's mind. Where Spike and his boys lurked. The beauties put me upstairs using a makeshift, not-too-sturdy-fireman's-hold, and called an ambulance.

Still plastered, I somehow remember being shipped back down the stairs in a stretcher. Nothing to be done for broken tailbones. After twenty-four hours, the ambulance staff reinstated me in my apartment.

You can bet Hebrew showed up in minutes with me stuck on the couch.

"Suzee, Suzee, last night you missed it, you missed the fulfillment of everything they prophesied. My wife and I were going to tell you, we decided you were worthy, but then you didn't come home." He wrung his hands, flustered. "Darn it, I wish my wife would get here." I remained silent. If only I could move.

"Oh shoot, they landed, Suzee! They landed on the roof of our building in the middle of the night and told us to get ready. Next year on Groundhog's Day the ship will return. Well, they didn't know it was Groundhog's Day, but my wife looked on the calendar after they left, and it's that very day! Isn't it ironic? Can you believe it?"

"Uh, wow, uh, no." Helllllllp.

"We're preparing to go with them, but they said to act normal in the meantime. You know, go about business as usual. You're gonna flip out when I tell you the whole plan. My wife should be here. Where IS she? Sometimes I forget important stuff."

You're familiar with the expression, a life or death situation? Considering present company, the thought remained poised, too close for comfort. "Hebrew, I can't keep my eyes open. I guess you noticed the ambulance, and in case you were wondering, I broke my tail bone and shouldn't try walking for a few days. The muscle relaxers and pain killers are making me so sleepy, I can't follow you very well. Can you give me some time to get better? You know, before you and your wife come over?"

"Oh, yeah, yeah, sure. You can't tell anyone, though. Wait'll we tell you the rest. You'll see. It's meant to be!" He hopped out the door. On both feet. I'm not kidding.

I arranged to vacate. Without delay. The truth is, Ted, weird and funny and all, made me sad. I felt sorry for the guy. Wished our Love could make him well.

Moving day came and it was speedy. Hebrew managed one last meeting. I kept my door open because friends were helping carry bags since I still couldn't walk well. Hebrew came stumbling down the hall. This time he held his head in both hands. "Suzee! I knew this was gonna happen. One of the tall cat's boys mugged me in the elevator. You tell him, you warn him, Hebrew has no choice but to have him rubbed out. I'm sorry it's come to this..."

As I made my getaway, I heard him whispering about some gazillion dollar drug deal coming down. They had plenty of time before Groundhog's Day. For a split second I wondered if 'they' used money where 'they' came from. I shook my head hard, like a dog after a bath. I was leaving just in time.

Ted kept sputtering. I could get in on the action if I wanted. Hebrew would arrange it.

POST HEBREW
STRESS SYNDROME

A BIG HOUSE on Downing Street in Denver was my next stop after deserting Hebrew/Ted and his banquet table of a wife.

Remember Gary of the LSD barn party?

Gary. He and Candy were very much in love which is what'd brought him to Colorado in the first place. He and I were very much instant best friends and I invited him to stay at Downing Street, too.

Gary had a friend, Alan, who'd made the drive with him. Some should not experiment beyond an aspirin dissolved in Coca-Cola. Anything more mind-bending will turn them into casualties like what happened to Alan from Florida. Just smoking part of a joint sent him to an edge where he teetered.

Then the curtain would lift on the following performance. You could count on it.

First, shiny beads of perspiration debuted on his forehead. Next a queasy grin, entering stage left or right, made a strange presentation across his lower face. The show stopper followed. Tying a noose around his neck, fashioned from whatever he picked up; a dog leash, a drape, a table cloth, baling twine. Grinning the awful grin, Alan traveled from room to room or sat in a lotus position, a silent production of himself, sweating and grinning.

In Alan's best interests, Gary bought him a bus ticket back to Florida. We heard he regained his balance, even stopped drinking Coors. This was a good thing.

Gary and I had no trouble entertaining ourselves with rash behavior during January of 1967. I think I'd be safe to blame my conduct on Post Hebrew Stress Syndrome. Regressing to age fifteen, we acted in an excessive, unguarded, and irresponsible manner. Ramping up Gary's Triumph, we hooted and hollered, carousing like rock stars. The car, an enabler, was like a friend who'd do anything to gain our affection, offering to accommodate our uninhibited conduct. That turquoise baby took mere seconds to reach warp speed.

We were responding to more than the call that reaches the ears of your common variety youth who think they're immortal and go wild, acting out dangerous teenage foolishness. We were chasing answers that our survival depended upon. But we couldn't have verbalized that.

Candy approved us to move into an apartment together and managed quite a few overnight sign outs (like the 'Get out of jail free cards' coveted in the game, Monopoly) from the dorm. Otherwise she remained cooped up there. Our apartment stay didn't last long. Neither did the apartment.

One night Gary and I were lounging in our pajamas on the moth eaten couch, smoking some pot while we waited for the acid we'd dropped to come on. Our ears perked up at the same time, catching the distant sound of sirens. Checking with each other to make sure they weren't drug-induced sirens, we pressed our faces against the window, scoping out the street below. Just as the LSD achieved lift off, fire trucks pulled up to our building. A chain of firemen ran inside the front doors, wielding a hose that grew longer and longer. Of course, they needed a long hose, a requirement even, but it looked otherworldly long to us. "The Never Ending Hose!" Gary said.

"Great name for a band," said I.

We were enjoying the drama until the Denver fire department broke in. Water shot out of what looked more and more like a sensuous mouth at the end of that unnaturally long hose. Upstairs, they fought a fire that incinerated the top half of our premises. We hadn't noticed.

The building burnt to the ground.

With us on the street. In our P.J.s.

DOWNING STREET AND MY KARASS

As Jackie Gleason would say on his TV show, "And awaaaaaay we go."

Like kick off in a football game, like getting the show on the road, or getting down to business; if my story about the Time-Of-All-Times was some type of ball, I'd say, "Let's get this ball rolling."

All the words I've been slapping down have been in preparation for a time in history difficult to believe.

P.S. It's easier to believe in the Tooth Fairy.

The meaning of that elusive 'it' is about to be decrypted. The book you are holding is your personal decoder ring.

First I gotta say, I feel like that little kid at the top of the high dive. Doing justice to this part of the story intimidates me like jumping off the end of the diving board for the first time. Can I do it?

We returned to the house on Downing Street. This move affected each of my choices ever after. I began making U-turns and 'spinning donuts' on the road of my life, finally boarding a tilt-a-whirl car that jumped the tracks. No barriers in sight.

The house was a big Victorian that accommodated twenty-five to thirty bodies. Those guided to the house were in the first bloom of such Love-hope.

I took a break from worrying about the world to become infatuated with John-John. Meeting John-John was like stopping at a railroad crossing and sitting there watching box cars whiz by. The train slows to a stop and out of a car jumps this cutie-pie. When I met John-John I found him connected to a long freight train of people. Every one of them members of my clan.

Gwenn, Morgan, Phillip, Eileen, Hank, Patrick, Pudge, The Kahn, Kurt, Randy, Gene, Tony, Spike, Jiminy Cricket, Chuckles, Mitchie Woo Woo, Jerry Miller, the babes from Temple Buell and many more...a very long train.

The talk of the town centered on music coming out of The Bay Area. Bay Area? What Bay? Huh? Little known to Midwestern me, this music had been around awhile. I'd been unaware. Until now. Sweeping not just the home of the brave and the land of the free, but the world.

The music offered a nub of thread. When tugged, this would begin to unravel the mystery of 'it'. Think of those feed sacks with that tricky piece of string at the top. It has to be pulled just right. Then lo and behold! All inside is revealed, there for the taking.

Made me wonder if now, with more music to feed them, maybe my parents could 'grok' the meaning of what was coming down. Their inability to comprehend still stuck in my throat, which is anatomically close to my heart where they lived.

Grok is a word coined by Robert Heinlein in his book Stranger in a Strange Land. It means to intuitively understand something.

Interesting when that girl from my hometown, Joanie, showed up at the house on Downing Street. She now went to college in Greeley, Colorado. Remember, we'd been girls-in-love-with-horses. I told you about riding our horses to town and sneaking out all night to hike to the riding stables in our uniforms consisting of flannel shirts and blue jeans. We revered flannel shirts and here I'd gone and forgotten to tell you about them. Anyway, our destinies were laced like a pair of Roper cowboy boots.

I've noticed certain relationships in life hold on to one another without my knowledge. One day, a person long gone, Joanie for instance, appears out of nowhere linking up for a moment or longer and then goes missing again. It's a safe bet they'll reappear later. Are specific people's lives somehow plaited into a pattern?

Aha, it may be what Vonnegut's character, Bokonon, refers to as a 'karass'. A karass is a group of people who, often unknowingly, are working together to do god's will. My clan was a karass.

Love for John–John spread out to include the whole train. It wasn't romantic, it was bigger. We moved as a single unit around Denver. We had slumber
parties. I remember stretching out next to my friends one night, stoned on
acid. Mesmerized, our brains in synch, we hallucinated a stampeding monster
herd of giggles thunder across the plains above our heads.

Our allegiance grew as did our family. The word got out about our open
door, open arms, crash pad.

One day I came home to Downing Street to find an amazing bus parked
in front of the house. The psychedelic paint job made it incredible. Not Ken
Kesey and the Merry Pranksters touring in their bus named Further, but
another band of Flower Children in motion.

Of significant importance to me, they hailed from the intriguing city
being mentioned more and more. San Francisco.

Every morning I awoke with a feeling of well-being that fixed a smile on
my face the second my eyes opened. My gentle clan flanked me, curled up in
sleeping bags on floors and couches, mattresses and beds.

Eager to live out each new day as impulsively as each moment might require,
our behavior often appeared reckless to those who didn't understand.

We were scouting the world together for unconditional love.

I had known that kind of love.

But, dear god, all families weren't like mine. This much–loved–only–child's
eyes opened wide in disbelief when she discovered the scarcity of unconditional
love. The realization became the capstone, the piece I didn't even know was
missing. After all my questions, all my experimenting, searching, and following
my heart, the answer crystallized in my mind's eye. Pure and simple.

Love.

Not emotional.

Not erotic.

Selfless.

Love.

As a little girl I memorized the saying, "Do unto others as you would have
others do unto you." Heavy! Could it be that simple?

It struck me. The good old Golden Rule, reverberating through eons.
Where had I been?

And the verse about sowing what you reap, implying the more I Loved others, the more Love would come back to me. If everyone did that, Love would, indeed, make the world go round. The Beatles sang: "And in the end, the Love you make is equal to the Love you take."

I felt like Elmer Fudd. Out hunting wabbits while Love had been stalking me. Shhh, Love whispered. I am hunting Suzee!

One day, feeling off balance and in the dark, I wandered around in a Denver park trying to fit all these puzzle pieces together. That's when baby beginnings of comprehension walloped me up side the head. Where had I been? I gasped. On my way here! To this eye-opener!

My purpose began to take shape in my mind. I was born to Love, to Love everyone because we are one. Related.

Yanking my head out of the sand, I made myself see people made of flesh and blood like me undergoing unspeakable damage, impossible agony. I'd stepped on a mental land mine.

I ran back to Downing Street and grabbed the first person I saw. I needed a hug. A big one.

I couldn't cope with this raw view of universal suffering alone. Calamity of such across-the-board proportion triggered panic in me.

We stood in the hall for a minute holding each other and then went to the large bare living room to sit on the floor and talk it out. Weren't all people brothers and sisters in the same trench, fighting an invisible war in the battle against Hate? Lies? Fear?

How had I missed it? The fact was, we'd been tricked into believing we should fight against other human beings. Brutal damage squared.

The more my friend and I talked, the clearer the truth rang. Others came, one or two at a time, and joined us on the floor.

No one in this vast family of humanity asked to be sick. Who would? But we were. We were infected with Terminal Misunderstanding.

The human race was barking up the wrong tree!

Would Love Be Enough To Fix The Catastrophe?

San Francisco...The Bay Area. Now I understood, they were the same place.

The road between San Francisco and Denver became the road more, not less, traveled. 'Missionaries' were arriving from Haight–Ashbury to the Downing Street house everyday. I thought of them as missionaries since they reminded me of those folks who go to far off places to help people understand god. After listening to these Flower Children on their mission of Love from Haight–Ashbury, converts, like homing pigeons, followed them back. We sensed this Haight–Ashbury district of San Francisco was our home, too.

We started referring to each other as 'brothers' or 'sisters'. Other names for us were popping up, 'heads', 'freaks', 'Flower Children', 'hippies'.

For those with inquiring minds, Haight–Ashbury is named for the intersection of Haight and Ashbury streets. Called The Haight for short, the district borders the east side of Golden Gate Park.

I sat at the feet of these missionary/evangelists from Haight–Ashbury captivated by Love, enthralled by their tales. Tales of peace and hope spilling over some unseen celestial dam to be experienced for real, here and now. Before long wouldn't the dam have to burst? Then, at long last, heaven on earth. This is what we hoped, waited and lived for.

An Amazon of a girl tramped into the house one day, also from The Haight. A big mama with moxie, she netted me right away, snaring my mind to fill it with tales of Golden Gate Park. She called it Middle Earth. Everyone read Tolkien, falling under his spell. Hobbits, enchanted fellowships of wizards, battles, dragons...The Ring. How could I not go there? Summer college break?

As blissed as I felt, I couldn't ignore the fact that in a few weeks spring quarter would begin at my next new college. This pesky knowledge flew around my head, bombing my ears, interfering with my sublime state. A professional house fly, with a Ph.D in Unswattability.

Expanding on the image, it occurred to me if a fly could get a degree, maybe somehow I could, too?

Two young men fated to profoundly affect me tumbled into my life. Crazy and his 'brother', Robert. From Haight Street, naturally. Like gypsies, tambourines in hand, they came romping unabashedly into my heart of hearts. Glamour (genuine, irresistible magic) dripped off of them, making an ample puddle of make-believe to goof around in, to dream in.

They wore colored beads around their necks. Bells tied to rawhide strings hung from wrists and ankles. One had on a cape, the other wore a hat with a feather. Braided yarn belts, a single home-stitched leather bag dangling from the side, kept their pants on. The bags held collected treasures, mojo booty. Most who came from San Francisco owned such pouches filled with prizes meaningful to their lives, particular to each child belonging to those glory days.

Our in-house, zealous, big mama enchantress asked if she could do some embroidering on Crazy's and Robert's pants. Embroidery was a big deal and these two were into more adornment, for sure.

Jeans weren't the ticket. Guys wore cotton bell-bottoms out of striped, paisley print, or Indian tapestry material. Girls were into hiphuggers, harem pants, granny dresses, short denim skirts and falling-off-the-shoulder peasant blouses among other things. Bright colors, definitely. Flamboyance.

For feet, sandals or barefoot worked. Headbands, patches all over clothes, more beads. Birth of a new word for clothes. FUNKY!

Pea coats were good. So were leather jackets and fringe.

Fringe, like beads, did not follow the principle of "less is more." No way. Love, glitter, twinkle lights, beads, fringe, lightening bugs, fireworks, things impossible to overdo.

Finally, most sovereign of San Francisco garb: Tie dye.

In the matter of a few hours I'd been diverted headlong from gentle John–John into the mad and dashing wake of this 'crazy' Crazy. He was a Pisces with a mischievous glint in his eyes, a sack full of yarns and a boyish grin like you've never seen (an exception may be Hugh Grant's). Ramfoozled, I fell in love. Craze was already in love, a lady cast her spell over him. Her name? San Francisco. He had to go back, but it was a given we'd see each other later.

Mom and Daddy were driving from Illinois to install me in yet another dorm (gulp) at one more University. Colorado State in Ft. Collins. The timing couldn't have been worse.

A Prayer Flop

My parents retrieved me from the house on Downing Street. I watched Daddy's curiosity and perceptiveness come to the fore, without being judgmental, of course. He interviewed everyone he met with a gleam in his eye and persistence. Thoroughly.

He wanted nothing more than to understand, gain insight into my life due to his Daddy-love for me. And I loved him with little-girl-love that'd never quit.

The problem lay in the separation of our minds. Not our hearts or our deep relationship. As I've explained before, I failed to communicate The Dream and it tore me up. With all he had, Daddy tried to mentally enter my world by my side, but he couldn't break through. My dad remains the most heroic and gallant man I ever knew. It still tears me apart to think of leaving him behind. Damn.

We spent the night in a fancy Denver motel, The Cherry Creek Inn, and next day they took me to another college, another dormitory. In Fort Collins, we went to dinner and to see Dr. Zhivago. Getting an early start the following morning, mirroring anxious optimism in one another's eyes, we waved goodbye as they drove away. Seeing their attempt at a positive attitude helped me almost believe I could pull this off. They were always in my corner.

Aware of unsalvageable pain and disappointment I'd cause if I bailed another time, I restarted my education at University Number Three. There was a sole acceptable reason to take this leap. Honest desire.

Not.

Ignoring my severe lack of motivation, I vowed to do this thing for them. I thought I could. After all, I was taking horseback riding for P.E. which inspired me, and is one of the few things I remember besides picking up an issue of a magazine a few weeks later.

When I looked at the cover, every nerve in my body switched on. An ineffable, groundbreaking 'something' was going on in San Francisco. My Siren snapped to, creating pandemonium in my brain followed by a yell, "Red alert, red alert. Authorization to move out." At that moment I knew I'd go AWOL from college again.

The magazine had done a spread on Haight–Ashbury, with pictures.

I read it. I studied the pictures, more attentive to them than any college class ever. I reread the article and laid it down on a desk. I fought to overcome the push compelling me to leave this new school. My emotions were out of control, what was happening in Haight–Ashbury won the fight.

Feeling the urge to pray, I gave it a go. I didn't know how so I started by folding my hands in front of me. I made the church with the steeple and opened the doors to see all the people, but I didn't know what to say. I was a prayer flop.

I felt as bad as a person could feel. I wanted to fix my college track record, make Mom and Daddy happy and proud, but I HAD TO GO TO HAIGHT–ASHBURY. Out of my hands, no stalling allowed...that Siren of mine was a tough cookie. What I want to be certain that you truly understand and even try to believe, as irrational as it sounds, is this: I did not have a choice.

After looking at the pictures again, I cried. Then I picked up my room phone and called my parents collect. And they cried, too.

HAIGHT–ASHBURY

THIS IS THE start of the Time–Of–All–Times, i.e. 'it', i.e. The Dream. The nitty gritty.

If I were to divide my life into halves, initials for the first half would be B.H.A. The other, A.H.A. Before Haight–Ashbury. After Haight–Ashbury. Because the most important moment of my life couldn't have occurred had I not gone to the Haight.

Writing about Haight–Ashbury is a daunting task since it's been a popular topic. However, a French movie director named Robert Bresson said, "Make visible, what without you, might never have been seen." I'll stand on that and show you the unique time through my eyes.

My Denver friend, Kurt, was a beautiful person. 'Beautiful', a front runner word in our evolving new language, was used by my tribe to describe a person, a day, an occasion. "Have a beautiful day!" Better yet, "Have a beautiful Sunday!" Sunday spent in Golden Gate Park was a transcendental happening. I'm coming to that.

To begin with, I had to get on a plane with Kurt in late March 1967. He'd bought my one way ticket on a United Airlines jet nonstop to San Francisco. It may as well have been a magic carpet. I know I had stars in my eyes, eyes Kurt knew needed to see Haight–Ashbury.

From the airport we caught a bus to Haight Street, disembarking on the corner of Ashbury. I looked up from watching my feet step off the bus. I'd been translated. My first view into another world resulted in an uncanny sense of homecoming. Goosebumps glided around my skin like fairies on point.

Altogether straight (i.e. not stoned) I opened my mouth, but couldn't speak.

I stood still, gaping at the scene passing in front of me. I saw what looked like thousands of individuals milling about. I stared down city blocks until the people became too small and faded into the distance.

Tranquility coursed through the air like a suspended stream of lavender water.

It was like I'd passed through glass, without leaving any hole, into the luminous atmosphere of a jumbo crystal globe.

First thing I remember? Lots and lots and lots of flowers and peace signs painted on street signs, windows and faces. Next a phantasmagoria of color and intoxicating smells of incense partnered with my senses. Next came kisses, hugs, smiles and Love vibes from strangers.

First impressions? Everyone wore their passion, their fondest fantasy. They'd gone the distance, not a shabby invention in any direction. A super abundance of velvet, the material of choice.

I watched wizards, Indian princesses, pied pipers, tarot cards laid out on the sidewalk, wood nymphs, jesters, pirates, gypsies, elves, many sprites, palm readers, people sitting on blankets throwing the I Ching, troubadours, jugglers, angels, dwarves, caped gentlemen and ladies from another century wearing laced dresses and ribbons, white witches with nice faces resembling Glinda the Good, medieval country wenches, fortune tellers with crystal balls, clowns, fairies with wands, hobbits. Endless pipe dreams personified.

The globe covered a space permeated with Love and peace. Leaving any of the neighboring districts, crossing into The Haight, you felt a transformation. The air changed. What was going on? Jefferson Airplane summed up this inexplicable phenomenon in their song White Rabbit. Gracie Slick belted it out, "Go ask Alice, I think she'll know."

Haight-Ashbury, a colony all its own, formed a small but strong nation. I found myself under a white hot spell of elation, shared by a fine collection of cosmic, trusting newborns.

Standing on the corner of Haight and Ashbury, I realized people were migrating in the same direction. "Hey, Kurt," hailed a few passers by, "you coming down to The Panhandle? Happy Sunday, man. Janis is singin'!"

Janis belonged to a band named Big Brother and The Holding Company. My friend took my arm, to stop me from turning in circles. He led me down the street to that part of Golden Gate Park known as The Panhandle.

We entered the outskirts of a crowd staring up at the flat bed of a long truck. Looking for where the noise came from, I picked out a whirring generator next to the truck. As we walked closer, I turned my head to see what was on the improvised stage.

Under no circumstances will I forget my first look at Janis Joplin. She stood there in back of a microphone, a funky grand lady, small, but commanding. She wore a short scruffy blue jeans skirt with a peasant blouse hanging off one shoulder. Scores of bracelets encircled her wrists and arms, scores more necklaces around her neck. Her mop of hair had a life of its own. Long, frizzy, untethered, it moved and shook around her broad face. This mane was on a leave of absence from standard hair care.

Freedom drenched her persona. Freedom from what? From tired norms. From lies. From fear. From despair. Freedom from hate. Freed to find individuality, where truth, faith, hope, and Love stood a chance.

Grinning and jiving with the company, this outlandish Raggedy Ann became my new groundbreaking off-the-wall hero of girldom.

Love saturated the soft candied air in the globe. The congregation breathed it in and blew it into the open when Janis hit her first note. Somehow she gathered that Love and sang it out to us in a way that changed lives.

Janis, charitable to a fault, held nothing of herself back, saved nothing for some future rainy day.

I said Janis Joplin changed lives. Her willingness to give till she collapsed added new meaning to the concept of selfless generosity.

Of course I'd been exposed to selfless generosity in reading true stories and hearing about saints on earth like Mother Teresa and in the Bible. My mom and dad were my supreme examples in this world.

But Janis was visceral and in my face.

I stood in front of a living extreme, a real person in front of my eyes. I'd never seen anything like this before. Nothing even close. ACCESSIBLE, she let us enter her soul, as she reached into ours. Turning herself inside out, raw and vulnerable along with graciousness, she returned our overwhelming Love.

FAMILY

WHEN BIG BROTHER And The Holding Company finished their set, another band climbed onto the flatbed truck. While they changed places, I leaned into Kurt to keep my balance. As he'd known she would, Janis bowled me over. She knocked me, rocked me, and socked it to me. My body remained standing on grassy ground. The rest of me had been beamed up. From someplace beyond the beyond I watched these 'Flower Children', as we'd been christened by the media. I knew then, I'd found a bigger family than I'd imagined existed.

Ever since the Time-Of-All-Times, I've been asked to contrast Flower Children and hippies. I noticed a ginormous difference which stunned me like a blast from Captain Kirk's phaser.

Viewed through my eyes, Flower Children were looking for god, spirituality. Hippies showed up later, liked what they saw and stayed. I watched them climb aboard to come along for the ride. Seeming lost, they raised the slogan 'Drugs, Sex and Rock n' Roll' more than a few bars. I did not voice my opinion. Hippies showed less inventiveness in dress and less dedication to the 'movement', yet many showed genuine respect for nature and in time headed for granola-ism.

Stepping on toes, I know, but here's my impression in one sentence, and granted, it's a generalization. Flower Children tended to become believers. Hippies leaned toward becoming yuppies often with a material focus. Drugged by the world and its skewed priorities.

Somewhere along the way I'd tagged myself 'Miss No One Nowhere' of Planet Earth. Now, in a pod of 'No One Nowheres', I found more live jewels summoned from the dark lands. These jewels, faceted with Love, shone like a light show on my heart.

Cradled by my new family, feeling dreamy, I swayed next to Kurt. What happened next snatched me back from beyond the beyond.

Two people I knew walked up to me. "Oh wow! Wow, wow, wow! Gary? Melliny? Hiiiiiiiiiiiiii!" I put my arms around them, touched and kissed their faces.

Yep, the Gary I told you about with bright orange hair. That same Gary from Iowa City who'd tripped the trigger of change in me, landing me where I now stood. Because of Gary, recognizable in 1965 as a non-robot, I'd been able to let go of who I'd been, to see who I could become.

"So how long've you been here? Where are you staying? I can't believe it!" I said.

"Suzee Creamcheese, far out! Figured you make it. We're living down on Divisadero Street," Gary said. "What about you? Hey Kurt, you guys know each other? Too much, man."

We sat down, and gave credence to our unspoken knowledge. Destiny had plans for the likes of us.

Coincidence? No way. We'd heard, and with blind faith, answered the call.

In celebration of this mysterious gift, we passed a doobie, cuddling one another with affection from our smiling eyes.

Angels watched over us.

"Are you hungry? 'Cause The Diggers just got here," Kurt said.

I came to find out The Diggers were Haight-Ashbury's own Goodwill Store/Salvation Army. They gave away clothes and meals for free. No end of amazements, and I'd been there a mere three or four hours.

Meanwhile, the next band took the stage and played for their extended family in Haight-Ashbury. Benevolent invisible hands in the ether signed our adoption papers.

HOME SWEET HOME

WHEN THE MUSIC ended, Kurt guided me away from the park, across Haight Street and up the hill. Love blew like a tempest raining four-leaf clovers on our heads and made it necessary for Kurt, my tether to this earth, to catch hold of my arm. It wouldn't have done to have lost me on my first day there.

He escorted me to a place where I could stay. A starter home! On up the hill we trucked until we made a right turn, and another, leading to an entryway. He knocked, and Cathi answered. She had a wide smile and a head of gorgeous dark hair. Cathi welcomed us, inviting me without hesitation to stay with her and the two girls she lived with. It seemed Kurt knew everyone in Haight-Ashbury.

Cathi and I became close friends and planned to find a place of our own. The following week, Spike and Gary from Denver showed up in our living room with Kurt, of course. Seeing them again warmed my heart. We hugged fast and hard.

I needed to find Crazy, who I'd met on Downing Street in Denver. Kurt suggested a place to check out. I found the address on Alma Street and knocked on the door. Adroit in his wheelchair, a black brother named Gypsy answered. Once inside the flat I was stunned when he jumped from the chair to lead me down the hall. I guessed he had a thing for grooving around in a wheelchair. We walked into a room cluttered with magazines, posters of bands, hookahs and bowls of beads on third hand tables.

As I asked Gypsy about Crazy, Robert arrived. Robert who'd come with Crazy to Denver. He told me Crazy, busted for pot in Los Angeles, had been put in jail. Bummer.

Crazy, the most playful boy I'd ever met, had nabbed my eager heart. Now he'd been nabbed in L.A. Not fair. He was one of the motivating forces behind making my break, following my heart. Because he personified Haight-Ashbury. Here I was in his city of Love and he wasn't.

Then the strangest thing happened. With no reservations I fell in love with Robert. He seemed like a lost puppy to me. We hung out for a few days before he told me it wasn't a good idea for me to be with him. Huh? He didn't get into details, but tried persuading me to go back to where I'd been staying with Cathi. I didn't wanna. He won.

We got stoned and said good-bye. Again, I didn't wanna. I thought he needed me to watch over him. I walked away, obedient for once in my life, and Robert walked away in the opposite direction. I did cheat, turning around to watch him go and I cried tubby, non-crocodile tears.

On my way back to Cathi's I became lost. I think it had something to do with being stoned. Intensely interested in the act of walking, I watched my funny feet. Looking up at times to say hi to people passing by, I noticed it'd gotten late. Where's Kurt when I need him?

I turned the next corner and ran straight into Robert, physically. Enjoying my feet so much meant I didn't pay attention to where I walked. He'd been doing some first-rate wandering himself. We stared at each other and started laughing, recognizing that this was a sign. We decided the situation was bigger than both of us and gave up trying to split up. We were meant to be, no bolts of uncertainty flashed in the air between us. All that flashed was that thrill of intense desire. It starts out physical and bores inward like a hot poker until your searching eyes sear deep through every layer. We were left standing there lost and obliterated by longing.

I asked him along to Cathi's for the night, assuming I could ever find the place.

I did. It was the first of many nights spent together since Cathi, Robert and I rented a flat up a long flight of steps on Hayes Street. Our new home, a few blocks away after crossing the Panhandle of Golden Gate Park, had two bedrooms, a kitchen and bathroom.

Merrianne, aka Merry Poppins arrived by angel-express. Cathi worked at the telephone company with her. Still Ma Bell, and a skyscraper, it stood like a big shot near Market Street. To this day I remain amazed Cathi held a job. I knew her to get on the trolley even after all-nighters filled with derring-do (it can't be coincidence, derring-do is also called Flower Flange, having more to do with flowers than anything else).

Merry Poppins, what a girl. I knew no one straighter and gigglier than Merrianne. The first time she came to visit, she caught us moving in.

Moving in is not exactly the right word since two of three had nothing to move. Cathi, on the other hand, qualified us since she had some moveable objects like a record player, albums, and a pile of groovy clothes.

Merry Poppins took us under her 'happy umbrella' and began furnishing our flat out of the goodness of her heart, bringing over the occasional odd kitchen tool or old metal porch chair. She liked hanging out with us. It didn't make sense then and never has.

Unconcerned by our extraterrestrial ways, she joined the club, meaning she fit in to the whole scene, the full Monty of the 'movement'. She became a most unexpected part of both families, the little one under our roof and the one swiftly growing in Haight-Ashbury.

Did I mention my parents sent me twenty-five dollars a month? Added to Cathi's paycheck and Merry Poppins' charitable contributions, we paid the rent, utilities, and ate food.

Finally settled, Robert, Cathi and I had a place from which to go out and come in. I began my expeditions and learned my way around.

FLOWERS

FLOWERS BECAME OUR symbol for universal Love. They were a big deal. Flower Children used them like badges to decorate themselves and gave them to everyone in sight. In the song, If You're Going To San Francisco, written by John Phillips, Scott McKenzie sang these words in April 1967:

"If you're going to San Francisco, be sure to wear some flowers in your hair.

If you come to San Francisco, summertime will be a Love–in there."

In a flash the song went worldwide. It bumped up the volume and acute urgency of the call. As fast as possible, Flower Children traveled to San Francisco from around the globe.

A dandelion's flower head changes into the familiar, white, globular seed head overnight. Fitting. Each seed has a tiny parachute, to spread its progeny far and wide in the wind.

San Francisco, a one of a kind lady, opened her arms wide because she, too, felt the call. Considering it her own destiny, like a mother she yearned to nurture these devotees whose hearts held seeds of Love. When San Francisco whispered her welcome, the seeds, like those on our dandelion, flew free into the air.

Landing, they rooted in the soil she'd prepared with care. After blooming, they loosed a fragrance so pure and sweet it caused a reshaping of the world. Thousands who caught a whiff dropped everything and made a bee–line for

San Francisco. Her Love-garden blossomed for an intense yet so brief a time it was heartbreaking.

Those who heard, but didn't come, created little Haight-Ashburys in the towns and cities where they lived. If each of these small communities was a dot and you drew a line to connect them, you'd see a crazy quilt road encircling the planet.

We knew about each other through the Love grapevine established by hitchhikers who made the rounds. Flower Children recognized one another and went out of their way to pick up and deliver a brother or sister. Pilgrims made the holy expedition to San Francisco, the city of Love, to pay homage. Content to return home, spreading Love on the journey, they dropped flowers along their way. A Trail.

In weeks to come, I sat for hours at a time in Golden Gate Park, my station where I made daisy chain after daisy chain from tiny daisies crowding next to each other in the grass like they couldn't get close enough. Could be they only grew that profusely for the spring and summer of 1967 to commemorate the Time-Of-All-Times.

I wore flower circlets around my head and gave them away to those mortals brave enough to venture off tourist buses that came by the droves.

That summer, tourists, policemen, Hell's Angels, and reporters consented to wear my flower offerings. The Trail grew longer.

TIE DYE

TIE DYE, COLORFUL patterns loose and free like us. We wore it with pride and became flags of tie dye on the move.

Tie dye

Ancient art

A Flower Child's I.D.

Lucy in the sky

Kaleidoscope eyes

Festive fashion

Liquid light show

Bursting impressions

Impact

Colors performing

Playing

Dancing

Grooving on the screen behind the band

Overhead projectors spread finger-painted goodies

Touched with motion and rhythm

Impassioned jubilee

Tie dye

Spreadable

Daze and dash

Splats

Amoebas on an outing

Rings around the sun

Voyaging orbs

Water–air

Moonlight mirrors

Fist eye–rubs

See inside there

Tie dye

Oily bubbles

Reshaping to the beat of the music

Intoxicating

Mesmerizing

Pizzazz on display

Aurora Borealis

Moving, moving, moving

Like us

Can we wear it?

YES

And we did

Tie dye!

What else this spice?

Where else this oomph?

This gloppy glory?

You name it

We tie dyed it

Hats

Shirts

Skirts

Gloves

Scarves

Headbands

Baby blankets

VW buses

Skin

And wallpaper
Tie dye's favorite cousin?
Paisley
Tie dye
The stuff dreams are made of
And still are
Check it out
Look around
There's a reason.

BEADS

YEAH, LOVE BEADS. Hours at a time, cross-legged on the floor, we strung them into necklaces. More handmade presents, like the daisy chains, to give away.

Handing out beads, another symbolic act of giving Love away. For free.

Beads were everywhere. Good-natured glinty eye-catchers.

Shops on Haight Street sold beads cheap or let us barter for them. I had a knack for embroidering on patches for jeans and jackets. Carrots were one of my favorite creations using the satin stitch. The running stitch worked the nicest for creating green carrot tops. I traded patches for beads.

All sizes. Big as marbles to miniature, bead drops winked with playful purpose.

I thread them on nylon fishing wire, higgledy-piggledy, no design in mind. They looked happy to be out of order. Like me.

Colored beads bopped out of my box, vying to be next.

There were shiny beads, octagonal beads, oblong, and pearly. Every kind. My favorite was a light-catching, round, inky-purple/green/indigo bead. A dark version of abalone shell.

Someone reading this is nodding his or her head with fond enthusiasm, recalling this certain bead.

We learned how to make beaded headbands, wide bracelets, curtains, little bags and the like.

Beads were good.

Beads were fun.

Beads put giant smiles on faces.

Most favored is still the single strand mix of different colors and kinds. Long enough to slip over my head.

Flowers, Tie dye, Beads: these were the distinct manifestations of Love we chose. With care. Sure, these things were pleasing in themselves, colorful, happy evidence of life inside the magic kingdom. But they meant worlds more. They were offerings, carried or worn to give away. They represented the Love, The Dream. Flowers and beads in particular because most people, if too shy to let us do it, put them around their necks or in their hair themselves. To us, they were putting on Love. The new kind.

THE DREAM

TAPED TO WINDOWS and tacked to poles, hand scribbled notices alerted us to concerts.

For instance: "May 14, 1967 Panhandle, Golden Gate Park, San Francisco (afternoon) Jefferson Airplane/others."

The bands playing that day were typical fare. I always stood up close to a speaker trying to hear it as loud as it got, to vibrate my ears off.

The music we claimed as ours sent warnings about the pride of man. It gave directives to teach our children well, to Love each other right now because the one who dropped us off here on earth would come back for us at last. Our music also imparted wisdom, "None are so blind as those who will not see." "Love eternal can not be denied." "Love is all you need."

Unplugged from the electrical current we'd grown up with, we plugged into Love. And each other. Free Love. Not talkin' sex, here. This was something bigger. For a minute in Bubble-Light Land, Haight Street under the crystal globe, everything was free including marijuana, LSD, mescaline and mushrooms. Either people handed out these goodies on the street or friends stopping by brought presents. From the Digger's free food and clothes to the Free Clinic to the Free Press to free music, The Dream lived. The Grateful Dead played just for us in our Golden Gate Park.

Mount Tamalpais was fertile ground for The Dream. Like Bali Hai, she drew us out of Haight-Ashbury across the Golden Gate Bridge, and then through a tunnel into Marin County. Painted with a rainbow around the opening, the tunnel symbolized entrance to a land where cartoon-like bluebirds flew. Since we claimed the mountain as our own, we used steadfast affection in calling her Mount Tam. Zip-A-Dee-Doo-Da!

An extension of Middle Earth, Mount Tam wrapped herself in crazy hairpin roads to bring us above the husky fog into the mother nature of god. Had the monolith from the movie 2001: A Space Odyssey returned to roost, marking another mystic boost in mankind's consciousness, Mount Tam would've bowed her head to its arrival. She would've made praying hands plus generous room for landing.

I remember a day I climbed toward the summit, following a path that wound through one of her live oak woods. Alone, I stopped, shut my eyes and breathed in sea air mixed with oakyness and eucalyptus. Someone distilled these smells to make the first patchouli oil. I kind of got off thinking I'd made a famous discovery. Tickled with myself, my eyes flipped open and that's when I caught sight of a tree off to my left I hadn't seen at first. Wow, that could be a Raintree. I knew it to be the sort of day it might happen. I walked down into a thicker part of the woods and touched the tree. Yellow clusters of petals hung from its branches.

Have you heard of the Raintree? It's a mythical tree with flowers of yellow. If you can find a Raintree you'll discover Love, the realization of dreams under a rain of gold blossoms. Paradise reinstated. "The Raintree is a state of the mind or a dream to enfold. For the brave who dare there's a Raintree everywhere. We who dreamed found it so long ago," (lyrics from a song named The Song Of Raintree County written by Johnny Green in 1957 and sung by Nat King Cole).

I picked some petals off the ground and stuffed them into my pocket. I felt a peaceful strength in the dim place I stood. Then a little Gollum-whisper in my head, "What's it got in its pocketses?" That did it. Peaceful or not I fled. I'm a sap for fantasies. What can I say?

Queen San Francisco and the Princess, Mount Tamalpais. They'd still need us, they'd still feed us when we turned sixty-four. We could count on it.

The Dream. The closest thing to Camelot; or Don Quixote's quest; or the lore of the Raintree, with one mind-blowing difference: like heaven, Haight-Ashbury is not merely a legend.

When roaming the neighborhood I'd lock eyes for a second or two with each passing person. My emotions tottered beneath the feeling of, well, let's call it team spirit. Sometimes I'd stop on the sidewalk to hug someone I didn't know who'd responded to the same urge. There were no strangers living inside The Dream.

My confetti-d eyes perceived Berkeley as swampeded by politics and Haight Street by Love. The lines were not clear, these agendas crossed over. Personally, I didn't see change happening any other way but through Love.

I used to hitch across the Bay Bridge to hang around in Berkeley, checking it out. It felt different. To me Haight Street citizens had Attitude, not a Platform. We were a 'movement'. We didn't want to exercise power over reality; we didn't want reality at all! Not the reality we were used to.

We were ranting and rallying against conformity.

Add war, to top off this sad scenario of a world without enough Love and what've you got? Bibbidi bobbidi boo, something Terrible.

Despair.

A gathering obscenity even more evil than war.

The end of the life and beauty of creation without any more. No leftovers.

Self destructive behavior resulting from lack of pain-free zones.

No escape.

In the eyes of certain grownups I knew, I'd seen puzzlement. Behind that I saw uneasiness. Did they suffer an emptiness since material comfort alone wasn't enough to provide peace of mind?

Maybe this uneasiness dove below conscious thought where it jabbed at their souls like an annoying beak. A woodpecker tap-tap-tapping twenty-four seven. Causing a festering sore, poisoning any chance for contentment.

Compliments of the dark side. That was my take.

Flower Children were living unfettered by rules of society. Our spirits overflowed with hope. The watching world would recognize a better way and sign on.

I believed this would happen, Scout's honor I did.

THE WAY WE WERE

WHAT COULD WE do to show the watching world The Dream? Believe me, the world watched, inspecting us through a souped up magnifying glass. No secret that Something was happening.

We knew the secret and reveled in knowing.

This 'knowing' rustled within us, but became indistinct when subjected to scrutiny. No matter how much dissection or analyzing, there were no explanations. It was what it was.

The consummate center of 'knowing' for Flower Children was Love. Our Dream in common began with embracing a new concept of love, creating an ember of its radiant peace. Fanning this into a tangible thing by our actions, we imagined a Love that would first enfold a single heart. Then a home, a street, city, country, planet, galaxy, universe. Expanding even more, growing, flowing, reaching...forever. Love that would wipe out hate, cruelty, injustice, war, eliminate all darkness and the swarming evil it heralded.

We dreamed of release. Deliverance of incredulous magnitude. Leaving a hushed brilliance to soak up, to steep in, to play in, to Love in.

No shocker a 'Love–In' celebrated the Summer Solstice.

We were believers.

The rub? How to share the notion. We waited for gentle direction. Ways to turn on our entire planet.

It sounded, er, sort of crazy.

In love with Love, we lived unrehearsed in The Now, The Moment.

Do you know how flexible flexibility can be?

A case in point. I'd leave home to go visiting. "Hey, Cath, I'm going to see Christopher Robin."

"Okay, tell him hi. Shine on!"

And I'd be gone for three days.

Go drop in on a friend and stay for days. Unusual? No, just inspired flights of abandon. We'd spend the time talking about Love, discussing The Dream and the music being made in its honor. Days spent in reverence.

Nicely–overheated–youth, we serenaded each other with Love songs.

Big thoughts spun like tops or handheld windmills, set in motion.

Example of Big Thoughts:

"Gwenn, here's one. If you stop and think about it, our beings mirror Nature. Aren't you blown away by how our veins match rivers and streams? Like blood, they carry life to the earth. Right? Oooo...sap! The same thing."

"Yeah, and how about tears, Suz? They wash away pain and sorrow the way rain cleans dust and dirt off growing stuff. You know, like trees and flowers."

"What about our breath? Isn't it so much like the wind? And when someone gets an idea? It's represented by a light bulb coming on, right? Just like a lightening bolt, blam. Electric energy."

"Okay, Suz, listen to this. The bitsyiest thing we've discovered is the molecule. It's got those protons and electrons revolving around the nucleus in the middle of the molecule. Which is the spitting image of the most gargantuan thing discovered, man, the universe. Same structure with planets and stars revolving in a path around the sun. Whoa."

"Hmmm. Then if we're created beings, maybe that's why people can create."

"Huh?"

"Well, my loveliest of Gwennlyns, wouldn't we have the same ability packed in the suitcases of our genes?"

"So? Where are you going?"

"Uh, a poem."

"Lay it on me, Suzee Creamcheese."

"Here goes...

Words to create what we'd like to see,

A beautiful reality.

Create, create create.

There is no war.

There is no hate.

Make your world beautiful today.

A public service announcement."

"Wow. I like that. Words are so powerful they can create life or death once they get out of your mouth."

"Sounds like a responsibility to me, but an exciting one, yeah Gwennie?"

"Precisely, my dear Creamcheese, precisely."

Things happened to happen. When it was some one-of-a-kind thing going down real cosmic-like, then it was 'a happening'.

Our language consisted of cryptic expressions going every which way. We were lively deciphering devices tuned in to one another, and the airways crackled with Love.

GOOD VIBRATIONS

WE WERE PEAKING! Can you dig it? And we knew where it was at.

We were blowing our minds and there was no one to bring us down. No one had to tell us to lighten up, 'cause we were already in that groove. No one was bummed or getting busted. Neither did anyone push their trip on anyone else. Outta sight for real.

Patchouli oil erased paranoia, leaving an aromatic contrail of peace and Love. You could do your own thing, get off on that and get into it even more.

We weren't uptight, uncool, nor was life a drag. Our acts were together. No bad trips. Mellow Yellow.

Heads were hanging out and handing out righteous grass, shrooms, buttons and acid.

The grass, bud, Mary Jane or Mary Joanna, dope, weed, pot, reefer coming to us in keys had personality. Named Acapulco Gold, Oaxacan Green, Blue Dream, Border Brown, Kona Gold, Michoacan, Panama Red, Rainbow, Punahou Butter, Skunk, Sinsemilla. Untampered with, wholesome as Mr. Natural himself. And nobody 'Bogarted that joint' on purpose, either.

Cleaning it, we removed everything except the leaves with care, but saved those scraps. There was always that chance you'd find yourself down to seeds and stems again, smokeable in a pinch.

We were hip to the Zig–Zag man. His face was famous, stamped on the package of papers we used to roll joints. With papers, the number was smoked down as far as possible until it became a roach. For which one pulled out a roach clip to hold the roach. No burned fingers.

If not papers, we used bongs, or pot pipes to smoke a bowl. Paraphernalia was abundant in head shops.

Freaks laid pure healthy acid and lids of grass on other freaks. The goodies became your stash and you were holding. If you traveled with your stash, you were holding and carrying.

Perfectly acceptable.

Carrying wasn't a big deal 'cause The Man didn't care.

Around every corner, enlightenment left sequined traces to latch onto, reel in, the catch of the day. Free and appealing, this trippy vibe even penetrated The Man's needy aura.

Cops had copped to it. No longer the heat, they turned cool. Might as well have been saying OM-m-m-m and meditating to get high with a big bundle of the residents. Not referred to as pigs now, just the new breed of friendly fuzz getting down. Taking a toke in front of god and everyone. Getting wasted with the rest of us. More than once, a police car pulled over when I hitchhiked. Getting out to open the passenger door, he'd remove his cap and tip his head to receive a flower necklace. Believe it! The Man, my chatty chauffeur, took care of me. A beautiful thing.

Spades were brothers and sisters, no problem. Who didn't admire their funky afros? We hung out, rapped, and spare-changed together. I loved hanging loose at Hippie Hill, listening to this one spade play a real bad axe. You can bet your sweet bippy the cat was boss. Kinda reminded me of Jimi Hendrix. The people in orange picked up on it and Hari Krishna'd in circles around him. Too much!

Hell's Angels, on some radical leave from being nothing but juicers, were our personal teddy bear bodyguards. Their expressions showed they didn't get why they were, they just were. It'd become their bag and their old ladies joined them in the same groove.

Everyone gave each other their own space so you could space out, roll with it.

The whole scene was one huge rush and no one was off the bus.

There was a noticeable lack of plastic people and the ones who came to be known as dealers.

LSD also had bitchin names. Orange Sunshine, Purple Haze, Microdot, Orange Wedges, Blotters, White Lightning (remember Aspen?), Keezy Wheezy, Blue Barrel, and Window Pane. Came as tabs, caps or contained in thin pieces of blotter paper soaked in an LSD/alcohol/water mix.

Get ripped. Sock it to me. Far out.

THE SUMMER OF LOVE

PROPELLED BY FLOWER Power, we could go with the flow and let it all hang out during that Summer of Love. Camelot. For sure.

A bombshell of awareness hit the bulls-eye in my heart. The town crier of my soul woke me up to the wake-up call. With spunk and attitude, like James Brown, he proclaimed Love had arrived. Love was here to make the rounds.

When individuals crossed boundaries into the neighborhood, how they changed! Everyday I watched their faces become defenseless, dappled with happiness. The crystal globe, acting like a shield, offered protection for the level playing field of Lovers living beneath.

The globe of the Haight had its own sky. A tie dye sky.

Some of us visited the back doors of grocery stores, bakeries, movie theaters, snagging food tossed after a certain date. Feasting together on the street was common.

An old man lived in an apartment above the restaurant he'd owned for years, long before we showed up. He brought out sourdough bread and a steaming pot of something to share. One evening the man sat on a small stool while he filled our bowls. The smell made your mouth water. We sat down on the sidewalk to the most scrumptious lamb stew I've ever tasted. From another generation, but he opted to stay.

We asked him, "Why didn't you leave when we came?"

"I got curious," he said, opening the soup pot to ladle more into our waiting bowls. "Been alive for seventy–seven years and never before saw anything like you children."

"What'd you see?"

"Connection, unselfishness, Love I guess. And why? I couldn't figure it. Where'd it come from? I stayed to find out. Now I won't leave no matter what."

"Do you know where it came from?" We leaned in.

"Not exactly. But it's powerful. The suffering in this old world heaps despair on a person. I hunted in the shadows for evidence of light ever since I met up with the darkness. The light had to be there."

We watched, waiting as he stopped talking and dragged the toe of his shoe along the top of the sidewalk curb. "Felt it, but couldn't see it," he said. "So when you showed up and I saw this little pinpoint of light in all your eyes, you better believe I had to identify that. I can't seem to look directly at it. Like fireflies, the light moves just when I think I caught 'em. Elusive, ya know?"

"Yes, yes! We saw it as a guiding star. And followed it to right here."

"Funny thing. What does that remind you of? Gotta admit, I never been what you'd call a religious man. Still..."

We watched big tears come from his eyes, dripping like oval see–through beads down his cheeks.

I remember feeling strong in my brotherhood with him and saying, "Religion. Can't it be a tree or a church or the sky or a train ride? A passionate time in a generation of devoted searching kids?"

"There is meaning," he said. "My hope had dried up forever, but I'm content now. And that's a first. You've brought hope that trails you like the tail of a comet."

I will never forget what my little man did next. He smiled and held up his left forearm to show us the black number tattooed there. I felt the air sucked out of my lungs as I realized his tattoo was compliments of the concentration camp at Auschwitz.

The guy got 'it'. The Lariat of Love lassoed him. Pulled him back, as it had the rest of us, from a crumbling edge. And, yes, to use the favored phrase, he was a beautiful old man.

SUZEE NOT BEING NORMAL

THOSE ARE THE words my mother would have chosen to name this chapter. With my dial set on high-frequency trust mode, I planned a solo expedition out of the Haight-Ashbury neighborhood. Wanna join me on that momentous twilit evening? Into the time machine with you. I have the dial turned to 1967 and typed in The Dream below the date...

San Francisco is my Fairy Godmother. To honor her the best I can, I've patterned my dress style after her. My adopted costume is your basic 'good fairy'. I love myself in this role (and it's still my favorite). A minimal amount of clothing is one of the benefits. Any night gown made of the frilliest see-throughish snow-white material works well. Flowing against my legs above my knees, the feel of my fairy garb gives me goosebumps. And freckles. I'm sure of it, and freckles make me feel charmed. Who won't adore a good fairy with freckles? Impossible. I mean, really!

Barefoot with rings on my toes, ribbons around my knees, bells on my ankles, beads everywhere, jangle bracelets up to my elbows and flowers in my hair made hitchhiking feel like the thing to do. I drop half a tab of acid and go on tour out of the Haight.

A long, pale pink car edges toward the curb and slows to a stop, adorned with a memorable amount of chrome. Since glitter shines and trickles off my body, I relate to the chrome. We bond. To me in my present state, this bodes well. A sign. Rare adventure must lie ahead.

The pink car carries five black guys. A smiley street light shows off their patent leather shoes, shiny like my new friend, the excellent chrome. Another fab sign. One of the men (they look to be in their forties) steps out of the car, and escorts me to the front seat. I sit shotgun next to the other two while he jumps in the back.

I have no qualms, not a one, and that's the truth.

These brothers are smoking pot, driving around the city, and listening to B.B. King on the radio.

Like sublime Queens, Victorian houses reign, approving of their city. Fog-bathed streets fasten a rainbow necklace around every light. Driving through the park, Middle Earth, we get out to goof around in the good-natured air. We hold hands and play London Bridge Is Falling Down. Two long ropes brought from the trunk are used to jump double dutch on the grass. We end up on our backs and watch the stars slide in and out of the fog layer. Then the Pacific, magnetic, draws us to its beach by Seal Rock.

Running around with older guys who know how to have real fun invigo-rates my spirit.

Later, close to midnight, my new friends ask if I want to go back to their pad. Of course I do. We park in a part of town known as the Fillmore District. Theodore turns the car off, and Jonesy opens the door for me again. The polite top-note menthol smell of Kool cigarettes introduces itself to my super hero nose, welcoming me. The Fillmore District is the designated Land of Kool Cigarettes. Here, Kools are mascot-like. I also smell Love, the solid base note of Haight-Ashbury. Love insinuates itself into the atmosphere of The Fillmore.

"We're home, Suzee Creamcheese," Jonesy says. "Follow us. Did anyone lock the front door?"

"No, man, sheee-it, I spaced it clean out." We laugh, giggling our way through the door and up the typical long flight of stairs into their San Francisco flat.

"Do you guys have any Chuck Berry?" I say.

"Uh-huh, loaned the album to the people across the hall. But how about Santana or The Chamber's Brothers, little lady?" says Theodore. Three of their names stick with me: Jonesy, Theodore and the one called Mr. Right On.

"Groovy...perfect," I say. "I saw Santana last week down at the Longshoreman Hall."

"Hey, I was there," says Jonesy. "Santana get's down."

"For sure. Do you have any Big Brother or Cream?" I say.

"Right on," says (you guessed it) Mr. Right On.

We pass a joint and dance around the flat.

"Who's hungry, man?" someone says.

Mr. Right On opens a bottle of champagne. "Grab some fancy glasses, this is the good stuff."

Theodore says, "I got steaks, who wants steak? And red wine?"

"Red Mountain?" It's one of the two wines I'm familiar with. That and MD 20/20. They burst out laughing. "What's so funny?" I say.

"You jivin' me? Red Mountain ain't no damn good, girl, wait till you try French wine."

I eat everything on my plate. There's ice cream for dessert. Time to crash, my eye lids, on strike, refuse to stay open. The men vote to put me in their best bedroom. Voting! Funny cats, these guys.

"Theodore, man, go put on clean sheets for Suzee, the special ones." I'm off to a king-sized bed with pink silk sheets. Clumped together in the entrance, they wave nighty-night in unison, blow kisses and shut the door. I revive to appreciate these sheets. I've never heard of silk sheets, let alone slept in any. These are fresh as sheets dried by sunshine on the clothesline in my Grandma Down's yard.

I burrow in. Sleek as a seal. Out of harm's way.

In the morning, Mr. Right On wakes me and offers a cup of coffee. "I don't drink coffee yet." I've never forgotten saying that because coffee turned me off and I wondered why I'd said 'yet'. Weird what stays with a person.

"Will tea work?"

"Orange juice?" I say.

"Right on!" grins Mr. Right On.

Breakfast is sausages, eggs, blueberry muffins, grits (my first ever) and gravy. We smoke a joint afterwards and my new friends deliver me back to Haight Street. A pack of Kool's in hand.

What's more, you need to know out-of-the-ordinary adventures like this happened lots. Since it was the Summer of Love, I wondered if the moon had something to with it?

ENCHANTED CHILDREN IN
THEIR BALLROOMS OF MUSIC

OUR MUSIC RESOUNDED through the fairyland named Golden Gate Park, it also jived and thrived in the ballrooms of San Francisco. The Avalon Ballroom, The Carousel Ballroom, The Fillmore, Winterland.

I can't count the number of times I saw Ike and Tina Turner, Little Richard, Chuck Berry, B.B. King, Steve Miller, Country Joe and The Fish, Jim Morrison and the list goes on. And on.

Little Richard wore a suit covered, and I mean covered, in what looked like gold doubloons. Each shiny round piece held by a single tough thread so when he shook his booty (which Richard did like nobody else) he became a living tambourine.

A musician named Arthur Brown came out of the wings in the bucket of a backhoe. The Arthur-filled bucket, held in high position, lowered when it reached center stage. After taking its time to touch down, Arthur would then step off, striding forth with the presence of a toreador wearing a tall metal helmet that spew a soaring flame of blue-tinged fire. The top of his head burnt like the Olympic torch. In today's pyrotechnic sideshow displays, a burning metal helmet is peanuts. But back then, all we'd seen prior to Arthur's head gear was Lawrence Welk and his bubbles.

The ballrooms opened their arms, dousing our souls with melodies and lyrics, foretelling the surprise of Dreams come true.

When one of our ballrooms later came down with the financial flu, Chet Helmes, trying hard to keep it well, received a WESTERN UNION TELEGRAM from The Beatles delivered to AVALON BALLROOM (OPERA HOUSE) SUTTER AND VANNESS (VN) SANFRANCISCO. Mimeographed and circulated, it read: WE HEAR YOU ARE HAVING DIFFICULTY YOU KNOW YOU HAVE OUR SUPPORT AND OUR LOVE FOR WHAT YOU AND YOURS REPRESENT JOHN PAUL GEORGE RINGO (THE BEATLES).

Looking back to the Time-Of-All-Times, I see me as the Speedy Gonzales of lizards flicking about. I darted in all directions, spontaneous and hot on the tail of any unsuspecting answer. Not intending to leave much untried or unexplored, I knew I'd be bound to catch all kinds of answers to my questions.

Janis sang: "Why's it all so hard?" In 1967 I didn't get that. I'd been too well loved and cared for to have experienced swampy pain sucking my soul under. So far.

Around any corner, waiting to surprise me like confetti dumped from a window onto my willing head, fell simple secrets. Like how to live in such a way to be moving toward creativity instead of dog-eat-dog competition. How to live with joy and Love, treating others as if they were you.

The headline news of our hearts? WE ARE ONE. Trust was the vanguard of every choice. Case in point? My night out with the five spades.

We hoped for an ending we didn't know was impossible, and we pushed as hard for it to be born as a woman giving birth. The child? Oneness.

Songs offered on the stages of our ballrooms were airborne notes to god. Prayers that the world of brothers and sisters would someday all live together in that yellow submarine in the sky.

The decision to deviate, hark to the call of that sassy Siren who'd hunted down the yellow submarine for us, took guts. It brought loneliness and tears. I met fewer people on my chosen path, but the ones I did meet understood the tears. In a way, we became human tears, crying for the long lost gone-ness of Eden.

SUMMER SOLSTICE

SPEEDWAY MEADOWS IN Golden Gate Park in San Francisco couldn't have been a better place to celebrate the solstice. As the bands belonged to us, we belonged to them. Here are names of some who gave us their offering that day: Jefferson Airplane, Big Brother and The Holding Company, The Grateful Dead, Quicksilver Messenger Service and Mad River.

These were legendary groups.

That day I saw the Airplane's female singer, Grace Slick, and Janis hugging each other before the Airplane started to play.

Red Mountain wine, swill in green glass gallon jugs, provided a cheap means to stay hydrated. Slung a certain way over the shoulder tilted the jug at just the right angle to line up with your mouth. This made guzzling effortless. Passed around the crowd along with joints, thousands of us sat on the ground, peaceful little monks purring in unison due to a pleasant buzz provided by the wine and grass. Like gifted creatures, we danced in the tall eucalyptus trees surrounding the meadow.

Besotted by Summer Solstice, this astrological event geared us up for the dawning of the Age of Aquarius. June 21 1967 was the Summer of Love's apex.

Quicksilver Messenger Service sang spiritual words to feed our souls: "Oh God, pride of man, broken in the dust again...shout a warning unto the nation that the sword of God is raised...you bow unto your God of gold, your pride shall be a shame." They go on to sing about god restoring the earth at last.

Now, realize this song was not being sung by a Christian band. Many of 'our own' bands sang what was named Acid Rock.

Earlier, I did my best to try and explain the far-reaching effects of dropping acid. I described how taking an acid trip opened a door into another dimension. For me and lots of us, it was a highway to god. Straight to god, no passing 'Go' where, if there was a Jesus, he'd be sure to camp, excited for visitors. From tidbits I'd heard in my Sunday School days, I figured that 'Go' would be a suitable site for J.C. to linger, being the go-between god and man and all.

The Desiderata, found pinned to most walls and taped to glass windows of store fronts, declared what could be considered our rallying call of metaphysical pursuit, our mission statement. "Go placidly amidst the noise and haste, and remember what peace there is in silence." It goes on to give glory to god, and for circling sheep like me (baaa), kept my thoughts rounded up. I bleated anxiously along toward the fold. Of course, I couldn't have defined how or why, yet I so knew Love made its home around there somewhere taking care of those stupid sheep.

Summer Solstice, a tribute to our impossible Dream. We tried to "reach the unreachable stars." I will forever believe that, indeed, "the world was better for this."

Today, when I close my eyes and go back to June 21 1967, I see dancers in the trees and smell the strong scent of eucalyptus. I see rag-tag singers on flatbed trucks and hear holy music. I see a congregation of radiant multicolored worshipers and listen in to gentle voices speaking our language of Love. I smell ocean and incense. I taste sourdough bread. My fingers sink into short soft grass, differentiating the smooth small petals of dwarfed daisies, so plentiful they're like ground cover. I see faces shining with a fine wonder, too innocent for this world.

Ironically, this great Love-in on a momentous day of celebration is the day I first detect a solemn cadence in my heart. I freeze. I know a dirge when I hear one.

Sniffing around the edges of our pretty little world, the beginning of the end has come. Watch.

SERGEANT PEPPER'S LONELY HEARTS CLUB BAND

NOT LONG AGO, an eight year old in a tie dye t-shirt let me know that her favorite CD is Sergeant Pepper's Lonely Heart's Club Band. Kids of all ages during every decade since the 1960s have been attracted to this album. What's up with that? Makes me wonder.

No other music tied us to one another during Spring and Summer of 1967 like Sergeant Pepper's Lonely Heart's Club Band by The Beatles. Sprawled on floors throughout The Haight, we inched closer and closer to speakers, devouring the lyrics. A new sound, concocted with symphonic orchestration and rich multi-leveled echoes, pulled us into each song. Words furnished us with fresh revelation about Love.Within You Without You, Lucy In The Sky With Diamonds (not about LSD by the way, John told me, well, in a printed interview that is), With A Little Help From My Friends, A Day In The Life, Fixing A Hole, to name a few. We scarfed up the implications. Yeah, we already belonged to a lonely heart's club and these songs were written about us, for us, to us.

Our generation of seers, graced with pluck and inspiration, made a quantum leap listening to Sergeant Pepper's Lonely Heart's Club Band. The leap brought us nearer to the spiritual world and its principles. Garnering information about life going on within you and without you, we better understood the intended divine design for living beings: human/animal/plant.

The creator called mankind the crown of creation. And Jefferson Airplane happened to write a song named Crown of Creation.

Someone put us on earth and Loved us more than anyone ever could. We were not nor would we at any point be all alone.

God's intention called for total acceptance of anyone and everyone. This by–now–blatant trueness caused a new fascination with humanity, even the grodiest samples of it. It felt like my mission, should I choose to accept it. Yes, I was so out there, but out there armed with tremendous transparent vulnerability. I knew being on call might hurt, but I always signed up anyway. Vivid example coming up.

I've said the end of The Dream is near. In fact, it's here. I loathe to write of the passing because unbelievable beauty turned into unbelievable ugliness.

Looking at my picture as it dries, I hope the portrait I've painted of the Time–Of–All–Times is complete, that the canvas shows you the real thing. It's a mural of a preternatural moment in eternity.

There is a perfect quote from the book, Raintree County, to use as my final brush stroke, illustrating Haight–Ashbury.

As Ross Lockridge Jr. wrote: "Which had no boundaries in time and space where lurked musical and strange names and mythical and lost peoples and which was itself only a name musical and strange."

NOT SO GOOD VIBRATIONS

BY JULY THE presence I'd felt sniffing around the edges pounced on our pretty little world with all four or six or eighteen claws or was it hooves? Nothing recognizable as feet anyway and it landed with a snarl and putrid breath that coated the crystal globe with sticky slime. The atmosphere became clogged with paranoia. People showed up behaving badly, focused on money, nasty drugs, and guns. Our coded language of Love turned messy in the span of one measly month. Just plain BAD. Listen:

BAD vibes abounded. Flower Children, confused, scared and scarred by dealers appearing on the street, lost the vision of Flower Power bringing universal Love.

The giving away of mind-expanding drugs became a thing of the past real quick. Needing big money for grass seemed bizarre and getting burned by these newcomers brought us down. Bummed us out. Being ripped off was BAD news, a hassle. Ripping someone else off, so bogus no one wanted that kind of karma.

BAD trips started happening as greed beguiled people to tamper with the purity of LSD. Dealers cut the drug with substances like strychnine. Cleaning up your act became a necessary phrase since crystal methamphetamine desecrated human beings, leaving them shells of their former selves. Hulls now, filled with demons feeding on scraps of what used to be their souls. Coming down was such a come down, you needed more or you needed downers to knock you out. Cotton mouth happened from dehydration caused by speed and by rapping: talking your head off. Crystal meth made people chew the inside of their cheeks bloody.

Uppers and downers, the new fashion in getting high. This unfamiliar way of life on Haight Street was a drag, gross, and people started freaking out. They hassled each other and many lost it. Some O.D.'d.

We saw those who became strung out become uptight, wired, dangerous. Uncool would be the understatement.

Hell's Angels turned back into being BAD asses, treacherous juicers, speedball junkies, no evidence left of their once upon a time protective teddy bear attitude.

People started yelling at each other to lighten up, get it together, get real, stop copping out.

Have you heard of the slang word 'outfit'? A hint to its meaning would be another slang word, 'fix'.

It has to do with what came along next that was BAD...really BAD.

The needle of death.

Bliss Blow Up

REMEMBER WHEN I described my self as (A.) a non-bystander, and (B.) curious?

Even before the BAD elements crashed our world, subtle tricky dangers lurked, sneaking their way into the globe. My curiosity pricked its ears, eager and inquisitive. Like the time Cathi and I hitched to Los Angeles that same July and ended up at the home of two guys who'd created a new drug. We didn't think twice, and dropped a pill apiece. They'd named it OSB. "Huh?" we said.

"Oh, it stands for One Step Beyond."

The night grew darker and weirder. When we found our way to the bathroom and discovered an assortment of different colored hot water bottles hanging off the walls, we ran out the front door. One of the guys chased us. I think he had a big dog on a leash. But we got away. See, that was definitely weird. It didn't feel like Haight-Ashbury, it did not feel like home. It didn't even feel as nice as Kansas.

We managed to find my old high school friend who lived in L.A. and stayed overnight. From bed we stared at our eyes in the dresser mirror till dawn. The irises had given up as the pupils staged a coup d'état. Our eyes were black balls in a sea of white. We almost called 911, but at last our pupils returned to normal and we hitched back to San Francisco. This had not been wisdom in action.

In my mind, the whole of Haight-Ashbury was like one gabled gingerbread mansion of Love. Our sad manor now had dry rot going on. Not apparent yet, but a faint moldering smell upset my superhero nose. I couldn't understand or tag it. So I ignored it.

At home on Hayes Street we'd been invaded by three characters. They were speed freaks.

Fred and Jerry showed up at the door with a bejeweled big spoon wrapped in tight-fitting colored ribbons. A mysterious object, that. They came on in because, of course, we invited them. They were decorated like family, likable, but they turned out to be marvelous con men. Fred claimed to be descended from an ancient Egyptian/India/Indian race of holy-men and carried an oriental-looking shiny box around, never putting it down. He was a tall black man, while Jerry was a short, gabby and frizzy-haired manipulator. Jerry considered himself a lady's man and tossed out compliments like peanuts to pigeons. "Hey baby, you're a twentieth century fox!" Both of them seemed entertaining and harmless (which did not apply to that big spoon).

The third character to enter stage left was an older black flash of a lady named Tasha, which she spelled Tajah. She made that fact known right off and reminded us of the spelling daily. She sort of moved in by bringing over certain scraps of her stuff, but never slept there.

Tajah could've been anywhere between the ages of 20 and 50. She stimulated her surroundings by appearing in character as a painted sultry Persian princess, or a wild Amazon woman, or a tall man posing as a transvestite (figure that one out), or an Aunt Jemima mammy type, kerchief and all. Tajah stole from me, instructed or berated me, and, in her low-pitched voice, told hair-raising tales. She had been a junkie most of her life, however long that'd been. She knew gangsters from Seattle, connections for big bad drugs, and most of the jazz musicians in the Bay Area.

Loud, bigger than life, unforgettable, she asked me, "Suzee, honey-girl, watchoo doin' here? With me? You're a good child. You got class, had some fine upbringin' and belong on the nice and pretty side of life, not here. Be careful honey-girl, if you got to has yoursef a look around anyway, well, let Tajah take care of ya. Tajah ain't gonna let nuthin' happen to you." And she didn't. Even though one time she found me a job in a smoky topless all night jazz bar. She walked me in, announced I was her blood sister, would not work topless, and nobody was to touch me or give me no smack (i.e. junk, i.e. heroin). Nope, nobody messed with me. I worked there one night for the experience. See my curiosity at work? I'll never forget that one night, nor Tajah. In the strangest of ways I respected her very much.

Fred and Jerry brought over some pots and pans. Next they showed up with silverware. Then they moved themselves in. Slick.

THE DARK SIDE

MORE DIFFICULT THAN you can know is what I must tackle to show you next. Think of a coloring book. Open to a page that attracts you, a picture you want to color. The main thing is to color inside the lines, right? If the colors are outside the lines, the picture will look wrong: not how the artist wanted it to look, not the way he drew it to look.

I'm talking about truth. To be true, I have to color inside my own lines of this story I am drawing. I'd love to fib, draw a different prettier picture somewhere else on the page to color in. But then we won't get to where we need to go.

We came to wonder if Fred and Tasha were the same person since we never saw them together in the same room. By the time our thoughts, in all seriousness, were capable of wondering such a thing, we'd been turned.

By August of 1967 I'd started seeing homemade paper signs taped to windows on Haight Street next to the psychedelic posters. The scrawled words on the new signs said "Speed Kills." There should've been a mate to it: "Speed Lies."

Some of us are born wise. Some become wise the hard way. I am one who learns the hard way.

Heaven fell headlong into hell. I've thought maybe even I, the non-bystander, may have had second thoughts if I'd read something like what I'm about to write. Probably not. Yet there is a remote chance some soul might escape the mental agony brought by my full-on stupid choice. So, I write.

I bet you already know what I did. I picked up the needle. I shot meth-adrine into my veins. I even gave smack a go. I had to know. What was it like? Could I describe it? Write about it? Try it out and let it go at that?

Heroin held no interest. It bored me. I saw strange things when I shut my eyes. Are you ready? I saw Huckleberry Hound going up and down a ladder time after time. In tweed. I threw up. I didn't get the appeal. Got the tee shirt and moved on to speed. Speed is a big awful LIE and you buy into it without question. Aren't lies the opposite purpose of life on earth? You feel clever and powerful and beautiful beyond belief. You are sure there is nothing bet-ter in the world than this feeling. LIE.

It's occurred to me a thousand times Lucifer invented speed. And used it. The deal is, once or twice is not possible with this substance. At first, coming down isn't so icky. You feel a little loopy, spacey and then you manage to fall asleep. Not so after a short time of using this drug.

The induced euphoria convinces you that you love anyone in the room to pieces. Even if that someone is hard to take, annoying, mean, or dangerous. You are positive you'll be best friends forever and ever. It could be Charles Manson and you are filled to brimming over with intense love for him. LIE.

Long story short. You become delusional. Musical lyrics from our mentor musicians of the time started conveying sly messages about doing speed. Of course the artists are doing it, just like you. LIE.

Paranoia takes over your thinking, you see things that aren't there. You hear things that aren't being said. Purple cloaked dark beings whisper secrets in your ear. Secrets you can't quite make out. But maybe if you shoot up again, you'll understand. And you do and then you stay up for days and nights and more days and nights until you are nervous, jumpy, fried. I used to think I could smell my brain getting too hot and the odor was disgusting. Enough?

Speed overtakes your world and before long, you're surrounded by speed. When I quit, I never ran into it, like the drug squashed its loathsome belongings into a sack and scuttled away. I am not going to get too far gone in all this but feel, for good measure, it's my responsibility to leave you with a couple of god-awful mind pictures.

One night I snuck along a back street in the fog, having done speed for days. I no longer enjoyed any of its lies. The thrill of those had been snatched and replaced by bad skin, among other atrocities. Even the mirror couldn't lie anymore. Fear, a shadowy specter, stalked me. It wanted to sweep me away into the tortured gutter of my mind. I made it home and wrote the following, laughing. It is hideous. But now I'm glad I saved it. For you. Because I Love you.

You are what you know
That's what I heard someone whisper
I listened hard—it was that kind of whisper
You are what you know.
Epilogue
The other day
while on my way
down the street
I chanced to meet
a man insane, talking and drooling
in the rain
and I understood
every wet word.

In case you're a non-bystander or a curious sort like me, I'll leave you with this final image in hopes you'll never forget.

I saw a person who, I was told, had used speed for over three years. He sat in a room in a house in a dirty corner, trash stinking around him. He hadn't moved for days and hadn't even touched methadrine for months. The damage had become permanent. He sat there, pulling what he described as long things from the tips of his fingers. He'd said these noodle-like strands would be coming out of his fingers as long as he pulled, and he couldn't stop.

COLLATERAL DAMAGE

Somehow (well, now I know how, and I'll come to that before we reach the end of this story), my needle days proved to be a special effect, not a lifestyle.

Still, the playing out of my time in Haight-Ashbury didn't quite end when I was done with speed.

Going to visit a friend I cared for, I decided to spend the night. He was quitting smack which meant he faced cold turkey withdrawals, I didn't want him to be alone.

We were in blankets on the floor when three men broke the door down. They had guns and wanted money or heroin from my friend, who had neither. Off the floor one of them picked up a glass pitcher full of water, dumped the water over my head and threw the pitcher at the wall where it smashed, shards flying everywhere. Great, huh? They split. For some reason, they just left.

A diagnosis of hepatitis helped make the final decision to go home to my parents. And Judi was the big reason I left. She'd come from Seattle to get Robert. She showed up with his baby son. They belonged together, spending the next forty-five years proving it.

Consequences. Lies. It couldn't get worse, or so I thought. Mom and Daddy sent me a plane ticket.

The beautiful and not so beautiful time ended. Not, gratefully, me.

Was The Dream Playing Hide And Go Seek?

I WENT HOME to Moline gladly, even though an alternate title for this chapter could be Guilt Revisited. What should my penance be for panicking my parents with what they saw as my sustained unsound behavior? Going back to college, naturally. Back, in fact, to Blackhawk Jr. College in the fall of 1967. More English classes and psychology and creative writing. I got a job, too. Desire for a Gibson B-25 six string acoustic guitar pushed me to become a cocktail waitress at a decent restaurant, The Boar's Head.

I found Anson. He tended a group of my kind living in Moline. I use the word tended because he had a home base we called The Hovel. Anson, older than most of us, lived with his wife and baby. He opened his doors and heart to fellow misfits. This was his calling.

A keeper of the knowledge I didn't comprehend until my Siren lured me into that powerful current of change, Anson already knew about the approaching flood. There'd been no one else around who got 'it'. Anson, a loner, had considerable influence on me.

He explained I couldn't truly love anyone until I loved myself, which came as big important news. Timely. Having never heard this wisdom before, it shook me.

Anson wanted me to be strong. Being strong was another part of his message. Not just for me, but for everyone including himself. Courage was his personal creed and he latched onto it. That is what I saw.

Anson, a walking, talking loving–kindness who cared, catalyzed my growth as a spiritual person.

I learned from him.

I trusted him.

Afraid The Dream had disappeared off the face of the earth, I sermonized to my friends about Haight–Ashbury. It couldn't die, just went into hiding or something. I kept wondering where it'd gone and how to bring it back.

Not ready to stop believing in the lost Dream, I starved for a lingering taste of its unearthly Love. I needed to fill up the emptiness left by its absence. There was so much I didn't know. I grabbed at everything resembling it, but came up empty–handed. I longed to find The Dream, wolf it down or squeeze it to my chest, into me. Something.

I realized what we had going on as Flower Children was a vision.

I remember trying to set my mom's imagination on fire.

We were in a car. So, as my captive, I told her about the vision. "Picture everyone loving everyone else."

"What in the world do you mean?" She wanted to know and I wanted her to know more than anything.

She'd asked for it and I was ready. "All my friends have the same vision, Mom, it's not just me, okay?" I felt, once again, I might be able to bring her along.

"Oh Suzee!" Alarm rearranged her face. "What are you talking about? Don't be silly." Her mind couldn't stretch, could not push out of its box, and there wasn't room for company inside there.

I turned to face her. "Look, Mom, just try and pretend Love could be on such a vast scale that every living soul Loved every other living soul. What if, just what if it was possible?" Bewilderment teamed up with the alarm on her face. She was in left field trying to catch a fly ball with a teacup.

She laughed, but it sounded nervous. Her brow furrowed and her mouth strained, forcing a tight little smile. Then she did what she did best. She changed the subject.

"Did I tell you Carolyn is driving to Odebolt? I'm going to ride with her. I think Aunt Dorothy will drive down from Austin at the same time. Aunt Vivian and Uncle Bill may..."

"That's nice."

"Oh, and I get my hair done tomorrow before Literary Guild. Then I'm taking dessert to Kings Daughter's followed by bridge at Doris's." At that moment my dream for her was to metabolize The Dream into her very cells so she could join a new kind of club.

I waited, quiet, giving her time to wonder about the silence, maybe backpedal to wonder about my words. We were crossing the bridge over the Mississippi River. "Oh, look at that barge! It's a long one," she said.

Disappointed, frustrated, but mostly sad, I turned back in my seat. I took solace that maybe a seed had been planted. In some slumberland place, perhaps the seed would sprout. She'd have a dream about The Dream and wake up 'there', or at least with probing questions that'd lead her to 'there'.

Reminded of the day I'd played Dylan's Like a Rolling Stone for them and how they hadn't heard the message, I stared out the window so she didn't see my tears.

New Year's Eve At Winterland Ballroom

AH YES, THAT New Year's Eve, December 31 1968.

Sometimes I'm afraid I'll run out of words describing things, especially phenomenal things like say, oh, the ocean or the starlit night sky. Or Jumpin' Gerald's shoes. Things like these use up all the primo words pretty fast. Then I remember the treasure hunt and start digging again.

I made it through the fall quarter at Blackhawk. Mom and Daddy watched me warily, wondering what might be going on in my peculiar brain. They found out after Christmas when I informed them Craig, a.k.a. Captain Cornflake and I were going to go to Denver for New Year's Eve. In truth we were going to San Francisco and would hitchhike there from Denver.

Craig became a Cornflake one night, sitting between Ken Kesey, author, and Daisy Dave, president of a Hell's Angels chapter. The two proclaimed Craig a cornflake. The Captain, even. Had something to do with being from the Midwest.

San Francisco, although not the same as when I'd lived there, hung on best it could as an iconic monument to Love. We didn't spend time on Haight Street. The Captain and I were there for the concert.

Our music memorialized The Dream. It was the closest thing to the real thing. I traveled this far for a reminder. And maaaaybeeee I'd catch a sighting?

We dropped STP, a longer lasting version of LSD. Once inside, we sat on the floor. Tumbling magic lanterns lit the ballroom. Music started and we watched, open-mouthed and mute, as notes played and bopped around in the air like porpoises. Amplifiers thrummed the music so loud we thought we levitated.

A long-haired blonde male appeared on a dazzling white horse at midnight. The man wore diapers and smiled dotingly, lofting doobies into the crowd. We looked at the ceiling where they loosened a billowing net, allowing thousands of balloons to float down. Inside the balloons? More treats.

Craig and I walked into the pale gray morning and wondered about a couple the age of our parents sitting on some bleachers. What were they doing there? Out of context, straight arrows, yet they'd been there all night. They talked to each other. What about? Had they known The Dream, too? And how could they manage conversation? We still weren't that advanced. And wouldn't be for hours to come.

Hitching to Denver over the Rockies, we scored a ride with a couple of heads in a convertible missing its back window. During the drive, a foot of snow filled the backseat floor. Captain Cornflake and I traded places on and off. When it was my turn and since I still played with very stoned thoughts, I entertained my cold self by becoming a favorite flavor of snow cone.

An Attempt At Recapturing The Dream

THE ONE WAY to make sure The Dream was over for sure meant going back to live in The Haight again. It hadn't resurfaced on New Year's Eve. I figured The Dream went underground when in truth, it lay buried in a sacred burial ground: my heart. People had died, gotten sick, split forever. Many, like our beloved Sarah, remain MIA. Lots of those, too. The music contained murmurings, but the Love wasn't its old formidable self, not visible in people's eyes. I discussed my plan like the adult I wasn't, but my acting ability won my parents' support. Merry Poppins would help me get a job at the telephone company on Market Street in downtown San Francisco. Wow. I impressed My's Elf.

First stop, Denver, February 1968, to visit Crazy. That's where I met Mindi. The minx, the doll-size girl who stole my heart and was destined to play a part in my life that will make you reel.

She had pilgrimaged with friends to Colorado from Los Angeles in search of (are you ready, you should be by now) The Brotherhood of The White Temple. Everywhere I looked in Suzee's world, people were searching, questing hard, on the case, looking through magnifying glasses like private eyes. The ordained connection between Mindi and me cemented, I later flew to L.A. with Craze where I'd meet Mindi's husband, Rusty, and little daughter Jayna.

Ahhh, Rusty. Our energy together? Different. We were like snap on tools. One look at each other's faces and whap, we stuck. Mindi came home from

Denver. They'd drive me to San Francisco. We pulled into the city on a full moon and the stars were in our eyes instead of the sky.

One afternoon with Mindi, I became convinced I'd found god. Mindi explained to me I'd 'sprung'. And maybe I had. I don't know what happened, but it seemed like god to me. Springing referred to going higher, closer to the truth about the meaning of life. The off-the-wall fact in regard to 'springing' was how it affected my reality. This phenomena, 'springing', manifested itself day after day. A stranger on the street or a person who picked me up hitch-hiking would know in an instant if I'd 'sprung' as I would know if they had. It was in our eyes. That's where we'd see it. I'd say, "Thanks for picking me up," get inside, look at the driver and say, "Oh! You've sprung."

"Yes, when did it happen to you?" And we'd go from there without need to explain. This lasted about a month. I hadn't been taking LSD, hadn't been getting high much. The recognition had to do with some ability to perceive an invisible trademark in another, and it linked us for sure. Almost like The Dream, maybe a residual part. But it didn't stay. Neither could Mindi. She went back to L.A.

Rusty, Merry Poppins, Cathi, My's Elf and Alex rented a flat on Stanyan Street. It rested on the corner of Alma Street, up the hill from Haight Street past the fire station. Alex, kind of special, maintained a perpetual bendy slouch, presenting like a long rubbery contortionist.

I will never forget Stanyan Street, the speckled stone steps outside the Scotch Tape–scarred front door and the clunky brown, half-carpeted stairs that announced visitors so well. Magnificent personable bay windows curved around my bed, sur-rounding it. Right away we discovered the jolly roof, the most bless-ed roof.

Tall French windows framed a perfect view of my city from the little back room off the kitchen. Down the back stairway lived a family that I thought of as mystics. All night long they studied the stars searching for concealed secrets about life. They baked the best macrobiotic cookies ever.

And it was through this family we met Sarah who we took an immediate fancy to. She joined us, a girl so made for this Time-Of-All-Times she had to have been designing costumes for her entrance into the globe of Love while still in the womb.

I got an orange rug and a job at the phone company. Haight Street pre-tended with all it had that The Dream never ended. We all did.

More Please? Oh, Please Please Can't We Have More?

CATHI AND I met a group of thugs in the park, trying their hardest to be gentle Flower Children. They were the gang from Ninth Avenue and Judah Street, ex-greasers, sort of. For months I ended up linked with them like their sister/ mother/brother/something-or-other.

I wanted to take care of them. Hmmm, I may be seeing a pattern taking shape here.

One day the cops closed down Haight Street. It never happened again. They did it so The Grateful Dead could play for free in the middle of the street on March 3 1968. The street became jammed with kids. Light shows bubbled and wriggled all over the buildings. My heart held out a butterfly net to recapture The Dream, but it had gotten away and didn't exist there anymore.

I turned twenty-one years old two days later at our home on Stanyan Street. This birth date of mine branded me a Pisces.

I studied astrological signs, birth signs, rising signs and what a person's moon sign might be. Getting a chart done by an astrologer was mandatory, enabling an accurate insight into yourself and others. Remember, we planned on the Age of Aquarius to top off the coming new human consciousness like a cherry on an ice cream sundae. I paid solemn attention to my astrology because I figured if there was a god, he made the stars. Even those wise guys found the Jesus person 'cause of a star. Made sense to me. So did the I Ching, an ancient Chinese book which, translated, means book of changes. This, like astrology, was used for divination purposes. To help a person know which way to go, how to survive, to understand and navigate changes in life.

We were dedicated searchers. There were riddles all over creation, and we meant to solve the whole puzzle of existence. Serious as dogs after hidden buried bones, we dug and dug. We left plenty of empty holes, but now and then we'd uncover a chunky knuckle bone of visionary direction. Likely happened when the moon was in Aquarius.

At our home on Stanyan Street, as you know, the roof ruled. Rusty played guitar there. We had lots of company, and we loved taking them up, showing off our big-hearted, unselfish roof.

It was in the rarefied air of the roof that we first heard The Beatles had presented the Straight Theatre on Haight Street with an historical something. A gala opening. On April 5 1968 their movie, Magical Mystery Tour, would premier for the first time in America.

The Beatles still believed in The Dream enough to travel to Haight-Ashbury. This calls up that 'nearly' word again to haunt me. They came. Did I run into them? No. Damn! But as might be expected George Harrison's third eye saw the pathos at first glance. And it grieved him.

I kept hoping. Pretending. Straining to bring it back.

Like that doggie in the window song, I kept wondering about The Dream. Oh where, oh where could it be?

An Impressive Bust At The Border

OH. MAY 1 1968 is a date I'll never forget, a real doozie.

Road trip! Play, stop fretting. Be free. Adventure. Laughter. Let's go. Maybe it'd take my mind off the haunting loss plaguing my soul. Or it could be that a search down the coast of California all the way to Mexico miiiiight turn something up? Around?

I had a three day weekend off, plenty of time to go and come back if we drove all night. Merry Poppins loaned us her VW bug. Steve, who I called The Walrus, Marty, and me, fortified with a plan and thirty hits of LSD, pointed the compass of ourselves south. I kept a lookout for signals, indicators of guidance to the secret land where The Dream hid, chilling out I hoped, preparing for a show-stopping come back.

Our destination, because you always need some idea of where you're going, was Mike's Bar in Tijuana. Someone mentioned it and we took that as a hint. Would there be a reason for going to Mike's Bar which would present itself like a newborn constellation?

We coasted down Highway 101, veering to the west to find a Pacific Ocean cove with tide pools. Miraculous thingies hung out in tide pools. I could rely on some shell or rock to beckon me. On that trip I found three matched round pieces of green sea glass to use for I Ching stones. Tucked into my little leather bag tied onto one of my jean's skirt loops, I'd save the required three for when I threw the I Ching.

About two miles before the Mexican border, we checked the car, making sure no droppings of pot peeked out from nooks or crannies. But Steve's thirty tabs of LSD amounted to a problem. He carried it in an engraved gold watch case and handed me and Marty several hits apiece, laying the tablets in our palms with care. I had three in my hand and the idea was to do away with the evidence by dropping the acid before we reached the border station. I'd never dropped that much at one time. Steve, on some spontaneous carnival ride of his own choice, dropped the rest of the stash. We're talking around twenty–four hits of LSD. Marty and I didn't know what to think about that move. Oh well. Steve seemed confident and calm. For then.

We pulled into the border station. "Where is your destination in Mexico?"

"Mike's Bar in Tijuana, Sir." We tee hee'd, acting like silly and harmless tequila drinkers.

"I'd like the three of you to step out of the car, please." Oh shit. Dear lord. Oh no! "What's the problem, Sir?"

"Just step out of the car. Now." We did. "I'd like you to enter the station with this officer here." We did.

Sitting inside under glaring lights, we fidgeted, wanting to get out of there before the acid came on. Grinning conspirators, like the–about–to–be–stoned three musketeers, we sat tight, knowing they'd find nothing to bust us for in the car.

And then.

A guard walked in holding a piece of kleenex as if tiny rare diamonds were taking a little siesta on the tissue. Not diamonds, but two tiny marijuana seeds rested there.

Huh–uh, no way, couldn't be happening. We were beginning to communicate among ourselves via LSD telepathy which meant one grim thing. We were starting to get off, beginning our trip right now, right there in an International Border Crossing. They took my boys away and handcuffed me to the back of a desk chair in the office. The guard left to check a car through. I played on the chair since it had wheels. The arms made it feel like a commander's chair.

I fantasized that I, an Admiral–ette, had 'the con' like on a submarine. Then a paddy wagon drove under the spreading roof of the station.

A guard unlocked my handcuffs. Another guard led the boys into the room and deposited us into the vehicle. There, behind a wire mesh screen, sat Steve and Marty staring at me with dilated eyes. I stared back and we talked.

Out loud this time.

"So, uh, Marty? Steve? This is weird, huh?"

"You could say that, Creamcheese, how're you doin'?"

"Gee, fine. At least I think so. You?"

"Not too sure, but okay for now," said Marty. "At least we're going back to California instead of to Mexico. Hey Steve? What about you?" No answer. Sort of to be expected considering his recent dosage.

After being stripped, showered, fingerprinted, and having a mug shot taken in my new outfit, 'the staff' had prepared me to spend the night in The San Diego Federal Women's Penitentiary.

My second stop after the shower and picture taking room was called The Drunk Tank where I met five or six females who were bombed. All I saw when I watched them barf and move around were paisley patterns. This was interesting and amused me. Like watching a play.

Next, I entered a cell block filled with different sizes, ages and colors of women. I mean, there were Hispanic and Oriental women in there, not colorful ones like green, blue, red, purple. Not like that.

One towering black lady approached me as soon as the woman officer who'd brought me there left. "Now, look here, little darlin'. I am your friend. Stick with me and I won't let anything happen to you. Whatchoo in here for? Stealing? What?" She sure reminded me of Tajah.

"No, I got busted at the border for pot and I am tripping my socks off. I took three, that's three, hits of acid."

The lady looked me up and down, said, "Damn, girl," showed me a thin bladed knife and said again she'd watch my back. I think I lay down on a bunk and hallucinated the rest of the night. So far I hadn't felt afraid, not even once.

In the morning when I'd started coming down, a woman guard ran a billy club down the bars of the cell as she passed. "Suzanne Carson," she yelled.

"Yes, here," I shot my hand up like a grade schooler who knows for sure they have the correct answer. I wanted to show obedience at role call. Now I began to feel a trace of the heebie-jeebies. What if they didn't let me go?

"Come with me," she said, "you've got yourself a little appointment with a detective." To my eyes, her smirk tried to imitate a smile.

I walked into the real thing, a padded room like on TV. The matron shut the door. I knew I was still stoned because the dark-maned detective, who looked like a Muppet with short black hair sticking straight up, said in a Kermit the frog voice, "Young lady, we are releasing you on grounds of insufficient evidence." I wondered if I should feel any concern as I watched his stuffed animal mane growing as he told me the good news. Concern? Naaaah. Leave now? Without a doubt.

On the street, standing outside The San Diego Women's Federal Penitentiary, to what did my wandering eyes appear but Marty and Steve coming to find me.

Marty led the pleasant-faced walrus by the hand. Although his body was in attendance, by no means was his mind in the immediate vicinity.

Later, Steve explained he hadn't spent the night inside any walls whatsoever, he'd enjoyed himself, out exploring the galaxy.

STANYAN STREET

MA BELL AND me got along okay until Greg, part of that thug gang Cathi and I'd adopted in the park, stepped on my foot, breaking it. Greg, an appealing brat, had made it necessary for me to quit my job in June 1968.

Since my foot with cast required healing time, I made haste to hitch back to Moline and gather all the kids I could to return with me to Stanyan Street. I thought perhaps more of the beautiful people thinking Love thoughts would charm The Dream, call it home.

Innumerable visitors walked through our door. Even Fred and Jerry. Fred accused me of stealing his false teeth. They still used speed. Sad.

Scores of visitors moved in or stayed for weeks.

We each had our own room on Stanyan Street: Cathi, Alex, Merry Poppins (still straight as, no, straighter than an arrow). Me and Rusty, snap on tools that we were, shared one platonically. She was magnanimous in the number of airport runs she made in her VW bug which became crammed to the gills with beatific cheery acid heads coming to visit Stanyan Street. If I had to make a guess, I'd say somewhere around 300 people came and went. We'd have welcomed more to combine our voices, making a louder call for The Dream to hear.

A visitor from the Midwest, John, came home from panhandling one day. He was a changed man. No, angel. His intensity: memorable. He'd transformed into the red angel who wore red clothes, ate red food and limited his fluid intake to ketchup and tomato juice. He was excited about his red life and extra-excited to bring new friends home. He was excited about circles, too. Everything was circular. Concentric at times. Micro to macro, I'm talking everything. Polite as a professional butler, he changed all the white thumb-tacks in the flat to red ones.

Then, the red angel disappeared. I saw him much later in Davenport, Iowa, and he'd turned back into just plain John. I think the color red was the color of an E ticket for The Dream Ride. He'd gone rather mad. Feeling the loss of The Dream, he lost himself and turned into an angel on a mission to find it again.

Marty, whom you've already met, had been among the first set to arrive from the Midwest. It kept getting to be more and more fun with each arriving guest. Marty was fun because when I grew weary of the cast on my foot up to my knee, he went with me to the ocean and waited while I attempted soaking it off. When this didn't happen, back at Stanyan Street, I laid my heavy leg on the kitchen table and Marty sawed that boring cast off. Dr. Marty! My foot was fine. Still is.

OUT OF OPTIONS

NEAR SUMMER'S END when we couldn't afford Stanyan Street anymore, everyone moved to Page Street. Except me. I started work as a babysitter for one of my favorite Ninth and Judah guys who was married with a child. And had a job. We called him Michelson. A happy-go-lucky fella, Michelson. I spent loads of time with the gang, going to the Russian River and tearing around. Always forgetting my contact lens case and soaking solution, I'd stick my contacts deep into a pocket and wet 'em with spit in the mornings. We'd sleep in a pile like a large litter of puppies after drinking vats of Ripple Wine. Ripple, believe it or not, was a step down from Red Mountain. God.

I gave up on the wine buzz. It didn't help.

Buzz went bye-bye. Like The Dream.

After I watched some of my freak family make the move to Page Street, I admitted to myself that the Love had moved, too. Haight-Ashbury was no more and, in truth, had not been for a long time. Many of us fled, battered and in mourning. Lots moved out of the cities, started communes, began to 'live off the land'. I'd been obsessed with one word, maaaaybeee. You know, like The Dream could resurrect itself. But, no, speaking of that, even the Jesus freaks left.

We'd been trying to dig up, or at least I had, something dead and laid to rest. It needed to be left there in peace. The loss ruined me. I even thought about trying to get some help from Jesus, which just goes to show how desperate I'd become. How had I ever believed in him? I recalled that, as a child,

I blew kisses at a picture of Jesus on my wall every night. How could I? He was much too uptight wherever he was and I didn't think anymore about it. I wanted nothing to do with him. He'd died a long time ago, just like The Dream, even longer.

Time to give up. Or was it? A sorry mess, I went home to Moline to think.

OLLY OLLY OXEN FREE!

MAYBE I'D OVERREACTED in believing The Dream was over. Perhaps it really was playing hide and seek? It hid, I sought and sought, but couldn't find it. I hurried to my safe place in August 1968, home to my parents who deserved a chest full of purple heart medals.

I assumed my post on my bedroom floor, inwardly calling olly olly oxen free, brooding and contemplative. The Dream might come out of hiding if I chanted this invitation with sincere determination. So I did while stringing chains of Love beads. I didn't know what else to do. I did know that Daddy feared for my mental capacity. Would I be reduced to a kind of state where I'd soothe myself with arts and crafts while creeping along toward autism? It's true I didn't talk liberally. I made beads, preparing to reenter the living Love world when The Dream came out of hiding.

I grieved, starting to process the end, but, still, maaaaybeee?

I wrote a love letter to Stanyan Street, the paper so wet with my tears it crumpled into wavy wrinkled sheets.

Daddy asked to read it and I shoved it across the table to him on an afternoon. He nodded, gave it to Mom to read and I saw a wistful look on both their faces. Daddy repeated for the umpteenth time I should be a writer of some sort. A journalist he said, more than once.

The day came that my parents talked to me. Yes, yes, my bead necklaces were lovely. But didn't I want to learn a trade? Something to fall back on to support myself (like with money) one day? Bless their hearts.

You know where this is going. Straight to college. Again. God.

Iowa City Revisited

The University of Iowa still had my transcripts, what was salvageable of them. I steered clear of manhole covers. The spies from 1965 were no longer there anyway. Very few friends remained. Dunc, John and Diana, Chuck Vinton with his unprecedented album collection, Edie and The Parson. Suzy Finch, in a big brick house, her good influence always ready at my side. Daddy nicknamed her Mother Finch years before. He had great hope that she'd straighten me out by osmosis if I just stood next to her. Had I kept standing by her I may have been in my fourth year ready to get my college degree, too.

I met new friends who were more or less positive influences. Richard, a real compadre as it turned out. He and Scotty (Dirty Duck) became my chief supports. Without Scotty, I'm not sure I would've mobilized the staying power. We ate dinner together almost every night at his trailer on the edge of town or in my tiny apartment on Jefferson Street. I first met David (Daddy Duck, the Duck Duck Duck of Earl) through Scotty. In the future these guys would become steady playmates of mine.

Joanie visited. Joanie of horse days long gone by and later of Denver and Stanyan Street. Sarah came, too. Sometimes at night, big-eyed with heartbreaking honesty, Sarah would run in the door describing how a gorilla chased her home. She had the fanciest fantasies. It was hard to resist Sarah. Elegant, she bloomed in big plumed hats and wore home-stitched finery the likes of which I'd never seen, even on Haight Street. She had it nailed. She looked like Jimmy Page or maybe Jimmy Page looked like her?

When she stayed with me, both of us distraught at what had happened to Haight–Ashbury, we listened over and over to a tune called Dear Mr. Fantasy keened by Stevie Winwood from the band Traffic. It helped us lament The Dream. All we had to hold on to for the time being was music to fill in the blanks of our hearts, enable us to cling to the memory of Love. We played it and played it. "Dear Mr. Fantasy play us a tune, Something to make us all feel happy. Do anything, take us out of this gloom, Sing a song, play guitar, make it snappy."

Led Zeppelin, on their first American tour, played in the same room The Moonrakers had played in two years before, almost to the month. That'd been the culprit night I'd accompanied them back to Denver, remember? All Veeder's fault. He and that twelve string guitar of his.

Sarah and me made a batch of bead rings to give Led Zeppelin band members as presents and went to hear them. I made Scotty go, too.

Beholding Robert Plant throwing his soul out of his mouth all over the room did something to my stomach, a 'droppy' feeling that was in no way unpleasant. When we went up to them after the show and gave them their valuable rings (har har), they were appreciative. Now, get back. Robert Plant kissed me. Yep, Plant planted one on my lips that threw me backwards. What a shame an amplifier stood behind me since I fell over it, landing on my bottom. In a trance, I could've cared less. When I popped out of the trance, well, I may have blushed. I may have started coming undone since they were packing up to leave. How could he? I'd never have been able to leave me after a kiss like that.

Led Zeppelin wrote songs about the battle between good and evil. They used references from J.R.R. Tolkien's trilogy The Lord of The Rings. We were on the same page with that, aware that the dark side had thrashed The Dream.

Sarah sewed some kind of ethereal white shirt for Jimmy Page and we flew to Boston to give it to him. How did we fly to Boston? Where did we find the money? I can't remember. We also traveled to Chicago to hang with them.

Anyway, we found remnants of The Dream in music and worshiped the music makers.

To honor Mom and Daddy I made it from September 1968 to June 1969, maintaining a decent grade point. Daddy was thrilled to the point of rewarding me with a cherry red Volkswagen bus. I believe he, himself, wanted one. That's how my dad was. He loved new things, the latest. He'd been first in line at a Dairy Queen and McDonald's when they opened. Even that restaurant chain called Der Weinerschnitzel. He'd try anything. I see his influence more and more as I age and know how to discern it.

A slow learner outside of the classroom, I schemed on returning to the Bay area because, maaaaybeee?

ROAD TRIP NUMBER 9?
NUMBER 9? NUMBER 9?

AFTER A BRIEF, oh so fleeting notion of summer school, my new VW bus wouldn't hear of it. I've lost track of the road trips mentioned so far.

This chapter heading comes from a Beatles song, Revolution 9. A studio engineer did a test saying, "Number 9," over and over instead of like, "Testing one two, testing one two." And I was doing my own test over and over. Testing The Dream. I dared and dared it to come out of hiding. Meanwhile I'd keep searching.

My pal, Val, and me (I know, I know, it should be "Val and I" but sometimes I'm into less formal) planned a drive accompanied by my cat, Judah, to San Francisco via Boulder and Los Angeles. We did all that and along the way I talked to her about The Dream. She hadn't been baited by that unrelenting Siren who had rearranged my life, so I dropped it. Val, like Mother Finch, had admirably earned a college degree and pleased her parents. We comprehended each–others–ness which worked just fine.

Casting my Love line out, trying to bait The Dream, had instead landed me five romantic relationships during the last year. Needing to blow up some emotional bombs, I wrote a composite poem for those loves. I like this poem so I'll share it because you've been in love and you'll relate.

Having waded, struggled and ached through countless
games of love,
some required,

others desired,

some surprises,

some illusions,

some popcorn and peanuts,

all extraordinary,

all necessary,

all beautiful pieces of the enchanting puzzle that put me

together for you,

and you together for me,

I came blundering into your purple–blue, odds–and–ends,

smiling part of space,

and often lost myself in your limitless eyes.

All of your deep captured, captivated,

hurled me spinning through soft breezes of desire

Rewinding reels of memory,

finds an image of you, dappled with raindrop shadows,

and recalls the waterfalls and rainbows I became being you.

Have you not seen through me to you and me,

and me and you?

In the high mountains I saw two trees that had grown together,

and joined, went about their business of reaching for the sun.

We stopped in L.A. to see Rusty. When I looked at him, I comforted myself with tatters of The Dream I saw in his eyes. I wished I could shake his head like a salt shaker to make the tatters sprinkle out into our hands. Maybe we could've thrown them into the air and, poof, recreated The Dream.

Val and I stayed at Rusty's best friend's parents' house, no parents in residence. Rusty's friend's name was Sommers. However, his grandma, Nang, stopped by every afternoon. She headed a gang of characters, the caliber of which were native to southern California. Sommers called them The Nang Gang. I had an inkling they may have had a similar Dream once upon a time and The Nang Gang represented what was left of it. They were cunning, dedicated fans of alcohol. I figure most alcoholics have succumbed to numbing some long lost dream. Gone down like ships weighted with frustration and blues too heavy to carry.

I remember two jim-dandy experiences in Los Angeles. Counting The Nang Gang as one, Sommers initiated the other. "Wanna go swimming tonight, Creamcheese?"

"Sure. Where?"

"This public pool I've tried before in downtown L.A. You'll like it."

"Sommers, downtown L.A. is dangerous. How late does it stay open?"

"Oh it closes before it gets dark, safer to be open during day time."

"Right," I said.

"It'll be an adrenaline adventure. Nang suggested it to me awhile back."

I adored Nang and her gang so I got excited. Anything having to do with the name Nang was okay by me. Besides, I was restless. I needed to act out and I needed a few good laughs, medicine for my dispirited soul. Sommers, a brother of The Dream, I could trust.

Leaving after dark, we drove to the pool. I wondered why there weren't a bunch of gates surrounding it. We left the car in the least lit corner of the parking lot and ducked around circles of light created by plenty of street lights.

When we got to the pool I understood why they hadn't bothered with gates. Standing in front of a chain link fence, I looked up to see how tall it was. Floodlights around the perimeter illuminated eight strands of barbwire, angled outward one on top of each other, to discourage juvenile delinquents like us from sneaking in for a moonlight swim. This represented challenge in its purest form. Without the tequila we'd never have made it.

After Val and I drove on up the coast to act like tourists in San Francisco, we pushed further north in the country. There dwelt a college by the name of Sonoma State. Well, why not this one next? Guilt drove me with a whip. God, I'd hurt my parents so much. The more college I could complete, the better they'd feel. Penance.

Completing the journey, I got a job in Moline at the legendary Plantation Restaurant to save money for another road trip. I also needed more time to rev up for my next run at higher education.

Higher education, it's less painful to write it that way instead of using the other word, the 'c' word. Even saying the word college recalled my guilt, bringing it out in full dress.

SCOUTING WITH MOTHER FINCH

COLLEGE PLAN IN place to enter winter quarter, I'd find a house to rent in Cotati, near Sonoma State, and start establishing residency. Mother Finch and I would do a road trip. Suzy deserved this adventure since she'd gone straight through college and become a teacher. What a concept.

Daddy was happy I was traveling with Mother Finch in preparation to go back to school, but not so happy because his shoulder hurt. He'd been able to retire early since he'd earned it and itched to hit those golf courses. I didn't like that the doctors couldn't diagnose his shoulder pain, but Mom and he encouraged me to 'make tracks' which they said when they meant 'get going'.

It was September 1969. We'd head north in the red VW bus to the Lake of The Woods region in Minnesota, cross the border into Ontario where we'd discover a different breed of beer right off, Canadian beer. A wonderful thing. Turning west, we'd traverse Canada to Vancouver, and make a left to take the coast road down northern California to San Francisco. Of course I had ulterior motives wanting to snoop around for any evidence of Dream sightings and Suzy understood because Suzy got 'it'.

We had a passenger for the entire trip. This won't surprise you in the least, it was a fly. We named him The Chief and became attached to his presence, to the point of being careful when we opened and shut the van doors. The Chief kept to himself, not disgusting like your run-of-the-mill fly or anything. He sat in his own place and never on us, even at night. He wanted out in San Francisco. His choice. FYI, Mother Finch will deny this ever happened if you ask her, but I'm here to tell you it certainly did.

Driving through the Canadian Rockies of Alberta in autumn convinced us the tamaracks, aspens, and evergreens deserved to take a bow. Mother Finch and I vowed to make a quilt out of the same bold greens and radiant golds when we grew up.

Before we'd left Moline to cross Canada, I'd made a plan for our first real stop to be Dogpatch, on the coast by Ft. Bragg in California. It was north of San Francisco and would prep Mother Finch for her first visit to the City by the Bay.

Suzy hadn't been baited by The Dream, but she understood it and her mind was open. I wanted her to meet a few of my friends who'd escaped when it started decomposing (or went into hiding?).

Dogpatch in its day was a sort of a wonder of the world. For me it'd become a 'Clampettized' version of a destination resort. Which is to say the architectural style of Dogpatch appeared jury-rigged: made to keep standing with duct tape and pieces of wire. Like that.

Dogpatch sheltered Robert, Judi, Sally, Tomás, and some other Haight-Ashbury refugees. Indescribable, really, so just try thinking Lil Abner, Mammy and Honest Abe Yokum, Evil-Eye Fleagle and you'll sketch out your own mental photograph of Dogpatch. Clap trap shacks with dirt floors and barefoot mamas. Judi sculpted a nest out of her browned country legs where she cradled newborn baby child after child. Robert, who I found and fell in love with that time when I sought Crazy, qualified as Judi's first child. He caught fish after fish, kept the outdoor fish smoker going and played with his growing number of children. I realized then that being one of Robert's kids would far outrank having him for a husband. He would always be a child at heart.

Suzy and I stayed long enough so that the world looked different when we left. Dogpatch tended to skew a person's world view. In a good way.

In San Francisco I showed Mother Finch historical spots commemorating The Dream and explained I was still hoping to hunt it down. Putting on her detective hat, she scouted with me. No luck.

Suzy flew home to chase Mike some more and maybe get a job. She'd been chasing Mike most of her life and the day would come when he let her catch him. Suzy was like one of those missiles that cannot be deterred. She was a Mike–seeking missile and he never had a chance.

I should've gotten on that plane and flown home with Mother Finch.

HALLOWEEN 1969 — "THE TIME HAS COME THE WALRUS SAID, TO SPEAK OF MANY THINGS"

I GUESS YOU recognize that line written by Lewis Caroll. The many things to speak of, like shades, have been waiting for me in a murky twilight. I never travel there in my mind. But, to tell the story, color inside the lines, I'm obligated to tip toe near the shadows, look in and show you what I see. I'd much rather start stalling about now, write some fluff, but I cannot.

The Dream still had a powerful hold on me. I didn't want to let go. It'd been too beautiful.

Lessons dealing with acceptance of responsibility were about to be learned.

Two girls I'd met before in San Francisco and I scored a small charming house to rent in Cotati. I spent time going back and forth to visit friends who still lived in the city, Cathi and Sarah, who shared a flat far from Haight Street.

I visited them on Halloween, still feeling I needed to pay my final respects to The Dream although I'd already done it how many times? Cathi put on her Indian Maiden costume, her signature fantasy, while Sarah dressed up as herself, which was more than sufficient. I went for my favorite role as good fairy. I did a primo job on my ensemble, a wispy opaque slip for the gown, sprayed silver glitter hair, stars and moons painted wherever they'd fit, and my very good fairy shoes.

Plus my wand. A lot of good that did me.

We took off for the beach on the Great Highway at the end of Golden Gate Park, bound to find a party or start one. The fog added a nice Halloween touch as we built a fire on the sand. Cath and I sauntered down to Playland Hall. The marquis read Hell's Angels Ball October 31, 1969. Fun! I'd had such great rapport with the Angels. They'd been Robin Hoods. Of course, they were no longer nice guys and I knew that. I'd been out and about now and tallied up some knowledge.

But, I longed for the old days and my naive innocence. I wanted it back. I was sad and so empty, too stubborn and reluctant that Halloween night. On purpose I forgot I'd been working at decreasing my substantial intake of denial.

That marquis hypnotized me.

"Let's get out of here," said the Indian Maiden by my side.

My baby growing–up–self paced inside my conscience and screamed leave. Now. But my starved–for–denial self puffed up and screamed stay! Must have more.

I slammed my rose colored glasses onto my face, clicked my heels together three times and said, "Nope, I am going in and I'll be just fine." Like a pitcher's best attempt at his fast ball, I'd thrown myself into my good fairy trip by now.

"Suzee, be heap big serious," said Pocahontas.

"But, they really like me in there. I look like Janis and they love her." I sounded mewly. She was starting to bug me, acting like my mother or something.

Cathi walked away into the fog. I stayed, willing away the danger vibes. They never had a chance to get through my thick stupidity.

There is a big difference between genuine stupidity and purposeful stupidity. And I was being an idiot.

I rode with the Angels that night, on the back of a huge Harley. The guy said they'd take me home. I knew they weren't going in the right direction. They took the good fairy to a house where a gang of them lived. Two men followed her downstairs. They made her lie down on a couch and raped her. She will never understand why there were not more than two of them that came down the stairs.

I learned something though, something true. While I faked being passed out, these two swaggered in, real tough guys. The one suggested they take turns alone with me. When each came to the couch, they changed into different people who tried to be tender, gentle, and kind when no one was looking. They whispered sweet words in my ears. They fumbled, failures at love. No one had taught them how.

I turned off my brain. Went for numb. I survived.

Later when I had to come to terms with this terrible thing that had happened to me, I found compassion within. Yes. Can you believe it? I could only see the truth of shattered lives, of men who'd never known love. I'd made a grave mistake that could've broken me. Now I had a choice. I could learn from it, not waste the suffering, find a way to see that something of value could result from it, or lose my mind. Could it be that I'd not be able to recognize other people's battle scars unless I had a few of my own? Having been through this pain, I could perhaps offer comfort and compassion that can't be sincere unless you've felt it for real yourself. The fullness of the lesson eluded me, but I did know it was my job to forgive those Hell's Angels.

Hank Williams wrote these words and I borrowed them to be my own set of memorized treasures.

"You never walked in that man's shoes, or saw things through his eyes...

But in their shame, they're all the same, these men with broken hearts."

I'd used up my last ace; none left up my sleeve. I mean, it was pure luck I wasn't murdered or worse. Okay, I knew there was a god. That didn't help much. Still running on empty, I hoped for more. Didn't there have to be more? I needed more, but I didn't know of what. Not yet.

ALTAMONT AND
OTHER SORROWS

ON DECEMBER 6 1969 my cherry red VW bus carried us to the free Rolling Stones concert at Altamont Speedway in northern California. A heartbreaker. I stood on a tall black speaker tower next to the stage, near enough to overhear Mick speaking softly to Keith. The Hell's Angels had just killed a man in the crowd below my feet. I watched it happen from my perch.

The vibes in the red–lit air were building to a dangerous level like a sneeze. You could feel it coming. Closer, closer and as panic rose, Mick began generating a peace that, by the grace of god, calmed 300,000 people. 300,000 very freaked out people. Imagine wielding that kind of power. Whatever anyone might say about Mick Jagger, at that moment, a short distance from his compassionate heart, I knew he'd used his power as a light against the powers of darkness.

Led Zeppelin came to town. Sarah and I went. Cathi came, too. I remember walking into their hotel room and having a banana cream pie land on my head as someone launched a fish into the hall. I'd always had a hunger for varied experience so I started eating the pie dripping down my face. Scanning the room for Robert Plant, I didn't find him and left.

I now thought of The Dream in terms of a relic, a fossil I wanted to dig up. Could one do CPR on a cadaver? Voo–doo thoughts snuck up on me sometimes and sent cold currents through my marrow. I didn't like it, made me think of when, as children, Janny and I buried a pet turtle in her backyard. We'd gotten it at Woolworth's in the small pet section along with a small plastic water park home: living quarters for the tiny. Of course it died, and after its solemn funeral we had to practice serious patience. We couldn't wait to dig it up. What a disappointment. Its shell had become soft and squishy, and it looked awful. I don't know what we expected? A scientific find? Maybe that it hadn't died and was 'turtle-sleeping' in suspended animation?

And so, in my consideration of digging up The Dream, I realized the disappointment I'd be asking for.

Everything kept going wrong. Halloween. Altamont. Pies on my head and worst of all, worse than the worst, Daddy had been diagnosed with lung cancer. I asked question after question, each one designed to trivialize what Mom said during that phone call to tell me the impossible and unacceptable news. I didn't cry because Daddy was going to be fine. I knew it.

DADDY

DECEMBER 1969 – JANUARY 1970. Rain has hung my heart with tears.

I already had my plane ticket for Christmas. Since I talked to them often and Daddy sounded fine, I'd persuaded myself he'd be cured. A little chemo and maybe radiation at Mayo Clinic, that's all it'd take.

On the plane I thought about Daddy. I felt his steadying hand on the back of my first bicycle seat as he spent hours until I learned balance. How he repeated his jokes if anyone laughed. How funny he could be and how stubborn. How much he loved The Red Skelton Show and puppies and debating. How people thought he was a sharp dresser. How the waitress in Estes Park, on one of our summer vacations, said he looked like Maurice Chevalier. How he worked so hard and used some of that money to buy me a horse which meant even more driving for him. Coming off the road as a traveling salesman, he'd take me back and forth, back and forth to the boarding stables.

Then there were the times J.B. (my best baby–buddy friend since diapers) and I would schmooze Daddy as soon as he'd walk in the door, beat and happy to be home. At eight years of age we thought ourselves tricky and clever schemers as we'd bring Daddy his slippers before he could even reach his chair to kick his feet up. Next we'd deliver him a Pall Mall cigarette and lighter. Then his bathrobe. But before he was able to enjoy any of it, we'd start begging our little hearts out for him to get right back up and drive us out of the city limits (fifteen miles or so) to our idea of heaven: Starlight Amusement Park. And he'd do it. His doting, self–sacrificing heart couldn't resist us.

How much he loved me and my mom.

Mom picked me up at the airport, said the treatments had worn Daddy out. She wanted to prepare me. Unsettled by the worry on her face, I hesitated before the front door. "Go on, honey," she said, "Daddy is waiting like a little kid, he's so excited to see you."

I opened the door and saw him sitting at the dining room table. When I hurried over to hug him, and looked into his blue blue eyes I saw that nothing except his eyes were like always. My daddy looked thirty years older. White-haired and too weak to stand, he had a walker next to his chair. A fucking walker. I wanted to kick it to the moon.

Daddy would die. No, huh-uh, no. Please. Shocked, I sank into a comfortable easy chair of denial and settled there. Then I discovered courage. Brave like a warrior, I'd fight the disease and Daddy would be one of the lucky ones. I'd begin the mending of him with positive thoughts and god would perform the rest, the healing cure.

Mom and me took care of him. I played songs for him on my guitar. One night a crowd of homies came over. Enter Sonja and Rusty, mainstays since they kept my ship afloat during many a devastating personal storm, and seven or eight other anchoring friends. I sat on the floor by the couch where Daddy stayed now. My friends went to hang out in our family room. I remember playing him a song about reincarnation that I hoped would inspire his spirit. He told me, "Suzee-babe (he'd called me that since I was a little girl), go be with your friends, you don't need to stay with me." After I played another song, I went to my friends and remember taking a picture of them in a group on the sofa and floor. They visited with him on their way through the living room when they left. Daddy liked that. He loved to talk.

The cancer spread to the base of his brain and wiped out part of his personality. He acted spacey and those blue blue eyes didn't always track. Aunt Florence took time off from her nurse job and came from Chicago to help. I made Daddy a colorful mobile out of construction paper and hung it from the ceiling over the couch so he could space out on the whirling shapes.

The day came too soon when he couldn't stand or walk. Aunt Florence and Mom and I weren't able to take care of him. Hospice hadn't come to Moline yet. Daddy went to the hospital in an ambulance. When they took him out the door in a gurney he cried. "Good-bye house, you've been a good house," tears on his face. This made me see the child in him. His words to our house brought me nose to nose with his death. I saw in his words how much our house had been his big dream and he didn't want it to end. I thought of life without him and it wasn't going to work. I remembered the all the times he'd held me and made me safe. When I was a little girl he was my first love.

I rode in the ambulance with him.

At the hospital I sat in a chair and embroidered flowers and stars on my clothes until one night, the nurse walked into the room, looked at the monitors and told us Daddy was dying. We stood at his bedside. Mom looked lost. I told her to hold his hand. She held his left hand and I held his right one. He'd been in a coma for three days. And about two minutes later on January 20th in 1970, he took one long rattling last breath.

I did not cry. I became Sturdy Suzee for Mommy. The god I didn't know very well granted me strength and strong faith in there being some sort of eternal life.

Jan came home from school in Madison, WI. The same Jan I'd gone to kindergarten and to see the Beatles with. Other old friends young and old came. There must have been lots of people. It remains a blur. My one memory is Janny standing behind my closet door in my room holding me.

I smiled at the minister the entire time during the funeral service, like I was reassuring the man, holding him up, helping him keep the faith. And he was the Christian, not me. Strange.

My memory switches from the church to the grave site with nothing in between. The last thing I remember from that day is an old friend of Daddy's. The man walked up to me on the grass at the cemetery on that cold, gray January day and took my hands. He said, "You've just lost your best friend." It hit me in my guts.

I've rediscovered that truth everyday since because there is no one who can take his place. I miss him. I miss his love for me like crazy. It's irreplaceable. On earth, if the daddy is a good one, an unmarred daddy, then there is nothing quite like the love between a girl and her father.

I miss him.

NOW WHAT?

EAGER TO STAY busy, Mom returned to teaching Latin and English that February of 1970. She wanted to face life, get the reentry part over with, take it on. Single now, she'd never date or marry again. She confided in me years later that she'd been given one kind and loving man, so special she'd never want another.

She told me to make tracks.

I begged her to buy me an Old English Sheepdog I'd seen advertised in the paper. I named him Wynken. I needed this dog. I was a lonely girl now, but I didn't admit it.

No college plan, I'd trashed that idea, honest for once. But not honest enough to tell Mom that quite yet. She had plenty to handle, finding her way through a death to start a new life.

No Dream.

No San Francisco.

No Daddy.

Sitting in the eye doctor's office, waiting to have a check up before I left town, I contemplated my future. I needed to go back to California and could stay in the rented house with the two girls. I'd get a job there in the small town of Cotati. I wanted to live in the country and regroup. Get a grip because my hold on the future was slippery. Hell, my hold on the present felt like I slid inch by inch towards the bottom of my rope and what would I land on? Not brave enough to even look down and see, I realized that for the first time I felt lost.

I invented things to shoot for. New plans. New meaning. New things to look forward to. I considered other friends who'd moved farther into the country that I could stay with for awhile.

It happened right then. I heard a voice. I'd never heard a voice in my head like this one.

The voice said, "Go to a high mountain in The Rockies of Colorado and learn how to live simply and how to survive." What? The voice insinuated I shouldn't lolly gag. And that was that.

I flew back to San Francisco, caught a lift to Cotati where I'd parked my VW bus, packed up and split. My new roommates were speechless as I blew in, loaded the bus and left. I didn't try to explain. I knew all I needed to know. This new direction, like nothing I'd experienced, made a fork in the road of my life. No similarity to my gunslinger of a Siren, this voice didn't just act like a big shot, it shoved with serious intent.

Wynken and I drove through San Francisco. Our affair ended, I needed closure. It had to be a real farewell and to do it right, I wrote a thank you note to my city that had hatched The Dream. I laid the envelope on the beach by Seal Rock.

what a royal sunset.

i'll be blunt, it may dull the pain.

good-bye.

you've been gentle, shown me patience and guidance.

i will see you again i suppose,

but no matter how many times, i'll always cry.

you gave me my first glimpse,

touched me with all the power of Love.

i wonder if you'll remember me?

i'll never forget you.

thank you, San Francisco.

it's time.

i must go.

I drove north and stopped in Grass Valley, California to say bye to Gwenn who'd bolted to the country. She knew. I told her about the voice, ate her homemade granola piled with fresh strawberries, and drove away. Waving me on, Gwennie came across as the spiritual cheerleader she is. I didn't even spend the night. Orders are orders, man!

When I came to the western edge of the desert, thinking about how far it stretched, I felt a little flutter. What was I doing? "Get going," that pushy voice reminded me. It made me think of that earnest rabbit in Wonderland with the watch, in a hardcore hurry. All the time.

About ninety miles past Reno I started to shake. "Wynken, are you alright?" I said. What could he tell me? He wasn't the one shaking. Am I alright?, the better question. He moved closer to lean his head on my shoulder. I didn't even know where to go except to some high mountain.

We drove on and on. The desert is a lonesome place. I did it, I asked for a sign, any teeny weeny sign. I advertised for help in an invisible newspaper. Teeny weeny sign would be most welcome!

In two seconds a car passed, swerving around my bus with a girl waving intently, signaling me over to the side of the road. I pulled onto the shoulder, she jumped out of the passenger side and sprinted to my window. "Do you happen to be driving to Colorado?"

"Yes, as a matter of fact," I said, "I am."

"Can I have a ride?" In a whisper she said, "Please?"

"Get in," I said. What was happening? Was it really happening? I stared at my hands on the wheel. Yeah, I'd been given a sign. So relieved to know somehow the voice I'd obeyed had put me on the right path, my body went all shapeless like a soaked soup cracker. Tension must've been holding me up in the driver's seat for a long time.

She had a small satchel and lost no time running in front of my bus to the passenger side and yanking the door open to let herself in. Now I could legitimately ask the question of a person instead of a dog, "Are you alright?"

"Now I am," she said.

"What's your name?"

"Ivy."

"I'm Suzee and you have no idea how happy I am to meet you. Welcome to my bus."

Ivy explained how she'd felt like she was stuck in some bad movie. When the car she rode in passed us and she saw Wynken and I, she told me it was like she looked though a little hole in the wall of the theater she sat in. And it looked like a great movie was playing on the screen next door. She wanted to be sitting in that theater instead, the theater of my red bus.

Seconds before, she'd seen my bus in front of them and prayed for help. Her prayer happened at the exact time I'd advertised for a sign.

Talk about instant best friends.

The guy who'd picked her up hitchhiking seemed hunky-dory, high tailing it to Boulder where she lived, driving straight through, he'd said. They sped along until Reno when he decided he wanted to rent a motel room and do some gambling. Ivy told him she'd continue hitching and he seemed very disappointed.

She scooted off, found a corner by the highway and sat there all night. No cars stopped. Until dawn the next morning when the same man swung over, got out, opened her door and said, "Get in, you'll never get to Boulder without me." He wasn't rough, but persistent so she got in the car. They were alone out there that early in the morning. Luckily he agreed to stop when she waved me down.

Now, no longer by myself out in the middle of the desert, I didn't feel so lost. In fact it was a revelation admitting to myself that I'd felt lost at all. Hope came glad-handing, but in a sincere way. Ivy invited us to stay at her house where she lived with a group of vegetarians. "Thank you," I said. I also said thank you to that voice, still trying to work out what or who it could be. Wynken and me were going to be fine, rescued. I'd been injected with something like a booster shot of faith. As had Ivy. She also understood the attempted assassination of The Dream. That in itself gave me great consolation. I felt stronger. Anson would be proud.

The voice played a major part in my destiny. I started thinking of the voice as a guide to be trusted.

I liked that. No, I loved that. Something, maybe the something or someone I began to realize I needed, was afoot. Had The Dream hired the voice?

BOULDER AND THE SEARCH

I LOVE THIS part of the story.

For one thing, I had something new to search for. Instead of The Dream I needed to find a place high in the Rocky Mountains to live in so I could learn the art of survival. I figured this meant living without normal amenities. Or maybe none.

The folks at Ivy's house were loving. The beer drinking, meat eating ones lived upstairs. The vegetarians and rigorous fasting/cleansing group lived downstairs. No one had any problems with anyone else. Plus they welcomed me as a stranger who might be an angel, you never knew, and invited me to stay forever if I wanted.

I explained I would contribute when I found a job and be leaving to live in the mountains when I found a cabin. They could dig it.

I broke this news to my mom. Nothing I did anymore seemed to worry her as much as before. She loved me, tried to trust me and besides, teaching full time took most of her energy. Her survival plan? Keep busy. Booked to the gills. The squares for days of the month on her appointment calendar looked black, there were that many penciled-in plans filling the space.

I began my search two days after I rested and cleaned up. First I walked around Boulder. Part of the day, I stuck my nose inside doors to ask about jobs and then I'd drive up dirt canyon roads on the look out for cabins. After three weeks of rigorous effort with no leads, I wondered if I'd blown it. My guide voice? In absentia. Then I had an interesting thought. What if the mountains were testing me, making sure I wanted to live in them and learn from them bad enough to stick this out? The thought carried a lot of weight and I kept looking.

One February evening I walked into a restaurant named The Little Kitchen, hungry after a wearying day of driving mountain roads. I felt blue, burnt out from hunting. Dropping down on a red stool, I rested my head in my hands and asked for a cup of ginseng tea.

I took a gander down the counter to my left and locked eyes with a boy who had red hair, freckles and a magnetic aura. I knew a character looked back at me. I thought, Oh yay, I could use a character about now. Characters held a high place in my estimation because Daddy had been one and as you'll recall, taught me the art of Character Appreciation as soon as I could talk.

I slid from stool to stool down the counter to ask him the question I fell asleep reciting each night. "Do you, by any chance, know of anywhere to rent up in the mountains or where I can get a job?"

"Nope," he said, "but why don't we get a bottle of wine, go to my place and I'll do a Tarot card reading for you."

"Sure," I said. I liked him right away. A lot. He wore a long coat like Jethro Tull and reminded me of a leprechaun. What's not to like? Also I recognized a hint of The Dream in his eyes.

By turning the Tarot cards face up and studying them, they assured him I'd find a cabin the next day, and spoken as an afterthought he said, "Oh yeah, a job, too."

I couldn't bring myself to believe that.

However...

WARD, COLORADO

NEXT MORNING, A Sunday in March, one scheduled stop included an old ghost town called Ward.

When combing the back roads I alternated between several routes. I'd met two of the eight or nine Wardians on my recent explorations through there, Jayne and Norman. One road curled through what remained of the town, landing a person at the top end on the Peak to Peak Highway. I'd been attracted to Ward right off since it fit the bill as a high mountain, around 10,000 feet. I yelled for Jayne who came out onto her porch and she told me like always, "No cabins for rent. Sorry, don't give up." I admired Jayne because she'd been at Woodstock. Sequestered in Moline with hepatitis, I couldn't go.

I'd also once run into Norman walking on the road through Ward. He carried a gallon jug of Wild Turkey in his Bluto-sized hand. The whole Norman was as big as Bluto, Viking style, because he had shoulder length blonde hair and a fierce expression.

I drove down Lefthand Canyon. The strong smell of pines rubbed in how I didn't live among them and depressed me. A truck approached from the other direction and braked to a stop as a dark-bearded, short-haired man rolled down his window. "By any chance would you be wanting to find a cabin to rent in Ward?" he said. He really did. He said exactly that to me in the middle of the road.

"Yes. Why? Yes I am."

"Turn around and follow me. I own a cabin by the post office. It's a miner's cabin, built in the late 1800s. It's old."

He showed me the most perfect cabin in the whole wide world. No electricity, no water, an outhouse, a coal storage room, a cookstove in the kitchen, a pot-bellied stove in the living room and a bed room with a brass bed. All of maybe 400 square feet, the place could be mine.

"And just in case, would you want to trade that bus of yours for my cabin and this 1947 Chevy pickup? I am moving to Alaska," he said.

"I absolutely do want to make that trade," I said.

"I have the title to my truck and the deed to the cabin on me. How about we do this now?"

"Why not?" I said. "Lets do it."

I chugged to Boulder in my new truck and I named her Sarah on the way down the mountain. She ran fine. I don't even remember the man's name, but he'd taken admirable care of Sarah.

Parked in front of The Little Kitchen, I jumped out and hurried inside to look for that boy who'd read the Tarot cards. The owner of the restaurant, Richard, a quiet, mellow cat, walked up to me and said, "Hey, somebody quit. Do you still want to work here?"

It felt like my eyes spun in circles. "YES! Yes, yes, yes," I said.

"Can you start now?" Richard asked.

"Sure I can."

Freaking out, I scanned the place for the Jethro Tull leprechaun. He sat, grinning, at the counter.

Reminding me of the plane ride to San Francisco with Kurt so he could introduce me to Haight-Ashbury, overnight my life had become a magic carpet ride.

I moved into my cabin.

WHEN I BEGAN WRITING
THIS HERE BOOK

I'D FOLLOWED WHAT I'd come to think of as orders from headquarters to get thee to, not a nunnery, although it would've upgraded my lifestyle at the time, but to the Colorado Rocky Mountains.

Once nestled in, I heard the voice again. The time had come to start the book.

Sitting by my pot-bellied stove across from the window in June 1970, I spaced out watching snow fall. Being summer according to the calendar didn't matter at this altitude.

That book. Now? For real?

O-o-o-o-kay. I spread the notes I'd begun five years ago in 1965 onto the uneven top of a crotchety table. I started reading. My records took me back to when 'it', the Time-Of-All-Times, started. Here are the first two sentences:

"I want to try to help you navigate through some of your changes; the hard ones, the lonely ones, and the confusing ones. Because I Love you."

Once and for all I'd make sense of these notes. I copied the two sentences on the top page of a thick pad filled with lined yellow paper.

Daydreaming, I remembered why I wrote those words and I remembered what those words meant to me in 1965. I gave my mind a vigorous shake. I needed to reenter 1970 and catch my breath. Embarking on holy ground, I couldn't just rush in.

I looked out the window. Corn snow pummeled the tin roof as my cat tried with all of his cat–might to sit smack dab on my pencil. Weather that high up was dramatic. I had all the time in the world to write my story. Or so it seemed, since I'd just turned a mere twenty–three years old. Adding enough sentences to fill the first page made me feel better. I'd begun. The voice sighed.

I lived in a dangerous town. You'll see.

THE WINDS OF WARD

SPRING AND SUMMER were a snap. It's a good thing they broke me in before winter of 1970 came. Wynken and me raved over the beauty and adventure. I burst into tears at the baby green of Aspen trees. Then came the first of the wildflowers. High mountain air doesn't play fair with how tickly it can be. Like kitten whiskers. Like the whole kitten bumping me with its kitty nose and tapping its little paddy paws on my cheeks.

We camped out under the clear star-dotted skies. Seen at such soaring elevation, there were too many. They made us howl at them.

I found out how to identify mushrooms and gobbled them all summer.

I would learn the art of survival in Ward, like I'd been told to do by the voice.

So would the three girls who became my mountain-women sisters. Sherry, Jennifer (Jenny) and Ruby. We did everything together. Rusty moved to Ward along with many others from Haight-Ashbury. The Bucksnorter's Hash and Incense Club was born as more people arrived. If we weren't tearing up the town in Boulder at The Sink wearing our hefty mountain boots and getting rowdy under the pinball machine, we and others of our kind from Ward would make it to Gold Hill and take over The Gold Hill Inn. The shortcut involved an hellacious drive on a non-road. We only went to Gold Hill to seriously drink and close the place down. In winter we'd creep home in a VW bug that barely fit on the narrow invisible path covered with fresh fallen snow. The drop off the ledge was a good 1,000 feet. Looking over was like looking out an airplane window. On our 3:00 A.M. trips back to Ward, I got out and walked. Not only to break trail so the driver could see, but to save my life.

Old things remained in Ward. Like Hazel. I met her soon after I moved in. Eighty-four and single throughout her life, she drove a red jeep, and wore a brown leather aviator's cap with flaps and a bill. A retired biologist, she messed around growing things inside and outside. I saw her outdoors every-day I spent in Ward. Hazel knew a mound of history and owned most of the town, had bought it up during the depression.

Aged buildings still stood, too, like Hazel. I snuck into a boarded and locked hotel with rooms intact. It reminded me of the Titanic. Clothes hung in wardrobes and the beds were made. Gave me a vibe of Miss Havisham from Dickens' Great Expectations. Creepy.

Ward is the third windiest place on earth, a documented fact according to Hazel. Sometimes the wind howled for weeks on end. Situated below the Continental Divide and nestled into a geographical bowl, Ward set a trap for the wind. Many a night spent sitting alone in my historic cabin built by long gone miners, the wind galloped around the corners, screaming and laughing, chasing its tail. Something went on in that wind. I heard tell it contained spirits of men, women and children who died in the fire of 1901 which reduced the population of Ward from over 9,000 to the ghost town I now lived in. A few times when the wind bellowed outside my cabin, I sensed a couple hoary miners discussing newfound claims. Pale forms hunkered over and their voices became low and secretive, like they knew I was listening.

When I walked through town by the ramshackle Odd Fellows Building on windy whiny nights, I heard tinkly player piano music. Haunting echoes and emptiness floated into the street. It'd served as the town's saloon and I even heard glasses break, barroom brawls.

Once I tried walking home from a party down the Peak to Peak Highway, but thanks to the wind, had to crawl a half a mile on my hands and knees until I entered the bowl. I'd been knocked clean off my feet by the wind. Another time, after eighteen days of shrieking, it squirmed into my mind like a worm and tried to possess me. The winds of Ward were not wimpy.

WINTERTIME IN WARD — NOT FOR WUSSIES

LET'S TALK ABOUT wind chill factors. The wind blew over ninety knots (just over 100 mph) during my first winter. The temperature fell to forty below zero. I don't know how to calculate wind chill figures and maybe I'm glad. Jayne told me to put tape across the keyhole of my front door in the fall.

"What? Why?" I'd asked.

"To keep the snow out."

"Aw, come on, you've got to be kidding." I looked at her hopefully.

"No," she said, "I'm not."

Jayne didn't kid much. Kidding didn't come easily to her. Living at 10,000 feet can do that to a girl.

Well, I forgot to tape the keyhole one night and in the morning I woke to a three foot snow drift in my miniature living room. Speaking of snow, like the wind, there was a lot of that, too. It drifted high over my roof and to enter my cabin I had to scoot down an icy slide, barely clearing my head through the top of the door frame, into the coal room off the kitchen.

When storms came through, the venerable Hazel warned me to never allow my fires to go out. I must tend the coal fire in both stoves all day and all night long. I took that advice to heart. Sometimes a Wardite would check on me. I appreciated it, but the full time work of keeping the fires burning kept me from getting lonely. Coal is impressive. I can still see those big jagged earthy chunks of black energy glowing red hot.

I acquired a chamber pot with a lid.

Ward...not for wussies.

Norman toyed with me, teased me in a gruff Norman way. "You'll never make it this winter. You're a Flower Child, not a mountain woman. And besides, there ain't a drop of miner's blood in you." Norman was a miner.

Spring doesn't come until May that high up in the air. As a trophy of sorts, I found an old fashioned, gorgeous, brown wicker rocking chair with big arms in the back of my pickup. Norman put it there. Then I realized he'd dared me in his own grumpy way to last through the winter. Norman, proud of the Flower Child, rewarded me.

I said I lived in a dangerous town. To show it will take some space. I lived in Character–ville. Some of them, like the weather, could be dangerous.

THE CHARACTERS OF WARD

MAGICAL SKIES, COLORS, clouds, stars, flowers, trees, air, mountains, ponds, people...Colorado itself. Perhaps The Dream wasn't dead or in hiding? Had it mutated in a way I didn't understand yet? I tried to pay close attention. The way the voice had directed me, the miraculous movings in the invisible world that had sent me to my cabin and job, gave me hope. Maybe The Dream, chameleon-like, had plans in the making.

Chameleon. A more perfect segue to bring in my first character does not exist.

Paul Dunn. I'd first met him late in May 1971 up on a hill off Left Hand Canyon. Someone suggested I look him up when I was searching for a cabin. I followed directions and hiked a trail to his one room shack. Before I knocked he said, "Come in, I knew you'd come." The blue in his eyes arced across the room, and touched me. I'd never been touched by an eye color before.

"Wow, what did you do just then, with that whatever it was from your eyes?" I asked.

He smiled knowingly. "Just something my eyes do when a Pisces comes into view. I can't explain it."

"How do you know I'm a Pisces?"

"I can't explain that either."

He had long greying hair, a salt and peppered beard, and looking at him through dust motes in the sunshine coming through the window, I swear his skin sparkled.

"Are you a wizard or something?" I asked.

"I don't know, and I can't explain what I mean by that either," he said. The air turned wavy and I thought I saw a tall pointed hat start apparating (thank you J.K. Rowling) above his head.

I told him where I worked and to let me know if he heard of anywhere to rent.

The next time I ran into Paul Dunn, he'd moved off his hill down to a shack near the road. He'd also moved out of Merlin mode. He'd done an about face, changed his address at the personality post office. Seriously. He wore a funky ratty old Gabby Hayes type hat, tied his hair straight back in a pony tail with leather cord, and had birthed a new image.

Meet Paul the Miner. He had a new vocabulary, talkin' silver, mica and gold in them thar' hills. Toting a verbal bag, he heaped mining tales on the table. This Miner version of Paul, a bundle of charisma, came to my cabin with a bottle of whiskey and named me Belle. Belle, the Belle of Ward. It didn't take much of a whiskey ticket to get on board the time travel train of which he was the conductor. His stories came from the infamous old days of mining in Ward, and sounded legitimate enough to almost make me believe he'd been alive back then.

I learned from one of Paul's girlfriends that in his prior life before Ward, he'd been a famous disc jockey back on the east coast. Didn't necessitate any leap of imagination to picture Paul Dunn rapping into a microphone, spinning vinyl over the airwaves.

Paul Dunn the Miner's next incarnation did not bode well. He assumed the identity of an outlaw. He got a horse, wore old style chaps, a neckerchief, spurs and rode around town with a shotgun shoved into a scabbard. He cut off his hair and shaved his beard. His stories now told of escapes lived by Jesse James and Kid Curry. His spun tales whirled faster telling of bank robberies and hideouts. This Paul Dunn, the outlaw, drank more whiskey than the miner had. He started riding his horse into the middle of the road in town, neckerchief up to cover the lower half of his face, to stop cars. He held up people in cars. "Hand over all your money or else." We thought he'd gone too far this time, but we hadn't seen nuthin' yet. He'd become Dangerous Dunn.

Drunk one night, Dangerous Dunn sunk into an irrational jealous rage over a young lady who'd put up her teepee near Ward. He'd seen her chatting with Bruce, a musical genius who played organ, piano and sang opera. Dangerous Dunn rode to Bruce's cabin later that evening, pulled out his buck knife and cut off Bruce's earlobe. He escaped on his horse and wasn't seen again for months.

Ward grew by leaps and bounds. Flower Children and hippies fleeing the cities, outrunning shrapnel from the detonation that blew up The Dream, found remote havens where they could nurse their wounds. Would there be a way to recover? If we abandoned The Dream, could we replace it with another aspiration, as holy? Like the grail?

Ward's population grew from eight or nine to seventy or eighty. It secured a riveting reputation as a hiding place from fallout and a sanctuary for rogues, even revolutionists.

Redbeard, a piratical ex–biker sporting a black eye patch, ferreted his way to Ward as did Patti Hearst. Ward had been discovered, attracting characters with a capital C. Every newcomer was an Advanced Character.

There may as well have been a border crossing into Ward: to gain entrance to the Province. The Ph.D you earned in the outrageous character development department of your own self would serve as your passport.

I realize the need to write a whole separate book to do Ward justice. Daddy would agree (being one) that it is characters that make the world go round. Actually, it's god doing the spinning like a divine D.J., but characters are spice. Judge–like, they overrule boring claims made by lawyers of blandness in the courtroom of life.

Hold on a moment.

I think I'm in trouble.

No, I AM in trouble.

I can't handle this chapter. Remember when I said the characters in my backstory wanted me to tell their stories and how they were all clamoring to be first?

Now they're jumping up and down, shaking the ground I put them on. I just stuck my head out my mental window and they have lined up outside the room where I'm writing and I can't see the end of the line, even when I squint my eyes.

They've been biding their time to gang up on me. I'm afraid it might mean more of these kinds of stories are out there, full of characters that I've forgotten or tried to forget. I bet they've written stories of their own. Just as important to them as mine is to me. What if they're even better?

Humility is not a bad thing.

But I'm pretty sure that doesn't sound like me. Selfish Suzee isn't all that much nicer than Dangerous Dunn. She could maybe sink into irrational jealousy over some writer's better story and cut his ear off.

A One–Act Starring The FBI

A FEW MORE details, a tad more fleshing out before I break free from the gravitational pull of those times and people.

I shared a job as Post Mistress in the shabby building across the way from my cabin that served as the Ward Post Office. Joe brought the mail, rain or shine and all that. As Post Mistress, I handed out mail to the characters, and shot the breeze for a spell.

When the FBI got to town, they trusted me implicitly. Post Mistress equaled Government Employee equaled ally. The agents came to investigate an allegation of hashish being brought into the country through Ward. Of course hash arrived regularly to a phony post office box, phony since the name of the key holder was fake. We'd set it up so delivery happened without a glitch. Duck soup. I didn't have to do much, just put a brown paper–wrapped box in a slot and wait until Bill stopped in to get it. Bill the lawyer received hash from Holland for fun. He didn't sell it or anything.

The FBI stood out like aliens from outer space. You could not miss them, even if you wanted to. They might as well have held signs high overhead accompanied by a megaphone to announce, "WE ARE THE FBI!! WOULD YOU LIKE AN AUTOGRAPH? OR A FREE PICTURE TAKEN WITH US?" Thinking they'd shrewdly infiltrated the community, dressed in checkered lumberjack type shirts so new the folded creases showed, these guys 'mingled'. Nonchalant, they sauntered into the post office, winking at me and wearing weird wool hats. Under the mistaken illusion they were incognito, they waited to spring their trap.

Residents who wore faded, patched, and sweaty shirts smelling of coal smoke couldn't get enough of these honest-to-god G Men. They were the best entertainment to hit town all winter.

As a stand-up government employed patriot, the FBI commanded me to point out any suspicious persons in the post office. I did. I passed messages tucked between letters to everyone who came to get their mail. In case they'd somehow missed the fact of the FBI, my notes pointed out the most suspicious persons in town, those well-groomed fashionable men from the Federal Bureau of Investigation.

OUR FINAL
HITCHHIKING TOUR

"For still there are so many things that I have never seen. In every wood, in every spring there is a different green." Bilbo Baggins said that. It also applies to people. I subscribe to his philosophy.

As if I hadn't gotten my fill of characters, Wynken and I journeyed to the Canadian capital of characters in July 1971. I suspected we'd find characters where I'd set my sights, but did not expect it to be quite the Character Central we encountered. Wynken and I took off on a hitchhiking venture of enormous scale. I didn't inform my mom of our plan. I called her from pay phones, but didn't share the full scope. Didn't mention that my call originated from Canada for instance.

Leaving Ward to make a serious loop, riding every roller coaster on the way (me, not Wynken), we'd hitch to Washington, north into Canada, and check out Vancouver Island. Somewhere along the way we met the Jethro Tull Leprechaun by arrangement and camped at Wreck Bay on Long Beach. Then we crossed the provinces to my true destination, Toronto, to find Anson. If anyone knew what might be coming next, it'd be Anson.

Oh, and we found a number of roller coasters.

The hitchhiking extravaganza proved to be so fine. No worries: my approach to a walk about. Wynken was a wonderful hitchhiker. Sheepdogs are very dignified, keen, aware and loving. They inspect and guard, on duty at all times.

I often think of Jesus as a sheepdog.

In the days, starting during the time of The Dream, when hitchhiking didn't scare me, I learned a thing or two.

Nine out of ten rides I got were with so-called 'lower class' nobodies in dumpy old vehicles, who abounded with a mobile neighborliness. These people were not in bondage to possessions.

I listened to their wonderful tales, wise sayings, and found out about forgotten home remedies that still work. I learned hundreds of songs I'd never heard before. One percent of the people who stopped to give me a ride drove big fancy cars. They either didn't speak or became animated telling me why they were so important and rich.

Janis sang: "Freedom's just another word for nothing left to lose." I've noted that people who possess the least are the most generous. If they have two dollars to their name, they'll give one away to someone holding a sign on a street corner. The more we have, the tighter we seem to hold on. Check it out.

There has been a mistake in regard to the terms 'high class' and 'low class'. Their meanings should be reversed.

We hadn't communicated for ages, but I'd been singing to Anson for years. Accompanying myself on guitar, I talk/sang to Anson, told him what happened to be on my mind, in my heart, asked him questions, sent ponderings in his direction. I didn't think he happened to be some ascended master or anything, I just missed him.

We appeared in Kensington Market Place, unannounced, at the small shop he'd opened. The circus that he unavoidably drew to himself assailed us the minute we stepped into his world. We entered an ongoing sideshow packed with a curious menagerie, an offbeat breed of individuals.

Older, wiser, more beautiful than ever, he welcomed us.

Creative, energetic, Anson is driven like most sensitive and lovable madmen.

The first associate of his we met, an older Jewish man named Pickles, stole my heart right off the bat. Pickles reminded me of a grizzled Mr. Mxyzptik.

Tell me you have heard of Mr. Mxyzptik, one of Superman's cosmic arch-rivals who materialized during rare instances when red kryptonite came into the picture. Anyway, Pickles looked and acted like Mr. Mxyzptik. He'd cut his hair, which had touched the ground, the week before. We hated to have missed his hair.

Pickles, no hoarder but an inventor and artist, created what he christened 'maharajahs'. He gave us a tour of his one room domain brimming with trinkets of every UNimaginable kind. Drawers, boxes, shoes, and closets overflowed with not only free floating, but jars and envelopes full of, well, junk. But not junk to Pickles. Walking into his room felt like walking into a giant bubblegum machine that has those little plastic encased toys in it instead of gum, or like a twenty-five square foot crackerjack box full of the prizes found on the bottom. Want more? I recognized marbles, glass stones, jewels, miniature balls, rubber bands, bangles and bingles, etc. etc. etc. Amazed and impressed, I wondered how he'd found Anson. Hmmm, that made me wonder about me, how had I found Anson and why did I maintain this loyal orbit around the sun-of-him?

To the maharajahs now. Teetering on mounds of treasure lorded Pickle's maharajahs, phantasmagorically shaped sculptures created from his trove of valuables. In the corner stood his latest masterpiece, a six foot maharajah made from hundreds of thousands of delightful things in his storehouse. He slept in there somehow. We didn't see a bed.

Next person in the cast we met told us her name in a loud brusque voice as she marched into the shop on determined stubby legs. "I am Myra!" In saying her name, she rolled the 'R' with attitude. This twenty-seven year old Myra was Russian, three and a half feet tall, and had the mind of a ten year old. "I, Myrr-r-r-ra, am here." She'd get louder. "IN MY FRIEND ANSON'S SHOP TO HELP SERVE YOU!" When she pronounced Anson's name she put a puff of an 'H' in front of it. So it came out, "Hanson." Myra the sales representative! Anson didn't say a word, but we could tell he thought Myra outstanding.

Everyday Myra peddled her small bike over to Anson's shop, where he made and sold pipes, creatures and various other things carved from soapstone. Customers reacted to Myra. Some fled, some watched her without losing sight of where she was at all times, some chuckled, some rolled their eyes and others were just plain awestruck. I appreciated her, found her impossible to resist.

She'd leave after an hour or two of 'work' having stolen something. Anson said she liked leaving with all the money in the cash register the best. If not that, she helped herself to some items for sale in the shop. Her parents always called to tell Anson what she'd brought home. Then they'd have her bring it back. Anson got used to it.

He had no knowledge to lay on me about the missing Dream or what would happen next. He had his hands full, living and loving life. To Anson, The Dream had taken up residence in every person he met. That fit...that worked. Anson embodied The Dream, accepting and loving the unlovable characters. I'd been able to empathize enough to do that part. But, more than that, he believed in them, and this bigger task of believing in them showed off the real nature of The Dream.

I needed to know exactly how he did it.

I had a problem, though. I didn't know why my heart still felt a longing. Shouldn't this have satisfied my search? Finding what had become of The Dream and where it was destined to take us as Lovers of the world?

Why did it seem something was still missing, out of reach? What else could there be?

I didn't even know how to ask the question. Not of Anson or myself. Yet.

DON COMES TO TOWN

I DIDN'T CALL Don 'the Desperado' when I met him. He and a batch of people rolled down into Ward about August of '71 from even higher up the mountain where they'd made a go at spending the winter near Brainard Lake. Don came to Colorado from Oklahoma. He caught my eye.

More than that, I fell in love with Don. One night at a party I watched him from across the room as he sat alone at the kitchen table. His huge persona was on break and his face, eyes looking down at the table top, showed vulnerability. A tired soft smile shaped his mouth. It seemed like he was far away, not in the room at all, and he looked sad, almost defeated somehow. My heart kneeled at his side then and there. He had no clue. This small time frame is a picture that has held its color and life as clear as if it happened a few minutes ago. And it's been over forty years.

It took about three minutes of staring at him without his knowledge for me to come to my solemn conclusion. I wanted someone to tame me and I sensed that this young man could and would.

He bought two horses. A retired thoroughbred racehorse called Hot Fudge and an Appaloosa for me named Cozan. We camped, heard mountain lions scream, shot and ate a beaver, fell more in love.

We planned to go backpacking around Europe. Jenny, my friend, would babysit Wynken. We gave the horses away.

I wondered if The Dream had given up its American citizenship. I couldn't stop my quest since there was still a vacancy in my heart. There had to be one more thing The Dream had that would fill it. Something waiting for me. Wanting me to come close enough to find it or near enough to be found.

Before we left, watching sightseers drive by Don's cabin, a school bus maneuvered the narrow path of a road. This black man stepped out to ask directions. He wore a long buckskin robe and a headdress. Three long eagle feathers stuck out from braided kinky hair.

I zoned in on his face. I'd seen that face before. Then he saw mine. We shrieked.

Out of nowhere, Fred had appeared. In Ward! Fred was fine. No longer an ancient Egyptian/India/Indian holy man, fatter and mellow with teeth in his mouth, he'd morphed into Three Feathers. Wow.

Will Fred come into view like a star on the horizon of my life now and then for the duration? Thinking of Paul Dunn I wondered, who would Three Feathers be next time?

Don and I got a ride to New York with Tom and Pam, a couple from Ward. More characters to savor in New York. At a corner bar in Manhattan, we met a giant black gent nick-named 'Hands' because he could clap each hand by itself. His hands were so long, they flopped over and made a clap. I saw this. And Columbus Mapp, an old man on a weekend pass from Bellevue Mental Hospital grinned and grinned. We wondered what made him so happy. He told us he'd found out a person could get on the subway at one end of the city and ride all the way to the other end. "But wait," he'd said, "there's more. When I get to the end of the line, I can stay on the subway and ride all the way back to where I started from!" This made his day. And his grin grew wider.

I wanted to believe in these characters to the point of them knowing I did, because I'd learned it was an essential implement in the toolbox of The Dream. Showing Love by giving attention. I considered suggesting that Hands and Columbus Mapp take a trip up to Toronto to visit Anson, but thought I should ask him first and he didn't have a phone.

In September Don and I boarded a jumbo jet to London, paying the fare that amounted to ninety-nine dollars round trip.

Going anywhere with Don turned into something like a training expedition because Don had been in Viet Nam. As an example, we came to a cliff on a trail overlooking The Irish Sea. He instructed me to dangle my pack over the edge with cord that he, of course, had brought along for emergencies. After it hit the beach, he showed me how to climb down the wall as far as I could and let go, dropping the rest of the way to land by my backpack. Most of the time I felt I was in boot camp undergoing jungle training.

I became pregnant in a field of flowers under an ancient oak not far from The White Cliffs of Dover.

We returned to Ward after three months in Europe. Wynken had done a perfect sheepdog job of protecting Jennifer, even saving her from a mountain lion.

Don and I got married in Moline on December 21 1971. People hitchhiked in from around the country. The motley crew almost fascinated my mother's friends. Dangerous Dunn showed up carrying a saddle he'd hitchhiked in with.

Mom had started to feel kind of special and open-minded. She'd become different than the others in her bridge club. She had a secret life!

Case in point, she took me to see the musical Hair in Chicago and took a toke on a joint I'd brought along. Curious, she came closer to acknowledging The Dream, not able to fathom it, but no longer afraid. She wanted to be part of the 'in crowd'. This was now enough for me. It had to be.

BYE–BYE WARD

IN EUROPE, NO Dream residue anywhere, Don and I felt the leading to take our survival lessons further and move far off the grid to raise our consciousness and the baby, due in June.

Betting our bottom dollar on this great quote by Goethe, "Whatever you dream you can do, begin it. Boldness has genius, power and magic in it", we hunted for land in northeast Washington state where we'd build ourselves a house. On our search we started running into, you guessed it, characters galore which meant more appreciation practice for me. Ending up by invitation at a Christian commune who called themselves The Family of Brotherly Love, I first met the character named Annita who would become a leading lady in my life.

Christians scared me, made me bad nervous. They kept showing up around the edges and trying to convert me. Jesus made for a great sheepdog, but in no way could it be true he was THE way, without exception, to the god I'd grown to like. What about all those other righteous card carrying prophets and teachers who'd been around since the beginning? Christians were pushy, stubborn and no fun. I thought some were brainwashed and prone to savagery. Jesus must've been a nice person, but leave me alone about the rest of that religious agenda.

I went into labor in the middle of the night on April 18th 1972, two months ahead of time to the day. Pollyanna, about to make her debut, unfinished like a cake taken out of the oven prematurely, broke my water. From the woods where we were camped, Don drove 125 miles to Sacred Heart Hospital in Spokane. I went for natural childbirth, the first ever at the hospital, and my baby entered the world weighing a hulking three pounds and fourteen ounces. She resembled a nice-sized trout. Confined in the preemie nursery for a month, they didn't allow me to touch her the first two weeks. Ouch.

Don, meanwhile, had converted to Christianity. Temporarily. He roared down the preemie hall with every intention of removing his baby and taking her to the commune where she'd be prayed over and then survive without doctors. Our miracle baby. However, if I didn't agree to get saved, he'd hide her away with him in a South American jungle.

I'd been staying in the nurse's dormitory and Don had gone back north to the commune. Annita, on the fringe there, tried to talk him out of this plan. After the nurses reported him, he left threatening the entire staff and luckily came down with hepatitis A the next day. They admitted a very ill Don to the hospital. That bought Pollyanna enough time to reach the hefty weight of five pounds, big enough to leave the hospital.

Waiting to close on a 120-acre piece of property we'd found in Rose Valley near the town of Republic in Ferry County, Commando Don, Annita and I made a camp by Big Goosemus Creek where we brought the baby. We gave five pound Pollyanna baths by heating creek water in a big canning kettle. She's a grown up now, so it turned out alright. As an RN, I shudder.

We moved onto the 120 acres, a chunk of undeveloped property cut from a 3,000 acre ranch. Our land lay within half an hour of the Canadian border. We named our place The Needmore Ranch. After setting up a permanent outdoor kitchen we worked on building our house, dug a well, an outhouse hole, stripped pine bark from logs, and chowed down in the outdoor cook tent.

Dangerous Dunn, now Just Paul, a regular rancher type and freshly married, pulled in with his saddle (still horse-less but I guess the saddle made him feel better) and wife. No road, but they found us in July 1972. You could've found an identical likeness of Just Paul the regular rancher in any farm or ranch magazine. He'd be the one in the tractor or best-feed-for-your-horse ad.

DELAY

ONE DAY DURING their visit, Don and Just Paul, his sidekick riding shotgun, took off for a horse auction in the next valley to the east by Deer Park. They rented a trailer and brought home a drop-dead-gorgeous animal...for me.

I heard the horse coming a mile away. They'd made the highest bid on him, a half Arab and half Quarter Horse youngster. A two-year-old gelding who'd never been saddled or ridden.

Delay was his name. The instant I looked at him I knew he thought well of himself. He stood in the sunlight, a spectacle, and shone like a newly minted penny.

With a fluttery heart (gaga), I fell in love. The horse was aloof, regal, and in charge, no chink in his armor of attitude, none that showed anyway. I, the adorer, and Himself, the adored. I accepted this role with as much grace as I could pull together. I had relationships with a number of horses, all teachers. One, a joker; a couple were show-stoppers; another, a pet, belonging to me.

Delay let me ride him bareback right from the start. He and I liked bareback best. As long as the ground had sound footing, we pranced, danced and tore at a gallop everywhere we went. Not once during the next twenty-seven years did he buck, rear, kick or bite. His dependability became the cornerstone of my trust. Delay learned to trust me, too.

But right off when I heard the name Delay it struck me as strange. I wondered what it meant. Names sometimes have significance, implications. Did the name Delay hold a message for me? Was I dawdling? Dragging my feet?

Two years later the answer came: Yes.

THE DESPERADO

ANNITA WATCHED WITH me as Don assumed Desperado-hood. I'm not going to go into great detail, but you deserve at least one illustration so you can get the picture. Day after Don hauled my horse home, he bought a dozen baby ducklings and put them in the creek on our land.

A couple of weeks later Just Paul, along with his wife, hit the trail and headed for Montana. After saying goodbye, Don took off to do some business in the town of Republic, nine or ten miles away. Sergeant Don ordered Annita and me to be on duckling duty. He charged us to watch them at all times so they didn't swim too far down the creek and get lost. I nursed Pollyanna day and night and it seemed Annita cooked in the kitchen as often as I fed the baby. What with this and that going on, the duckies paddled down the creek. We could still hear them, so didn't worry.

Don came back in our old beater Dodge truck. A four-wheel drive, it came crashing along the rutted path. He shouted, "Where are those ducks?"

"Oh not far, listen, you can hear them."

"I ordered you to keep them closer, remember?"

Before we could get a word in, Don had gone in our tent and come back out as the Desperado. Shouting obscenities, he held a rifle. I ran to the edge of the hill with Pollyanna in my arms and he fired that gun high over our heads to scare me. I thought Annita was going to take him down, tackle him around the knees. She'd come straight from Texas to Washington. And you know how people from Texas feel about being from Texas.

217

But the gun scared her, too. I heard her yelling and cussing at him with all her Texican might as she repeatedly poked him in the chest saying, "If I was a man I would beat the shit out of you!"

That was the beginning of the end, the start of the coming attractions played out by the Desperado making sure it became necessary for me to leave him.

DELAY AND ME

THE REMORSEFUL DESPERADO artfully bent my brain into a shape he'd use as a leak-proof container to fill with pity. For him. Yes, compassion always worked to change my mind. His problems as far as I ever figured out had to do with Viet Nam and some other issues. Always sorry to the point of getting on his knees, fat tears coursing over his high cheekbones (Cherokee blood in him), he'd beg and plead for my forgiveness. I knew he meant it and counseling therapy never occurred to me...too new-fangled. So I hung on. Better to try my damnedest to keep this marriage going than have Pollyanna grow up without a daddy. My consolation prize for hanging in there turned out to be my horse.

Every few days I rode Delay five miles to our mail box. Three-month-old Pollyanna rode on my back papoose style. Sometimes I'd hold her upright on Delay by herself and he'd pretend inconvenience, but I saw right through him. This arrogant, no-nonsense animal took the smallest of steps, pacing himself and treading softly, mindful of the cherished cargo on his back. If he thought I wouldn't catch him, he'd sneak glances at my baby, checking her out, checking on her. When he caught me watching, he'd snort with disdain and shake his fine head, acting sassy and bored with such tomfoolery.

Did you know some horses let little babies crawl around on the ground through their legs? That shows how special certain horses can be. Gypsies were known to leave a chosen horse in camp to protect their children and belongings.

I learned Delay could jump creeks, picnic tables, cattle guards, spin on a dime, cut cows effortlessly, and barrel race: turning around 'them barrels' supernatural-like. Yet he'd had no training. He was born talented. That summer he even put up with my urge to try out a goat tying clinic so we could enter that event at the county fair. Blessings from horse heaven found their mark in his huge heart.

People noticed my horse. A fifth generation rancher offered me $5,000.00 for him. Did I mention Don shelled out $125.00 at the auction?

Friends asked to ride him. The truth is anyone could ride Delay, just not for very long. He simply loved to run. Off they'd go. Off they'd fall. Most of them anyway. I wondered if I took it for granted others would be sensitive to his calculated movements. I decided even though he had a smooth run, his speed caught riders off guard. Then again, could've been his habit of stopping dead in his tracks when asked or whirling his turns in one spot when nudged by the reins. Delay had come with power steering. He was responsive.

You'd think we'd learned to read each other's minds. This know-how didn't happen all of a sudden; it grew out of our sameness. We'd see a long slope, stretching earnestly towards the top of a hill, seeming as if it wanted to take in the view, too. Without asking each other, we'd find ourselves sitting at the tippy top of that long reach staring at the sky, panting from the long run. I always got out of breath after a stiff gallop, like my spirit ran with my horse's body. Simultaneously we'd notice a log in the woods and next thing be airborne, jumping it higher than need be.

Horse and girl so connected physically and spiritually, to onlookers it would appear like telepathy. It's a gift not given to many and I cowed before it, knowing my place before such an offering.

I wondered why this horse made sure he moved to keep himself under me when, gawking at a cloud, I'd slightly lose my balance. What caused him to take that job on? You can't teach a horse to compensate for a spaced out partner. He just wanted to. Was Delay smarter than any of the other horses I'd built relationships with? No, although his instincts may have been more finely tuned. Could he somehow understand the words I used to remind him that I was small and he was big and he needed to be careful with me? The answers to questions like these are not available to the likes of us, but the fact is he showed me he was there for me. Other people saw and wouldn't speak of it because what could they say? "Gee, uh, there's something about you and your horse." Yeah there was.

Delay wouldn't hold a grudge either. Horses who do can become danger-ous. Not him, he always showed me mercy. Once I cinched a saddle so tight that he fell over riding up a steep mountain since he couldn't get enough breath. When I loosened the cinch, he stood up matter-of-factly as if to say, well that's more like it. Get back on now, we're fine.

He went anywhere I asked him to take me even if he felt skeptical about what I wanted. Like walking in between boulders or large rocks. Sometimes they scared him. With his head down and his eyes opened so wide, my horse took stutter steps, wagging his neck side to side snorting at the rocks.

He gave me his full trust as I gave him mine. It wasn't thought out, it happened on its own. Why? I know what our relationship looked like, but it's beyond my human understanding to explain it. We were together for a reason, that much I knew. And one day I'd be let in on a little secret.

We finished the house that summer of 1972. It looked out from the edge of the forest with pretty views in each direction. Snug and sheltered. Such a nice house until The Desperado burned it down. But that comes later.

CHRISTMAS

NO ROADS LED into our place so, when winter came, Delay agreed to pull us in a toboggan along with groceries, laundry, Christmas tree, and kerosene for lamps. Out the window of our cabin, white-covered ground spread as far as I could see. The snow was deep.

Our house stayed warm. Dutiful Don made sure we had more than enough firewood for the cookstove and the heat stove. He was one competent soldier at heart. Properly channeled, his charisma and proficiency at survival could've molded him into a world-class hero. My husband knew how to make a person feel safer than anyone anywhere. He also had the ability to make that person feel life-threatened in the wake of category five Hurricane DON. It depended on the level of his crazy meter at the time. I never understood the barometer of his insanity. I did know that inner fear raised the pressure. Irrationally terrified of losing me, this fear made him hold on so tight he squeezed the love, like the way you crushed oranges to make juice, right out of my heart.

Those self-fulfilling prophecies are buggers.

Pollyanna's first Christmas couldn't have been sweeter. The three of us plus my mom spent it together. Relaxed Don let his guard slip since there was no one around to steal me.

Getting Mom into our remotest of homes was kind of cute. First she flew from Moline to Spokane. Family-oriented Don drove some jeep to pick her up. The jeep became ours through the principle of diminishing returns. See, a brand new Volvo had been a wedding present. Dear Don mangled the clutch, killing it dead—dead.

Not being a motivated worker—bee type, High Roller Don considered wheeling and dealing his true gifts. He acted like it was his birthright. No one was going to make him work at a petty job. Certainly not.

So, of course, he had no money to get the tight and tidy expensive car fixed. Instead he traded down for a used car which he traded down for a more used truck that got traded down to an old red rusted out Jeep.

I try to imagine my mom on the 150 mile drive with Son—in—Law Don in the piece of junk jeep honing in on our wilderness abode. I can see her watching houses and humans get farther apart until the landscape turned blank. Not a country club in sight. Shivering fact.

We managed the installation of Mom into our fresh built house by first hitching up a team of borrowed Percheron draft horses to an ancient hulking four wheel drive truck that didn't run. Strategically stationed down below the mountain where the rutty road ended, my good sport of a mother found a way to settle herself onto its lopsided front seat. I can still see that seat which had lost most of its innards although still had pieces of gray greasy stuffing peeking out like sweaty Italian mice. I don't recall any seat belts in that old truck. I gotta hand it to Farmer Don who drove those draft horses pulling the chariot through the snow all the way (two miles) to our front door. My mother'd been delivered unscathed, but with her hat on backwards.

Oh, Mom.

THE FIRST ESCAPE

DON HAD A dear side or I wouldn't have fallen in love with him. It made me sad how little he appeared in his own eyes. Big Don had to show up to cover Little Don's tracks. Then no one would discover how small and unloved he felt.

The Dream developed a bad habit of not coughing up the missing piece. I'd been ninety-nine percent sure having a baby would fill the hole, but no.

In April 1973 before Pollyanna's first birthday, Don had a court date. There'd been a comedy-of-errors marijuana bust the autumn before. A feeble-minded cop or two had shown up at our garden. It was a big "HA! GOTCHA!" moment for rural constabulary, even though it'd been some timid gone-to-seed-yarrow weeds they'd yanked out of the ground. You should've seen the victorious look on their faces. Right proud of God and Country. I think they reconsidered as they watched us clutching our sides trying to hold in the laughter. That's when Officer R.P. pulled out a plant identification book and proceeded to find a few undernourished pot plants.

I was over smoking dope. Beer took its place. I'd forgotten how I'd taken to beer once upon a time. Hit the spot.

Blustery Don came home from being a fool in court and began a rage that lasted hours. "I'm going to kill all the cops in town, one by one, like Gooks. I told em so, too."

That proclamation on the heels of shooting a gun over my head scared me into planning an escape. Officer R.P. stayed away from our garden henceforth.

Getting away from The Desperado took Houdini-like skill. And it took assistance. Like someone with a truck who, as afeared of You Know Who as we were, would volunteer to help anyway. The escape had to happen in the deep dark night and the brave designated driver would need to hide me, Pollyanna and Wynken under a tarp in the back of his pick-up. Then our assistant had to break the speed limit and haul ass out of the neighborhood.

We went back to the county next to the one Don lived in and moved onto another commune, not Christian, thank you very much. I'd met these people before and they welcomed us with an invitation to pitch a tent on their land. The commune people were hippies. I couldn't find any Flower Children. Although I'd once thought Don had been one; he'd mastered playing that game at first. Funny, now I didn't feel I could trust myself anymore.

Uncanny Don located us. He had a way of doing that. Don of the silver tongue. He could twist words around unsuspecting friends of mine, glean info and figure things out. He stalked us in a syrupy way, well aware that more flies are caught with honey than vinegar. I'd have none of his manipulation and I told him so. But at least I managed to have Delay brought to me.

What do you s'pose Sugar Don did in the meantime? That spring he invited dozens of very nice hippies in the valley to live on our land. He designed this plot to affect me in a fail-safe positive way. "Look, baby, all these wonderful friends of ours like me and trust me so much they've chosen to move in!"

To which I'd reply with uncontainable emotion, "Oh Darling Don, may Pollyanna and I please come home?" Assuming grovel position I'd then beg, "Puleeeeeeeze!"

It didn't work. But words like "Uncle" or "I give" were not words in his vocabulary. Next he set about adding onto our house what he made sure I knew about...a Christmas Tree Room. Good Neighbor Don persuaded all the new people who'd set up camp on our land to help him cut down more trees, strip them and build an adorable log addition. They helped chink it and move a wood stove in. It had an upstairs like a dollhouse.

Okay, by now you could guess how I might feel about Christmas and be right. My mom and dad told the story of a day when Daddy was on the road selling Johnson and Johnson Band-Aids and Mommy was at bridge club. I happened to be home alone, grade school age. I hear I got out every Christmas decoration we owned and did the entire house. Lights and all. In July.

That did it. Pollyanna and I, Wynken and Delay greeted all the new neighbors and camped in what we called The Hidden Meadow. From there the four of us watched Candy-coated Don, the new and improved Don, putting finishing touches on The Christmas Tree Room. I remember the tour he gave me of the new room, painting a picture in the air of the tree and our little family gathered around. In my own painting I saw it as a booby trap.

Don, Hard-Working Don, was working hard to convince us he'd changed.

Alright, so Christmas Don won. Don Juan.

Thing is, all the new neighbors trailed off. Promising Don and his unkept promises of giving them property led to the mass departure.

But Christmas in The Christmas Tree Room was worth it. My mother didn't come. I couldn't blame her.

THE GREAT ESCAPE

As soon as The Christmas Tree room had served its purpose, Dastardly Don re-became a real Dastard.

I wanted the man to go to work. You know, get a job. This didn't go over well. I waited until after the new year arrived, hoping 1974 would be the Year of the Provider or something like the Chinese had going, naming them the year of this or that animal. No. Dictator Don stamped and commanded me to never again tell him what he should do. Ever! Or I'd be prosecuted for, for... (spit flew out as he found his word) INSUBORDINATION. Yes, that was it. In other words, I'd be going to get it. And he'd be the one who'd give it to me. I should tell you that Don never laid a hand on me or Pollyanna. He ripped up my clothes, sliced shoes into pieces like jerky, tore up my books and put his fists through walls, but not once did he hurt either of us physically.

You'd think I would've laughed, but no matter how ridiculous he acted, he scared me silly. Hoodwinked by In-My-Face Don. Time and again he convinced me he'd do what he said. Full of baloney without a doubt, but a bossy sausage who reminded me he could disappear with Pollyanna and I would not see her again for the rest of my life. Like I said, he convinced me.

Needing to be made certain of his masculinity, he'd started hitting on several girls around the county. He'd even invited them to our home. At first strike he'd call the girl on hand 'Baby', real casual-like. His Oklahoma accent wrapped around that word like a slinky and flexible portable bed. 'Baby' danced a devilry in the heart of many a girl. Well, somewhat below the hearts would be more accurate.

One January night, a 'Baby' hiked in on snowshoes. She'd come for dinner. I couldn't believe it! Drooling Don filled her wine glass as he entertained her like nobody's business. Charisma Don gushed out like Old Faithful, drenching each story with allure. She sat supporting her chin in her hands, taken by every word. He flirted like mad, hypnotizing her while I did the dishes. Our guest left after dinner. Smooth Don watched her snowshoe across the winter landscape in the moonlight. Standing there like a overheated engine, he fogged up the window. Oh yes, and she had a gun strapped over her shoulder since she liked to hunt squirrels. Don was acting so squirrelly himself he should have been embarrassed.

I wished I had a gun. Make him dance like in the old western movies. Rooted, he held a fixed stare out at the field. I got bored and went to bed. I didn't like it. I didn't like him. And I didn't like her.

Because she reminded me too much of myself. It already felt like a lifetime ago that this 'Baby' had been put into that same trance. She made me aware of how stupid I'd been. I wished I could warn her, but she'd never believe me. I'd been warned myself.

The predictable thing came to pass. Don Juan began accusing me of lusting after other guys. Why? He had to. Self-guilt creates distrust of others. He fastened his lustful desires onto me. In psychology class, they'd called it projection. The problems started when he started believing this delusion. He did a Don move and locked me and Pollyanna in the house.

There was one window that opened which happened to be on the second story. Trapped.

Realizing he wouldn't win a popularity contest if people found out, after a week Daddy Don decided to take Pollyanna with him wherever he went. He knew I'd never leave without my child so he let me out. Boy was I glad to stop using the chamber pot day and night. I waited to see what would happen. He loved his little girl, but a desperate con man can't be burdened with a full-time baby on his shoulder.

The residents of Ferry County, Washington, enamored with Good Time Don at first, did what people did everywhere we'd lived. They stopped believing him. And they discovered his latent instability. He made people a little jittery. But they smiled at him a lot. It was better that way.

So when he assigned our closest neighbors Pollyanna duty, they didn't argue. They also didn't argue with me when I suggested running away with my baby, and, in fact, helped me make the plan. It had to be good. No, nothing short of stupendous.

Due to Admiral Don's knack for sensing mutiny we'd need to create a technically coordinated plan paralleling a world war military maneuver. We decided on the nondescript pick-up truck, tarp, and cover of darkness tactic. Plus, to cover their butts, I made them promise to tell Don I stole her when they weren't looking. They appreciated that.

They were up for that. Two nights later we'd do it.

I knew Delay would be fine at The Needmore. I said good-bye and told him I'd be back to get him or send for him. He munched on his hay.

Now I was ready to make our break.

It came off without a glitch. At least at first. The Desperado-escaping-tarp, designated driver named George and deep dark night, all fell into place. This time good neighbor George's pick-up would race over Sherman Pass, not stopping until it reached the train station in Spokane. We knew there'd be snow on the pass. Feeling like a phony, I prayed anyway.

The first thing to go wrong...Don came back from the bar earlier than usual to get Pollyanna. Drunk Don. Not good. The babysitters watched him put a large hunting knife between his teeth and thunder off, crashing through and into trees, looking for where he'd left his truck.

Unfortunately he found it.

The next glitch happened when our driver passed Officer R.P. on graveyard shift. What he thought he was doing motoring along like a little old lady was anyone's guess. But my driver, fearing Tracker Don at large in the same county, didn't even notice Officer R.P. until he passed him doing 90 mph and the siren started. Flashing lights made a display in the rear view mirror. Either outrun the police or pull over. My mouth started watering in the bad way. Agggh. Fear-barf. Incoming. Because I felt Don The Bull, seeing red, on our trail. Getting closer and closer. I just knew. We slowed.

"George? That you? I know your truck. Step on out now," said Officer R.P.

"Uh, hello. Sir. I'm in a powerful hurry. Sorry about the speeding. It's a serious hurry."

"What you got in the back of the truck under the tarp, George?"

Oh shit, I thought.

"Hey, looks like an over-the-speed-limit type of night. See them head-lights way up Trout Creek Road? Man, someone is blastin' outta Rose Valley. Ever since them hippies got a road up top, more of 'em moving in all the time."

I'd had enough. No time for barfing. I sat up forgetting about the tarp. I heard his boots scrabble backwards and stared into the totally freaked out face of Officer R.P. I threw the tarp off. Pollyanna woke and stared into the beam of R.P.'s shaky flashlight.

"Whut the...?" said Officer R.P. squinting hard.

No time to waste. We'd reached critical mass. "Okay, it's me, Don's wife, and he's figured out I'm running away from him. You have to let us go RIGHT NOW. You know him. And you know he's crazy. We gotta go. To Spokane to catch a train. NOW!"

He looked at George and then at me and said, "Good luck. Yep, that's Don's truck alright. Looks like he's half way down Trout Creek Road. I see them lights." He pivoted on his heels. "Think I'll head on in to the station. Now, git. Good luck!"

An hour and a half later I still looked over my shoulder as Pollyanna, Wynken and I boarded the most beautiful train in Spokane. We'd made it. The Empire Builder, a great legend of a locomotive, would take us to my Mom. I breathed normally again. "Choo choo," said Pollyanna.

SWEET SPOT

POLLYANNA LIKED THE train and slept in a canvas crate thing strapped to the wall on each end. It swung with the rhythm. Clickety clack, clickety clack. Wynken performed his impressive shrinking-dog act and fit alongside me in our berth. We slept many of the miles across Montana, North Dakota, Minnesota and Wisconsin. Pursuant Don had exhausted us.

When we reached LaCrosse, Mom was waiting on the platform and we fell into her arms like never before. It was more like we'd collapsed on her and she could scarcely stay on her feet.

Sheltered at last.

Then she drove four hours to take us home, my Moline sweet spot.

Such a relief, and her house so clean. I loved that part. Being able to plop and roll around on the carpet in the living room felt luxurious. Like being a movie star at a spa. No splinters or pebbles or grit. I did get off on nature and outdoor living, but oh, that carpet. I played on it to the point of feeling self-conscious, a touch sheepish. I could and did stoop to use my child as an excuse (like blaming your own fart on your dog). "Gee, look how Pollyanna loves the living room carpet!" Mom cooked and did our laundry and spoiled us. Pollyanna, learning to talk, called her Grammy. And from then on, until the end of her time on earth, everyone called her Grammy.

My fear wore off and the familiar antsy feeling came on. I took care of the appointments I always made when I went home, the dentist, eye doctor, routine gynecology matters.

I thought it strange when I had to argue the gynecologist into doing the annual pap smear. He kept trying to talk me out of it.

Weird, I was under the impression doctors had a thing for money.

It started when I reminded him at the end of my check-up, "Oh, and I believe you've forgotten the pap smear."

"You had your baby less than two years ago," he said. "Everything would've been checked. You don't need one."

"I want one," I said.

"No, at your age you don't need an annual test."

Grrrrr. "I want one anyway, okay?" It felt like a battle zone. I was familiar with battle zones. He had no idea.

"Look, young lady, you'll be wasting your money. Forget about the pap smear. You're fine."

This pap smear suddenly became what I must have. And I now wanted it more than anything in the world. "GIVE ME A F—————— PAP SMEAR."

So he did. And life went on.

By February Finagling Don figured out our home-free shelter and called. Crying, he said the house burned down by accident. The stove in The Christmas tree room started a fire.

It was the stove's fault. The stove did it.

"When are you and my little girl coming home?"

"Are you out of your mind? Never." With over a thousand miles between us, I turned into a force.

I grew balls!

My friends from Ward, Sherry and Jennifer, had moved to Ferry County after we did. Sherry called me in Moline. She wondered if I wanted to rent a house with her in Spokane. Being that she was one of my best friends ever, I had no qualms about living with her in Spokane and keeping it a total secret. We'd be 150 miles away from the Desperado. No one would tell him. I knew that was true. Plus I'd feel better being in the same state as Delay. And Sherry and Annita and Jennifer. Sometime ask me to tell you about the Chipmunk Pickles that Jenny and I won a blue ribbon for at the Ferry County Fair.

Pollyanna, Wynken, and I rode The Empire Builder back west. We found a house and I started classes in acting and creative writing that spring quarter.

No secret that Children of The Dream gravitated to the arts, so I positioned myself in the most likely of places. I'd be ready on my carousel horse of hope to catch The Dream, like hooking the brass ring, when my chance came. I still needed the missing piece (i.e. peace).

The Fates provided a nice lady with a six-children family who ran a day care next door and agreed to babysit my child.

I jumped in to the theatre life with both feet. I got to be a vampire in the play, Dracula. That's where I crossed paths with meant-to-be-Marilyn. She stage-managed, and watched me attain creepiness and drink my victim's blood for nights in a row. Through Marilyn, characters in single file entered my life from stage left and stage right. She, herself, made for a great one. And would reappear.

Pretending to be a vampire, something I'd never imagined. I recognized the positive fallout from vampirizing and wondered whether, if I made the most out of my acting power, I could scare The Desperado now?

Sherry and I had gotten a routine going, doing fine when the call came. Mom said she'd heard from the gynecologist's office. They wanted my phone number. "What? How come?" I said.

"They said you should get another pap smear. The results came back unclear. They said to do it right away. You'll do that then?"

I said I would when the quarter got closer to being over. "I'm okay, that doctor told me I was in good shape. For once college feels right and I'm getting A's. Plus I'm in rehearsals." I snagged the first available appointment with the Dr. who'd delivered Pollyanna. I couldn't get in for some weeks, but that'd work.

I found out I had cervical cancer, and when Mom flew out to help with Pollyanna I had a hysterectomy. What if I hadn't made that Moline doc give me a pap smear? God crossed my mind. He seemed to do that more and more often. Jesus freaks showed up on our street, tripping the light fantastic up to people's doors, inviting them to meet Jesus. I told them, "Hey, I'm cool with god, but Jesus makes me jumpy, edgy. None for me, thanks."

My life had been saved and at the same time it was certain I wouldn't bring any more lives into the world. But gratitude filled the emptiness of a missing womb because I focused on how lucky I was to have a child at all. It meant I'd joined that most virtuously-ranked of clubs called motherhood. And I'd experienced giving birth. So one baby would be enough. Falling in love, being loved as a wife had fallen flat on its face. It was a crying shame since The Dream had included living happily ever after underneath a rainbow with wildflowers floating in the air like snowflakes.

I felt displaced, gone missing, and became one scared little cookie. In actuality I was being prepped for what was around the next corner. And it would involve the message contained in Delay's name. I was about to stop dawdling and dragging my feet.

After healing, I got cast in a play at Spokane's Civic Theater. But then an ovary abscessed. Another operation removed it, and the surgeon grabbed my appendix since he happened to be in the neighborhood. Lordy. I made opening night, though for the rest of the run I shared shows with an understudy.

Wondering what my next step should be, due to disconcertingly believable reports about the Desperado, we moved back to Ferry County. Friends told me Don seemed less-off-the-wall. Plus he made frequent trips out of state. These friends also donated a teepee for Pollyanna and I to live in. We headed to the hills and Delay hauled our water.

Don made his forays, but kept coming back to what was left of the house we'd built. So far, he'd left us alone.

March 5 1974 - At The Lost And Found

OUR TEEPEE HAD no phone service and computers belonged in science fiction movies. So when I trotted Delay to the mailbox and grabbed Mindi's letter, I tore it open right away. I loved Mindi and who didn't love getting mail? What she'd written in her letter froze me to the ground. I couldn't move and could hardly breathe. Next to the news about Daddy, it contained the most dreadful news I'd ever received.

Pollyanna, Wynken and I had to make an emergency trip to California. We rode with Sherry who, as luck would have it, had planned to visit her mom in California. I needed to rescue Mindi, who, as I saw it, happened to be in a menacing situation. Sinister, even.

Mindi, sweet Melinda, my Mindi, soulmate, like-minded Flower Child Mindi, had become (gulp) a Christian.

Noooooooooooo!

I knew what I must do and I had to act fast. Go to California. Save her! The letter made it sound like she wanted to save me. She didn't say that, but I knew; I knew these Christian types. They were deceived, overzealous, pushy, self-righteous, sneaky and a danger to themselves, other people and children. Besides, Mindi the little minx was a Jew. Jewish people can't be Christians. It's either/or. Anyway, maybe I wanted to be Jewish.

We drove straight through. It took forever getting from Washington to Mindi's house in northern California. Sherry understood the disaster. She even knew Mindi. We broke the speed limit. Hours later, we pulled into Mindi's driveway.

Frantic, I jumped out, ran to her door, and entered without knocking. "Mindi? Mindi, where are you?"

A voice said, "At the piano. Who is it? You sound so familiar."

I walked around the corner in slow motion, afraid of what I'd find. She saw me, whooped with delight and ran across the room. We hugged and I held on for dear life, finally pushing her back. She looked the same.

"Oh my gosh! Suzee! What are you doing here?"

This sounded like my Mindi, moved like my Mindi. Maybe there'd been some horrible mistake.

Mindi ruined everything when she said with unbounded joy, "I know, it's a miracle! God got you to come. He wants you to know his Son!"

What? I had to fix her. What if I was too late? My pulse raced and my stomach knotted.

"Mindz, you're brainwashed, Mindz. Who did this? Listen, you've got to be deprogrammed. There are professionals who know how to help people like you."

She cracked up laughing.

"No, Mindi, you're seriously lost, like airplane luggage in the rings of Saturn. My cousin says that's where it ends up, in fact, he says that's what the rings are made of. And also..." I was stalling, but warming to my subject. Anything but that other upsetting subject.

"Suzee, do you trust me?" she said.

Poking my conscience, this imaginary little hedgehog tried to get my attention. It talked! In an innocent Disney–baby–animal–voice it squeaked, "What if she's right? Are you honestly happy? Haven't you been feeling a smidgeon of despair? Aren't you the one feeling lost, off course, without meaning anymore? No more Dream to live for?"

The situation wasn't coming down the way I'd rehearsed. I had doubts I never knew existed in me. Thrown off balance, I said, "Mindi, are you kidding? Of course I trust you, more than almost anyone in the world."

"Perfect. Sherry, it's great you're here, too. And Suzee, it's your birthday. How old?"

"Twenty-six Mindz. Hey, Pollyanna is asleep in the car, you've never met my baby. You know the Wynken dog already."

"Yep. Go get them. I'll call Taffy now. She's my friend and prayer partner."

"What? Why are you calling her?"

"It's because of Taffy I'm saved. God used her to explain the good news to me in a way I could understand, you know, 'get it'. She lives down the block. You guys will love her."

"You mean this chick is coming over now? But we just got here. Can't we hang out awhile first?"

Mindi jounced and giggled like she couldn't stand keeping a surprise, not one more second. I wondered. Could it be a birthday present? No, of course not, she hadn't even known I was coming.

Rolling my eyes, I sighed, "Mindi, supposing you did feel lost? But supposing you weren't lost. Supposing because you turned into this Christian thing, person, whatever, means someone tricked you and now you are lost, saying you've found Jesus." I wiggled my eyebrows like Groucho Marx, "Har har, did you find him in the Rings of Saturn?"

Flat ignoring my attempt to lighten things up, she kept going like the energizer bunny. "Suzee Creamcheese, I have big news. We don't find Jesus. Jesus finds us. He found us before the earth came into being."

"I knew it. You're certifiable."

We brought the baby and a few things in from the car. Wynken slept next to Pollyanna, but he'd woken up, nose against the glass. Pollyanna stayed asleep so I laid her on Mindi's couch. Later, we compared notes. Sherry and I were on the same page. Skittish, not to mention freaked. To each other our faces appeared palsied.

The Taffy person walked in, glowing with goodwill and smiled at us. "Hi, you must be Suzee and Sherry," she said. "Mindi, this is so cool, shall we get started?"

"Started? Wait a minute. What's going on?" I said, feeling my twitching face muscles accelerate into overdrive.

"You are about to cross over the Jordan River by faith into the Promised Land. Don't you want to?" Mindi said.

Unlike my face, she didn't flinch. "Suzee, Jesus is real. He is the answer. He is better than The Dream we held onto as Flower Children. He is True Love, more than you can know until you believe."

She could not fake this peace shining out of her eyes, the windows to her soul. I knew her. I still knew her. Looking all our lives, needing the answer to why we lived, Mindi and I'd sampled every religion, occult method, drug, you name it. We spit each one out because they didn't satisfy for long. Now, though, her contentment showed in the relaxed way she moved. Her voice, calm with peace, soothed my jumpy mind.

I wanted it. See, I trusted her. Mindi wouldn't lie. And if she was right, then...oh crap. What if it meant I'd be a Jesus freak without being able to help it?

Like she read my mind she said, "Suzers, think about it this way. What have you got to lose?"

That did it.

"Alright, how do I do this?"

Mindi patted the bed with her hand. "Sit here. Taffy and I'll stand behind you and pray. Sherry, come on, go for it. You'll be born again together."

Born again, I hated that term. Like peacocks, TV evangelists strutted through my mind. With oversized hair, they wore gold necklaces and gigantic rings that had to have been lifted from the Royal Family's crown jewels.

But I sat down on the bed and Sherry sat next to me.

Mindi and Taffy prayed out loud, although I can't remember what words they used. Something happened. In one second my mind changed. Emptied of every well-constructed argument against Christianity, it'd been rearranged. I couldn't even find my excuses or defenses.

I recall blinking a lot.

I don't know what happened. I know I did nothing other than take hold of a gift handed to me. I didn't assemble faith, or belly up to the Belief Bar. I simply accepted the reality of Jesus.

I'd heard the Bible quoted, made fun of it, put it on top of my head, taken a religion class. The words never made sense. They were just words.

Now I wanted to take a look at that Bible book right away. Mindi handed me one. I opened it to the book of John and the words there shocked me by doing handsprings off the page, fully clothed, decked out with meaning. These were the same lifeless words that had endlessly sat there, naked and still. I'd gone to Sunday school, church, memorized scripture, and read parts of the Bible. Without a great enough thirst, the words held no water. And they certainly had never before caught my attention by doing acrobatics and wearing clothes. Talk about living words!

Sherry and I couldn't put the thing down. No kidding, I wondered briefly if someone had rewritten the Bible when no one was looking.

We had so many questions, and like the words in that book, we'd become brand new.

Brand new.

We couldn't stick around, needing to stay on Sherry's scheduled visit to her mom.

Mindi and Taffy looked like mother hens whose baby chicks might be leaving the nest too soon. At the same time, they knew they could trust us to God's Daddy–kind–of–care.

God had given me a transfusion, which, being who I am, made me think of that rumor about Keith Richards of The Rolling Stones having his blood changed (for different reasons, ahem), but that's where the comparison stops. My blood got replaced with Jesus' own blood. The tainted blood of poor ol' Adam that'd been flowing in my veins was exchanged, and with that change went the sting of death. He died so that I don't have to be afraid when I die.

Minutes later, they waved as we drove off, upgraded creations no longer desperate for the Dream.

We'd found something better. We'd found the answer.

Peace at last. I smiled for a thousand miles.

GOD THE OVERACHIEVER

ONCE I SAW it, I couldn't believe how apparent and available God makes himself to the world. His presence is engraved on the whole thing. "Hey, here I am! Look over here, it's me again. Now up here, way up here. Yoo-hoo!"

But we still miss him all the time. So he gets more into it and starts showing up in some strange places (Can you see me now?).

From what I've seen, I think God is happy to be recognized as anything.

For instance, get a load of this. There are similar stories, but this is one of my favorites.

I picture it this way, however it could've happened differently. Down New Mexico way a woman is making dinner. It includes tortillas. She blends the corn flour and starts pressing out the masa dough. Lo and behold, and I mean LO AND BEHOLD, she sees the face of Jesus in plain sight imprinted on her first tortilla.

And suddenly, there in the village, a multitude of the heavenly host drop in, praising God and saying, "Blessed is the tortilla of God."

The word spreads. A migration of pilgrims begin the trek, however long, to view Jesus on the holy tortilla. The tortilla makes believers of men (and women).

He has made guest star appearances on linoleum table tops, deep fried fish sticks, the chimney of a suburban bowling alley, and in strands of spaghetti on a Pizza Hut billboard. Ten years ago a woman found the toasty likeness of Jesus on a grilled cheese sandwich. A priest enshrined a thermal paned window in which God used mildew like finger paint to etch his own face between the two layers of glass.

It doesn't matter if you believe or not. Maybe it wasn't meant for you. But these things really happen. God is serious as a heart attack, going to great lengths to reach his kids. What's not to love?

I'd looked everywhere for Love. He'd used the Love and made The Dream live for a few moments in Haight-Ashbury. He knew that, just as the little Jewish man did in Haight-Ashbury, some of us would follow the tail of that comet as it streaked across the tie dyed sky and that I'd be down every path looking deliriously for it after it disappeared.

I thought my finding it again was all up to me, all about me. I didn't know what grace meant. I couldn't believe God would give me anything. I didn't deserve it. Some people thought I was a good person, cool and caring, but my motivation for being 'good' sucked: I wanted to be loved. And changing myself to be more like Jesus as the Bible taught? Forgeddaboud it. That happens from the inside out, not the outside in.

He changes desires. Nothing to do with my measly efforts. No brownie points to pile up.

Looking around I knew this. God was a workaholic! Look at the creation for starters. Pick it apart. Dolphins. Birds of Paradise. Seahorses. Planets. Finally I grasped his off-the-charts over-achieving when he accomplished finding me. But I had to be in the fold looking out to fathom it. When I'd been outside, following dumb sheep like me over cliffs, it hadn't registered.

Hard to think whilst falling, never mind being a sheep trying to think. Baa.

The many avenues I'd explored, well they worked, at least partially. Astrology, for instance. The stars and moon affect us. Check out ocean tides. The moon governs them and we're made up of a lot of water. The problem is, astrology never eased any of my fear or guilt or pain or feeling alone. It didn't love me. Astrology is interesting, but I can't talk to it or bond with it like I do with God and Jesus. I could come as I am, be my real and crummy self, a renegade, and no demerits. That's Love for ya, that's grace.

Reminds me of those 'come-as-you-are' parties. An unsuspecting victim, you'd be grabbed and thrown into a car as an honored guest with your acne cream caked on, your shorty pajamas that showed your legs with The Nation of Cellulite's flabby flag flying high, and ghastly night braces strapped to your head.

This was a chick kind of party which started freeing me up to think of God as a He or a She. I figure that by fashioning guys and girls, He'd need to know the baffling behavior behind the brains and emotions in both sexes. Couldn't that qualify God as a He or a She when the need arises?

God has never insisted that I delete or rope off the characters in my life. Relief overcame me when I realized one and all are invited to enter my new life. It took me awhile, but then I got it (Baa).

I figure Jesus as a renegade, too, who met me on that level. I knew I'd have a problem with what seemed mandatory: being 'reverent'. But he straightforward required me to understand he wanted a relationship with me THE WAY HE MADE ME in all my irreverent glory. My present husband and I have come to the conclusion our mission might be to not attend church! Churches are buildings, not necessarily necessary. Wherever believers get together is church. I prefer a living room or a field. Churches scare me. Many Christians scare me, which I bet you've sorta figured out by now. I still Love them. We each have our own path and shouldn't be nosing around others, making opinions, assumptions or judging.

God is untamed and unrestrained and he's smitten with me. And you. And everyone else on the planet Earth. No matter what. Forever. I feel warmly wrapped in one of his baby blankets, cooing in his nursery.

I'm worthy of this unchecked Love and didn't know it, let alone believe it. Just like those guys on the yellow brick road. They were already their own dream come true, but the wizard had to help them know and believe it.

God does Oz? That's a look inside my brain for ya.

I don't worry about people who don't see this the same way I do. Every true search for meaning and Love has a happy ending. Love wins. Love rules. And that's all I need to know.

Talking about this makes me uncomfortable and I get turned off by my own self. Preachy. Uck. So I don't do it and won't unless somebody asks me a direct question. Otherwise it's not my bag. And God realizes that about me. 'Cause Jesus put on a skin suit so he could, you know, 'get me'.

Maybe he wasn't crazy about preaching either. He did it anyway. He saw the whole enchilada and I just don't. Not from my seat. It's a bad seat and there's a pole in the way. It's called my human nature and I'm fine saying, oh well.

When I started writing my story in that dangerous town at 10,000 feet in Colorado, I knew what I thought it'd be about. I'd be a messenger. The world needed to know that once there'd been a Time-Of-All-Times which I call The Dream. It'd be enough to know just that much.

And the story would have lived happily ever after. But I didn't know then that the story would show how The Dream was the kindling for the spark of True Love. And after that, my spirit engulfed, the fire of God's Love turned me into a red hot mutha of a whacky believer.

Go figure.

I Am New...Or Am I?

Pollyanna, the Wynken Dog, Delay and I returned to my teepee. Sherry'd rented a small cottage outside the nearby village, Curlew. Population ninety-nine. Not long after being born again, I dropped into a bar I liked in this same village. I climbed onto a bar stool so I could visit with Mike, the owner. Bartending suited Mike 'cause he was congenial and a master philosopher.

This guy, cute guy, joined me and said he'd heard I'd been in California the month before. How was my trip? I told him and wonder of wonders, he asked me direct questions about Jesus. Man, I sat on that bar stool slurping beer after beer with grace chasers, witnessing my head off. I thought I did pretty well until I started feeling more and more attracted to him and my old self wanted to keep going with that. It wanted out!

Through the window I saw my friends Sherry and Annita, my sisters in Christ coming to get me from the bar. Horrified, I swung to look at the clock. I hadn't noticed the time, 2:15 A.M. Past bar-time already. They were like angels in pajamas and robes with big curlers in their hair. Although they were considerate sisters in the Lord, I felt indignant. I'd had such a brilliant Oscar-winning testimony going. Even though maybe I leaned in closer and closer to the guy as I witnessed.

We moved from the teepee when I found the greatest little shack on the Kettle River. Someone named the road to get to the cabin Dump Road because the public dump lived on the left hand side. You passed by that before the dirt lane ended at my place. When my baby and I set up shop in the little cabin I noted it came equipped with yet another outhouse for our wintertime pleasure. Ha!

Delay served as our car.

I cleaned a beauty parlor in Curlew to pay our cheap rent.

Delay carried me the few miles to work, dropping Pollyanna off at Sherry's cottage on the way.

Summertime found us three playing in the deep, wide, rushing river next to our cabin. It's where Pollyanna and I bathed and washed our hair. During a bath I'd dive down to gulp a drink of water, cold and pure.

Delay liked to swim. I wrapped my arms around his neck as he swam, feeling power surge through his body. He was an athlete and I an honored guest on his lunging back.

Wynken preferred guard duty. We were, after all, his herd.

Friends of ours lived on the other side of the river. Dropping in on them meant finding a shallow place for Delay to cross.

When we visited other friends who lived in town, it would often be dark when we rode home. Delay used a civilized lope reserved for when Pollyanna was on board. More than once a bear waddled in front of us. Delay would snub him because he had more important business at hand.

Nights there, sparkling and clear like the river, were all lit up with stars. First time I saw the Northern Lights I thought the Lord had returned, just as he promised. Rays rippled across the sky, reminding me of those huge lights set up at car lots to lure people in for a sale. But these rays lived and breathed white, green, yellow and blue. I waited, quaking, but Jesus didn't show up. Next day people told me I'd seen the Aurora Borealis.

That summer a group of local young cowboys noticed us. Sons of dyed-in-the-wool rancher daddies, it became obvious they could not stand that some Flower Child throwback from the 60s owned a fast horse. Worse, the girl with all that big bunch of hair flying, charged around bareback flaunting his speed. This horse had grown a reputation of being able to outrun any other horse. Rumors spread, declaring no one except me could ride him. The cowboys stewed over the fact, and slowed their pickups to watch us canter on their roads. I knew they didn't happen to be there for any other reason than to check us out. They'd about plunge into the ditch they'd be staring so hard. I'd just smile as Delay offered to go faster. Then faster still.

I kept riding to town, patronizing the Curlew Tavern. That's where it got arranged.

THE BIG RACE

ONE SUMMER NIGHT at the saloon, the most strapping, smuggest, flashiest cowboy whoever sat decorating a stool, made a brazen challenge. "Welp, Girly-girl, I gotta say it looks like you have yourself a pretty fast horse. I also gotta say mine is taller with bigger muscles. And faster."

"Might be factual about your horse being those things compared to mine, but I know it's not true when it comes to your horse being faster. And my horse's heart is bigger because he's got a lot of it. So there." I wanted to stick my tongue out at him. He looked around the bar at his buddies who chimed in with their good-ol'-boy comments in support of said braggart.

"Yup, ain't no doubt about it. His horse got you beat standin' still, sweet thing."

"Sure 'nuff. That's God's truth there."

"Love to watch women get beat." Guffaw, guffaw.

"Come on now, wouldn't be fair takin' advantage of a little bitty female on her skinny little horse."

"I'd make a wager anytime against a girl like her. Bet she burned her draft card."

I burst out with my own take on a guffaw at this last statement. As if I'd ever been issued a draft card. What a dork. Lord have mercy.

At that precise moment, like it was in the script, my challenger's father strode in wearing the biggest hat of all. "What's that you say? Something about a wager?"

"You bet Pop, we're just talkin' about whose got the fastest horse around here's all."

"What say we have ourselves a race and find out?" said the dad.

"Sounds like fun, Mister," I said sending my voice into its most innocent high register.

"Where shall we do it, Dad?" The flashy son looked my way with a smile that would've swaggered if it had legs.

"I believe the airplane landing field outside town should fit the bill. I'll make a call to be sure. Hows that sound?"

"Dandy, when?" I couldn't wait. Eager beaver, you know.

"Coming Sunday okay?" said the big rancher.

"Oh yeah!" I said, refraining from bouncing my bottom on the stool and clapping like a little kid. "And I bet a case of beer my horse wins." They loved that.

Father and son snickered. "That'll be just fine. Bring your money, Girly-girl," said flashy cowboy. Leaving at the same time, plenty of backslapping went on between them.

My heart went pitter pat. "Oh boy!" I said to Mike the bartender and ran out to tell Delay.

Sunday came. Fathers, sons, relatives and a whole lot of other folks lined each side of the grassy airstrip. The cowboy sat upon a brawny, powerful-looking Quarter Horse. But that didn't matter to me and Delay.

The burly rancher took charge, and after lining us up to his satisfaction, he took his hat off, using it as a flag, and bellowed, "GO!" And the crowd went wild, ladies and gentleman! Music to my ears.

Delay won of course. We beat them badly.

Huffing and puffing with indignation, his rancher dad galumphed over on bandy legs to demand another race. He maintained his son hadn't heard "GO!" (Stetson too big?).

Delay and I, loving nothing better than having ourselves another full-tilt gallop, went again, whipping Biggest Flashiest Cowboy on Charles Atlas Horse even worse than before. We could've run and won that same race over and over. Till the cows came home.

This meant not one, but three cases of Washington's finest made its way to me and all those locals rooting for Delay. Two from the ranchers and one from our fans. I even shared with the cowboy set.

Tsk Tsk

Sincere local Christians, wringing their hands, paid me a visit and informed me I had to be with other Christians because I went to the tavern and needed help. It would be closer to the truth if I used the word exorcism instead of help. These believers had come across a prophet, brother such and such, to run their spiritual show. They told me he had the lowdown on righteous living. They told me the next step for Sherry and I. We must be baptized. The prophet teacher baptized us in the Kettle River.

He explained that, according to scripture, it was unholy to read storybooks which contained pictures of or words about animals wearing clothes. The Man Of God instructed such children's books be burned. We're talking Mickey Mouse Classics here, for Christ's sake (and I mean that literally, for his sake). He doesn't diss Disney, not his style at all.

My well-meaning brothers and sisters in the Lord filled my fear tank full up to the top. When they expounded on the evils of Halloween, I ripped my decorations off the walls on the double. No way did I want to suffer fearsome consequences of disobedience.

What worked for them, I found spine-chilling.

Next thing I knew, my Lord stepped in to set me free. First, he knocked me out of that bunch. He was all for my rebelling against their man-made rules. Rebelling came naturally. He, of course, knew this about me and worked with what I already had going for myself. He also showed how I could glorify him by just being me.

I will add a quote by Thomas Merton to illustrate this.

"A tree gives glory to God by being a tree. For in being what God means it to be it is obeying God. It "consents," so to speak, to God's creative love. It is expressing an idea which is in God and which is not distinct from the essence of God, and therefore a tree imitates God by being a tree."

What a concept. But we want it to be harder than that, don't we? We think we must do something more. But we do not!

What a relief!

I started asking questions that worried my poor little fellowship group. I was de-fellow-shipped. I didn't get mad at them. It might take a lot to make a Flower Child mad. I mean if I didn't get mad at those Hell's Angels, no way would I be mad for being disenfranchised by Christ's kids. I felt sad for what they missed on the subject of grace.

God appointed me 'Freelance Christian'. Then he hooked me up with like-minded believers around this country and the world. He did this by sending me to unconventional kooky Christian camps, where his grace and Love wrapped around me like a lead lined cocoon, blocking the deadly rays of subtle control. It breaks my heart when God's sons and daughters buy into well spun lies: terrible lies designed by our enemy to wound and divide.

I knew nothing much about the Trinity until the Holy Spirit entered my mind and introduced his own self as The Big Ho. That felt friendly. Times have changed. 'Ho' has become gang slang for a female of ill repute.

I wondered if he preferred another nickname, had others to choose from? The Big Ho said, "I do. How do you feel about Lovey Dovey. Like that one?"

I adore this person. Holographic at times, he projects himself into a vision like Princess Leia from Star Wars did when she had a message for Obi-Wan Kenobi and Luke. Sometimes he enters my mind, and, like a radio ham, transmits important info from God. And then there are those times when he puts on his Caspar costume and flies across the sky.

WHACK

NOW IS WHEN I should warn you: there is something to know about me, providing you with a choice. Either keep reading or, in the words of Meatloaf, from the song Paradise By The Dashboard Lights, "Stop right now...before you go any further..."

I admitted earlier being a Whacky rendering of Christian believer. I became Whacked as one of the faithful when God, in His mercy, made it known I needed to lighten up.

He kept me entertained and protected inside his grace with wild stuff. He sent a vision of the trinity appearing in the heavens, just for me! He orchestrated this with himself as R. Crumb's robed character, Mr. Natural, striding across the sky sporting a long white beard. Accompanying him were Jesus as Superman, and the Holy Spirit as Casper the friendly ghost. God aims to make me laugh out loud at his jokes.

There is his parallel universe the angels call Whack. This happens to be heaven, by the by. When I am out of Whack, I long to get back in, since it's where he lives. Being in Whack is the best!

Think of me as a citizen of Whack, as someone you know who is a Whackee. As you can imagine, all the tortillas in Whack, along with everything else have the laughing face of Jesus stamped on them.

The kingdom of Whack is within. I take that to mean we have at least a kind of passport to vacation there. Of course I won't get my permanent visa, my green card so I can stay, as long as I'm a resident of the Suzee body.

Whatever, Whack is within me and I go on retreats there. When I remember. Remembering. Now, there's the hitch.

All righty then, if you've decided you can hang in there with that going on, then please continue.

MEANWHILE, BACK AT THE RANCH

WE'RE UP TO November, 1974. The Desperado had been in Alaska. He returned to The Needmore where he seemed to hole up. I say 'seemed' because he had a talent for throwing his body around like a ventriloquist throws his voice. Who knew where the genuine Don body dwelt? I wondered more than most. Not seeing him out and about or being the recipient of one of his schemes made me more apprehensive than if he'd tried something Don-like.

Finally, he showed. Having heard about my being baptized, he came to tell me that, glory be, he'd been saved, too. Yes. Again.

Looking around, pretending to be interested in the door frame and roof, he mentioned the other reason he'd stopped by: God told him to. "God's primary commandment says we have to live together as a family." He looked up, heavenward, and saluted. I looked down, hellward, and shuddered.

"Gee, Don, I think God's first commandment has something to do with loving him with all our heart, mind and soul."

"Yes, and along with it he says to love each other. That's primary." His stick-on smile got scarier looking. Like a character's might in a Stephen King book.

"I'm pretty sure there's more to it than that," I ventured.

"Oh no. NO NO NO. Not correct. It means that you and I are supposed to love each other. It means Don and Suzee. God told me. I know the Bible backwards and forwards now. I am a preacher in Alaska. I lead a congregation."

Pollyanna stood behind me, shy, peeking around at her father. A spring of hope roiled up inside me. What if Don is a new person? I knew God could do that. What if he had? I had more doubts than Carter has pills. Duh. But, what if? My brain went haywire.

I did it. I let him in the door, my first mistake. Pollyanna bit my hand, she'd never bitten me before nor has she since. Looking back, maybe she'd wanted to tell me something.

CH–CH–CH–CHANGES

REMEMBER THE CHRISTIAN group run by The Man Of God? The careful people. Full of care. Their womenfolk wore long skirts and dresses topped off by head coverings. The men better not be caught with their noggins covered. I swear one time I smelled the heady aroma of burning baseball caps. Well, anyway, the ladies showered me with beatific smiles of approval. I'd returned to my husband. The wayward tavern–going sister followed the rules. Baby Christians are interesting specimens. That includes me. If I refer to those brothers and sisters of mine as care–full I can tell you I, myself, could've been viewed as care–less. Whatever. We're all the same, each a case of grace. Maybe care–free is attainable while still on earth? I'm not so sure, definitely not full time. Since Eden, things have gone south. I'm looking forward to better homes and gardens.

Don exuded good will toward men. And women. Things in our Godly ordained family scene went downhill fast. Pollyanna, me and Wynken returned to Moline on The Empire Builder. We wanted to be home in time for Christmas. No great escape, can you believe it? We had the leisure to make normal–people–plans to leave, like get reservations on the train. In advance!

Don had other fish to fry. He'd run out of sidekicks and buddies and had some sort of wheeling and dealing that, more often than not, kept him in Spokane. I think he became bored, so while we were at Mom's for Christmas 1974, he skedaddled to Alaska, a sizable wilderness which suited a dude like him.

Familiarity is a big deal. It'd been four years since I'd been home for Christmas. Those last three words cry out to my heart when I write them, more than any others I can think of.

We stayed a long time. The living room carpet and I continued bonding. I don't know about Mr. Carpet, but this girl saw it as a good relationship. I needed a good relationship under my belt, even a familiar carpet would do the trick. We got to see aunts, uncles, and cousins. This gave Pollyanna what she needed, like Mr. Carpet gave me: belonging. Our place in the scheme of things gave us new stamina.

Christmas at home meant being with friends I'd had since grade school and before. Irreplaceable. A full circle reconnection placed in motion. Not so many world-views apart anymore, we made up for lost time. It didn't matter so much about how different were the paths we'd taken. What mattered was what we had in common. Our roots.

We'd grown up breathing the same air, drinking the same water, smelling the same earth and woods. Playing in the same puddles, the same snow, on roller skates that needed keys, and indoors skating to organ music. Ice-skating by the fire station with the warming hut next to the frozen pond. Boys and girls discovering girls and boys. Swimming and going to the hamburger stand to eat by far the best tasting burgers in the world. Either because of splashing in the pool all day or because they were. Our hormones changed in harmony with each others'.

Slogging along toward becoming an adult. I think that's what was happening to me. Grow up? Never. Get it together? About time. Mom and I discussed my future. Perhaps I'd become a registered nurse. Can you stand it?

Christmas that year strung singular precious memories, like tree lights, around the center of me. I'll not take them down.

An Indoor Toilet At Last

I DIDN'T MENTION this but the previous year, while living by the river on Dump Road, I applied to college in Spokane. To become an RN. That is when I'd had my transcripts sent. Sending them to Spokane Community College required a leap of faith because, if accepted, I'd have to commit. As we know, I wasn't college material. They scheduled me an appointment with a woman in the admissions office. I caught a ride with a friend from up north who needed to do a routine big–city run for supplies.

When I walked into the interview the woman pulled out my paperwork and told me it looked good, except for one thing. There was a problem with the math requirement. Great, how I loved math beyond measure. Right. Worse, seems I needed a year of college algebra to enter their nursing program. A whole year. The news gave my plan four flat tires.

Until the next year.

After talking to Mom at Christmas I decided to reapply. Maybe they'd changed the math policy? It happens. Again, I made my little appointment with admissions. At the admissions office I faced the same woman as the year before. This discombobulated me. Somehow I found the chair, sat and looked at my lap. Hair hid my face. I had to raise my head when she addressed me. "Welcome, it's nice to meet you," she said and reached to shake my hand. She didn't remember me. I couldn't believe it. I was off to a good start. Here comes God. She flipped through my many transcripts and said, "You have all you need here to be accepted into our nursing program. In fact, you have enough credits in various classes to be able to skip some of the prerequisite courses. You can finish in two years with one summer school class." I had begun to sweat.

"When does school start?"

"You'll receive the information in the mail and seeing you've attended several schools, it won't be a problem for you to register, you know what you're doing," she said.

I felt like saying, I do? Thought better of it and said, "Thank you." The page which had lit up in her hands the year before must have stuck to another page! I didn't have to take algebra. They'd accepted me. I was in. Given the way God arranged things, I breathed easy.

Where to live? I've told you about my friend, Marilyn, who I'd met when I was a vampire. I hope you remember or you'll wonder if you missed some super duper bizarre chapter of my life. In the middle of completing the registration process Marilyn called me from Spokane, asking if perhaps I wanted to rent this groovy house she'd been living in. She planned to move. Not knowing what I had in mind, she'd given it a shot, just checking. I'd told her at some point about my nurse idea.

"Marilyn, you won't believe it. I'm looking right now for somewhere to live in Spokane because I'm going back to college."

"Suzee, this house is six blocks from the school," she said. "I think it's God doing that thing he does for you. Don't you love it?"

We moved to Spokane and leased the perfect house in 1975 so that I could acquire a trade and have an indoor toilet. I'd been a free spirit (you noticed). Now I had Pollyanna who held my heart, and Delay who managed it. I'd enrolled in yet another college with a vengeance. I would become a registered nurse, dammit. I had a baby, a horse and a dog. They needed me.

The college provided day care for students' children. Pollyanna rode on back of my bicycle and played not more than 150 yards from the class rooms where I learned to be a nurse.

Delay stayed comfortable with trusted friends up north and I visited him whenever possible.

I made it through a whole year. I'd done that once before. Now it was spring of 1976. Then I held it together through summer school. Gasp!

I'm trying to leave something alone, leave it out, very not put it in my book. Drat, I think I have to. Hand me my crayons. I've got more darn coloring inside the lines to do.

Divorced from the Desperado, I fell in love with a Toddler. An alcoholic Toddler. Worse, I married him. I must've been off my rocker. Never more than a bratty little brother to Pollyanna, he could be considered invisible. In fact he thought he was and said so. What I tell you next is just so classic it's embarrassing; I believed he'd change. Oh alright, even more classic, I thought I could change him or he loved me enough to change. All that is sick, but true and common. He pestered me, wanted me bad enough to do as much as necessary to get my attention. This youngster stopped drinking for a year, stopped smoking and went to a fellowship of pretty groovy believers the Lord had pinpointed for me. He read the Bible. Not the Lord, the Toddler. The Lord had read it already.

Late afternoon of the day we married in the backyard, the Toddler toddled out, saying he'd be back in a minute. He came back carrying a twelve pack of Old Milwaukee beer, and a carton of cigarettes. He never picked up the Bible again. Well, once, when temporarily under duress.

I'd never known a person could put on a charade of such longevity, go to the lengths he'd gone to pretend he was someone he never intended on becoming. What to do? I held on to one hope, that he loved me. I squeezed the hope tight like a charm held in my hand.

Here's the rub. I vowed in Jesus' name to stick with the Toad, er, I mean Toddler, in sickness and health till death parted us. Those words meant something to me. The next ten years or so I spent wishing. Wishing I may, wishing I might, turn the clock back. You might compare my mindset to: "Praying for the end of time," as in that Meatloaf song I seem to be fond of quoting, Paradise By The Dashboard Lights.

Delay Gets a Taste of City Life

THE TODDLER, COMPLAINING he felt invisible, convinced me he was. It suited to regard my situation with the singular 'I' and when I thought in terms of 'we' that meant Pollyanna, Delay and the Wynken dog.

Before school started again in September 1976, we migrated out toward the city limits. I found the house in a neighborhood where we could fence off an oblong area between houses. Delay moved to town.

I located some quality pasture, a real treat, but getting there required a daring five-mile ride to the outskirts of Spokane. Daring because Delay needed to carry me across a bridge spanning I-90, the fast-moving, vehicle-infested interstate. You can bet he rolled his eyes at me that day, like he asked with exasperation, "Oh good grief, Suzee, what now?"

I reminded him that once we made it to the small farm, he'd be able to eat all he wanted. I'd come everyday to see him till he'd finished the pasture. Then I'd ride him home, back to the fenced place and back to eating hay.

He pranced gingerly down the exact middle of the bridge while a couple of cops made cars wait on either end. Below, the noise of traffic created a deafening roar. Swinging his head back and forth, Delay peered down, white-eyed. Cars sped beneath him on his left, and zoomed out from under the bridge to his right. But he let me know he forgave me. How? By giving me what I asked for the next time I wanted him to be brave, by going out of his comfort zone is how. His big-hearted unselfishness on my behalf. And he always forgave me. See, that's the thing.

CLOSE TO HEAVEN ON EARTH

WHEN NOT STUDYING for school, I researched the Spokane library to find where land in the Midwest grew the most oaks and maples. I missed lightning bugs. I found what I wanted in Wisconsin, the lush rolling hills and hollows of southwest Wisconsin in particular, within three hours of Mom and Moline. And the necessary Hannemans plus other friends (Duck Club friends). Two counties looked the most promising, Crawford and Richland. The Toddler liked the idea since the creeks carried lots of trout and the lakes were home to blue gills, bass and sunfish. I knew he'd catch me catfish, too. The boy could fish.

Determined to live on a farm, I dreamed of the one we'd buy. I even embroidered a detailed picture that took up the whole back of a light blue work shirt. You'll notice I spend plenty of time showing off the farm in chapters to come.

God had used Grandma Down's farm and family to train me up in the way I should go. He pulled those passionate memories out of a hat again and again to keep me on track, albeit barely, I'd have to agree.

I needed to raise Pollyanna on a farm. It would be the best start I knew how to give her. Other than introducing her to Jesus, shepherd and sheepdog in one. No wonder I was drawn to sheepdogs, just another visual aid tossed onto a spiritual overhead projector.

The years spent in Spokane in nursing school had, but for a few, been characterless. I stayed focused. It wasn't an option to notice, let alone hold court for characters. But when I'd finished with school they came rushing in at me like the tide. More like a flood. I knew my destiny contained insurmountable numbers of characters.

After graduating in June 1977, onward to one of the counties I'd targeted in Wisconsin. Come to find out there existed a very full cast of characters in Richland County. Now, anywhere I moved I expected an abundance of characters.

The first one I encounter head on is Frank the realtor who shows us the farm. He is in his seventies with white ear hair spiraling out into the light of day. He has a gold tooth upstairs in the front. It sparkles. God's truth.

Picture this. Me and Frank walking the forty acres looking at the woods, stream, pastures and house. I'm in front while Frank pads behind. Trailing me in silence. He knows the place is romancing me. I'm thinking love affair until the end of time. Sweet. No, sweeter than sweet. The sweetest farm I've ever seen, even better than Grandma Down's because of the tall mounded hills covered with hardwoods waiting to go bonkers with fall colors. Misty hollows. It's quiet as can be. I stand like I'd been built on that spot centuries ago, too in love with what I see to speak or move. Frank, quieter than this present quiet, has positioned himself behind me. Close. His head is one inch from resting on my shoulder. But I am not aware of this since he's mastered soundless tiptoeing. I have no idea how long I've stood when I hear Frank's whisper. It doesn't jar me, doesn't move the air around my left ear where his mouth hangs suspended. With well-honed patience he's waited, innately knowing the exact moment my receptiveness reaches its zenith. Right on the nose he murmurs sighing words.

"This is it, Suzanne (dramatic pause), yes, Suzanne, this is it."

No one calls me Suzanne besides my mother. Until now. Until Frank.

How does he know? He's reading my mind, I thought.

It wasn't until long later when I recounted the story of how I found the farm that I realized it sounded like I'd been duped. I may not yet have seen it except that the people I told were yukking it up at my expense. "You have got to be kidding, right?" Bob said, coughing up laugh-mucous.

I may just be the prototype for the first blonde joke.

ALL LIKE SHEEP

WE MOVED IN when the farm family, who'd lived there for most of their lives, moved to a smaller home. Pollyanna grew up on the farm from age five starting in 1977. She went to first through sixth in the small rural grade school until 1984. The school didn't have a kindergarten so I drove her to Richland Center, fourteen miles away, and dropped her off at the town school while I started my career as an RN in an eighty–bed hospital.

I'd explained to Delay about Wisconsin, where green grass grows thick and tall as a horse's belly. I'd told him about how it rained when it should, no irrigation needed for horse pastures. I doubted he believed me, being a Western horse and all. After we were settled into work, school and the house, Delay arrived in a big semi truck. I'd hired a company who transported horses to bring him. He'd turned seven that July on the 7th.

Life proved grand for Delay in those lush, Midwestern pastures. Pastures that must take the shape of legends in horse dreams.

My faith stayed on target in the heartland, even when the Toddler found girls other than me to sleep with. Or maybe because of it. I knew now where to find help and was learning that my faith had a tendency to grow like Jack's Beanstalk when I was pushed to the limit of emotional or physical stress.

Yeah, I took it personally for a minute. Well longer actually, but I asked him to move out, and in time I grasped he had an inferiority complex. The situation had to do with his insecurity, not about me not being enough. It felt all too familiar. Hadn't the Desperado behaved identically? What was up with me? Seemed like I couldn't make a good choice. Pissed me off.

I knew chances the Toddler could handle his pledge of loyalty to our marriage were smaller than that bug called a No-See-Um. And, by God, I believed that would be my last ticket to ride on the matrimony train. The end of the line.

I'd gone and picked another one, this Toddler who moved back in, bleating.

He asked for another chance. I thought about how I'd been accepted without any conditions. That scripture about everyone of us being like a pitiable sheep whose gone astray stuck in my mind (and my throat). Being a poor sheep myself, I figured I owed him.

One dumb sheep to another.

FARM LIFE

So Pollyanna, the flailing Toddler, and I took farm living seriously. We got chickens, pigs, barn cats, a cow and a hamster. Hamster? I guess the hamster and barn cats weren't livestock. I got carried away.

Autumn, my stars! The oaks and maples came through as I'd known they would. Sumac and Bittersweet, too. Fantasia colors. Famed fields upon fields of pumpkins, apple festivals with fritters so good they should be against the law. Or maybe create a twelve step program to overcome fritter-craving.

Cantering on Delay in that fall air, smelling the sweet leaf-must as piles were thrown high by his happy hooves. Farmers tied their corn into shocks that dotted the land. Sounds of geese flying above our heads.

It's hard to think of feeling any better than I did in those days.

I learned bowhunting and Delay helped me get up into tree stands by letting me stand on his back. He'd stand nice while I hauled my archery stuff up by rope. Holding still for hours, he waited as I waited. Twitchy squirrels and chipmunks became unaware of me and flitted over the bow lying in my lap. That's how still I sat. One time a squirrel stood on my arm, staring at my face for a few minutes from a foot away. Woodstove fires began to fill the silent hollow with haze.

Two images stay, as real as the day they were shown to me. I doubt I can do them justice.

The first. From my perch in my tree of choice one dusky twilight, I glanced in slow motion (all movement had to be gradual when hunting with a bow) across a hilltop pasture and down into a small vale full of, and saturated with, back light the color of burnished gold.

Time stopped. I looked through sensual waves of ether into another domain. To call this vision pastoral doesn't cut it. Cows stood in deep grass that was still green from springs wetting the hills. Autumn trees like sentinels encircled the field. Nothing moved. Peace rose and came to me slow but sure, like a lover. Muted to a softness, air-brushed in the country of spirit, what I gazed upon was not of this world. I'd seen staggering landscapes and skies to knock me back and make me choke, but this was immeasurably more. I beheld a back drop for heaven, watercolored by God, that was so fresh on the canvas the paints hadn't even dried. Not once had I been first on the scene. Never had a look into heaven like this before. Never have since.

When I could look away, when it became too much to handle, I turned slow to stare in front of me. Had any deer ghosted into my woods? That's how they appear and disappear, like ghosts. No deer, but a particular oak with leaves turned to the color of chocolate dominated the forest. The setting sun reached the rim of the hill behind. A single ray shone through the oak's twiggy branches and dark leaves.

This second image utterly sent me. Heaven kissed earth with such passion, it caused a reality shift. Where I'd only been able to see the dying foliage and twigs of the tree, I now saw only the spaces in between where the sun shone thru. The non-substance became substance: the light traded places with the leaves, so the tree was hung with stars. Can you see it? I'll never not see it and for this I thank that God guy.

Lovey Dovey facilitated it somehow, I know that because it represented the shift in my own life. I'd been remade, had come back to life from being dead. What had been unseen to my earth-bound eyes I could now see with my spiritual eyes.

Mom loved the farm. Did she love the Toddler? Not so much, but she, like my daughter and I, tried to. We tolerated him, that's the best we could do. Until I couldn't anymore. The day came when God gave me leave to ask him to leave.

Like in a storybook, I can look at the Thanksgiving page and see Mom with Pollyanna and me in the big kitchen, cooking like mad and laughing. We had such a good time.

SUGAR BUSH

NEVER WOULD I have dreamed I'd make maple syrup from scratch. Learning that folks called a stand of hard or sugar maples a sugar bush, we found just such a clump near the bottom of our hill in back of the house.

Spring signals line up early in southwest Wisconsin, and the parade begins in February. Red Wing blackbirds arrive to land in leafless trees. The racket they make sounds like an auditorium full of blipping, ping–ponging computers. Snowdrop flowers jut out of the snow. And sap is deployed.

One sunny day in February of 1978, the roots in our maple grove give marching orders. "Sap, move out. Hup, two three four." Sap troops up the trunk, but then, br–r–r–r, night comes. Temps plummet and so does the sap.

The main thing here is that it's moving. Wooden spigots carved from a Sumac or Ironwood shrub are pounded into the maple's bark, no more than two per tree. Big buckets are set under them. Tree juice fills the buckets which you pour into something like a galvanized wash tub until you've collected about forty gallons. Then comes the fun part.

Forty gallons. I seem to take note of things that used to slip by me. Like the number forty. The Bible has a bunch of that number, forty, going on. Forty days and forty nights. Those Israelites wandered around that long to be refined in their faith. Like me. God, all the time boiling the debris of me to the top and skimming it off until what remains is the pure stuff, the good stuff. Him.

The kingdom of heaven, where he dotes from his throne of desire. There sits God, a royal fanatic crazed by Love, obsessing over us. Downright shocking, isn't it?

Here it is, February with patchy snow on the ground. You build a great big bonfire, use rocks to balance the tub over it, and pour in sap. You're outdoors again after winter! Hotdogs on sticks over the fire. And marsh mellows for s'mores. Smiles stretch across red faces that tingle from cold air. There's a job to be done.

Sap boils down and you keep adding more. Forty gallons of sap should make a quart of maple syrup. And you feel real good the next winter when you see that sealed quart jar of clear liquified amber standing on a shelf in the pantry.

'Cause you remember.

DEVOUT BEES

WHEN YOU WALK in the woods the spring parade continues before your eyes. Wild fruit trees are all over the place. The blossoms attract so many bees, their heavy thrumming vibrates the air in a monk-like drone.

One spring the droning sent me straight to my knees. Kneeling on new light-green grass, it seemed proper to join in. I buzzed and hummed along with the brotherhood of devoted bees.

Some things you never forget. And these are the things that make life, with its promised times of suffering, worth living.

Nature kept bringing me alongside Christ. Or did Jesus keep bringing me alongside nature? In the company of devout bees for instance, I'd lay on my back, drunk on woodland scents. Drowsy enough to ease up on my thinking. Relax the hyper thoughts that run inside my brain most of the time like mice on a wheel.

That's when I consider grace. I can't get enough of that sugar-grace. Grace consummated that Love which The Dream had taunted me with. Grace is the answer I searched so long and hard for. It's all that keeps me from going crazy. Really.

This is what grace looks like to me.

Once, in the spirit (don't ask me how it works), Lovey Dovey showed me a close up of Jesus' face as he walks above Peter on his way to another trial, a set up to frame him. Peter, below, tries for the third time to convince some locals barbecuing or hanging around a campfire of sorts that Jesus is news to him. Peter'd never heard of him. Jesus who? Here comes the close-up shot. Jesus winks at Peter, letting him know it'd be cool, he'd been forgiven before he even opened his trap!

In the Bible book I'd seen the words, "Jesus wept." But Jesus winked hadn't been recorded. And even if he didn't, I felt sure he'd have thought about doing it.

See, Jesus wants me to know, on some level, he's a regular chap in that he gets everything going on inside humans.

And he's not upset! More than that, like his Dad, he loves me with fiery ardor. Longs wildly for me, is hot for me even (check out Song of Solomon). Which creates longing for him in me.

This is hugely important or I wouldn't be able to stand My's Elf.

Never Say Never

ALSO, SOME LESSONS come easy and some do not. Blind to self–righteousness in My's Elf, I held a hoity–toity spiritual notion or two. Professing humility and proud of being nonjudgmental, I considered myself above being tempted by certain things that 'other' Christians (a lesser brand?) were tempted by. No problem there. I wouldn't be caught dead falling prey to such error. This in itself should've made for trembling. To the point of teeth rattling. Because in a back–handed way I was saying I was better than. Looking on from their home in Whack, angels stood or flew sobbing because I was clearly asking for it.

I quit my hospital job after a year because patient care made me feel awkward. I lacked confidence for things like moving patients in bed while changing sheets. In my mind I imagined I was hurting them more than helping every time I gave a bed bath. Like I'd move the broken leg or arm at just the wrong angle by mistake. Or turn a patient in a way that tore all their stitches out and they'd need another operation. Stuff like that. I did not have the Florence Nightingale thing going on.

So I thought perhaps I might be better bantering with old folks who often are left alone. Being out of our sight they lose their place in line and are too easy to forget. Visitors come less and less.

Plus nursing home staff got to take them on hayrack rides. Much better and less dangerous than bed baths. And intensive care units.

One day at my new job the autumn of 1978, I heard talking in the activity room. I stopped outside the door. A girl spoke to the residents as she tuned her guitar. Then she sang. And that was it. There was something about her voice and, I promise you, you'd know what I mean if you heard her. I walked to the door, compelled, and looked in.

There she was. My own unbelievable-to-my-eyes angel from heaven. You might think I'm kidding. But on this point, I would not kid. Sideswiped by the fluke of all flukes, I flubbed and fell in love with the girl in an instant. I didn't mean to.

I didn't tell a soul, not even myself. The sun shone brighter, colors became so intense I had to sometimes avert my eyes. And I heard the birds in the sky singing. As though for the very first time.

The whole nine yards, cliche or not, a real mind bender.

She was much more honorable than the Toddler. Being tall and thin with short tousled hair gave her a boyish look. She took care of her mother and she took care of me in the fashion women are meant to be taken care of. She, unlike the poor Toddler, showed Pollyanna and I the greatest of respect, told the truth, opened doors, carried groceries into the house, checked to make sure we had everything we needed. And most importantly, that we felt safe. Shielded. Secure.

So why did my lovelorn heart make this flub? These affections sure didn't line up with hitting the mark. Having these feelings wouldn't work for me. But there was this big problem. I not only liked these feelings, I'd grown attached to them.

Yep. Uh-oh.

I cannot and will never judge anyone who deals with the feelings I faced. This was My Own Private Idaho. This had to do with me, Suzee, and my relationship with the God I thought knew.

The greek word for sin is also used for when an arrow misses the bulls-eye. Maybe the arrow hits the target or even lands in one of the circles, but it misses the center where the best peace and plenty pours out on you when you hit it.

I knew I could have good. I knew I could even have better, but I wanted best. And I knew God wanted me to have his best, too, because it shows. Then people notice and sometimes might want it for themselves. I think this may even be the reason I'm here on the planet.

God never spanked me, punished me, or threatened me because I felt the way I did.

I talked to her about my bigger-than-life-dilemma and she got it. I warned her I asked God to take these feelings I had for her away. He hadn't, but he would and when he did I wanted her to be prepared. As yet I didn't understand there just isn't a way to be prepared for loss. Or to prepare another. She didn't believe for a minute anything would change.

Meanwhile, I'd come to know a girl named Janeen, someone I don't believe I could've made it without. Able to talk to her unbridled, I held nothing back. Her understanding of grace allowed me to be myself without reservation. God knew I needed sweet-hearted Janeen. I felt better, stronger and more certain that the things that seemed out of control were part of a plan.

In Janeen's friendship and acceptance I found some relief.

But geeez, I'd reached the end of the rainbow, solved the questions that The Dream had posed, found God and the truth. And now I'm in love with a girl?

BINGO!

THAT YEAR I worked in the hospital, prior to my Pine Valley Nursing Home job; I was in charge of the coronary and intensive care unit. Me. Egads. Doctors called me Nurse Nonchalant. It was my ruse. Terrified of life and death responsibility, I covered it up with appearing too relaxed. So loose I could hardly stand up. Like a boneless cat. I floated from the nurse's station to rooms, easy-going, cool.

I had one unforgettable patient, Character Royalty. We became fast friends. Turned out he didn't have a heart problem. Upon being discharged he made a point of inviting me over to meet the pride and joy of his life, his sons.

He told me he owned a beach house on an island in The Bahamas and said I could vacation in it. This struck me as non-coincidence as it gets, because I still had $10,000 dollars Mom had turned over to me at Daddy's death. My fancy in regard to that money involved going to a place where I could see ocean water as blue and clear as glass like in a swimming pool. The kind of water I'd seen in magazines. I visited my ex-patient to meet his sons and let him show me pictures of the Bahamian water.

Bingo.

Getting to the little island in the sun made for complex, complicated travel plans. Being hard to get to turned me on even more. The fact that I'd become something far far less than an intrepid flier ate away at my brain. I replaced bad thoughts with happy blue water thoughts. I looked for my good fairy wand. Had to be around somewhere?

By February of 1979 I had some vacation days so I invited a friend from California to meet me in Miami.

I traveled by train from Wisconsin to rendezvous with Eileen.

She is known by many names such as Aunty Em, The Pineapple Princess, Olive, The Pimento-ed One...all beside the point because I'm stalling again.

But, truth be known, as this book keeps demanding (pushy thing), the reason for train travel stemmed from an extreme fear of flying. I hadn't stepped foot on a plane for ten years before I braved those planes to get to the island. Except by boat there wasn't another way. And no boats went there. If they had it would've taken weeks. In addition to costing a ton of money.

You may well question the veracity of my faith. Why didn't I just trust God? All sorts of reasons came to mind. All-wet reasons. Like, you know, human error. Or, God can't pay attention to everyone at the same time. Or Holy Moley, look what he did to his son? I banked on Eileen's faith to fix mine. We'd tackle my phobia in tandem.

Lack of faith used to embarrass me. No longer. I now use the 'Sheep Defense'. Baaa.

Our first plane ride ended up being on a strange transport aircraft with no windows. I handled it with prayer and a cocktail.

Flying further across the ocean in another plane, smaller but with four seats facing each other and big windows like in a van, we stared down at inky black water. What happened to the lovely light-aqua color?

The pilot shared that we were passing over The Tongue of The Ocean. It's where the sea floor drops off a ledge to become 6,000 feet deep. That, you realize, is more than a freaking mile. I thought, number one, planes shouldn't have transparent openings the size of picture windows that rattle, and number two, our stupid plane shouldn't be flying over such bottomless water. I added a Valium to my prayer/cocktail mix.

The third and final plane to take us to our island had room for three people. I sat in the cockpit and as we taxied for take off, the Bahamian pilot started handing me scrunched up Wonder Bread sacks to stuff in the holes on the control panel. I wanted off. I gulped another Valium. There wasn't anymore booze to wash it down. Our plane was having a terrible hard time getting off the ground.

A classy lady, about eighty-five and wearing heels, sat on suitcases in the tiny rear of the toy plane with my friend. They were shoulder to shoulder, leg to leg and torso to torso back there. The woman said, "Oh, it's always such an adventure getting to the island!" She was loving it.

"You've done this before?" I wondered if she had escaped from an assisted living home.

"Yes, yes, been coming to the island since my parents brought me as a teenager." She was loving it more than ever. "I live in Hyannis Port. Where are you girls from?"

"Wisconsin and California," I said. It occurred to me this person had gobs of money. Maybe a Kennedy. A Kennedy from a five-star assisted living facility.

The plane completed its struggle and lifted off. We flew the rest of the way fifty feet over the water. We landed on a cracked runway. Smashed up planes lined its too short self. "What happened to those planes?" I asked, then wished I hadn't.

"Them planes, boss lady?" The toothless pilot chuckled, "They been lookin' that same vay lots years now. Sometimes another one crash down, too. They wrecks up real good here. Then they comes haul it out the middle to one side or the other. So's more planes can land, you know?"

He cackled up a storm, inspiring me to ask hopefully, "Bet that happens during hurricanes?"

He grinned at me with a look that said he'd like nothing better than to pack me a snack box full of cinnamon rolls and sugar cookies. "Nope, happens all the time," he said.

The lavender-colored Custom's shack held one counter and some Bahamians leaning against walls and draped over luggage carts. Relaxed, mon. We passed through. The lady from assisted living in Hyannis Port knew every person by name and asked that they keep an eye on her husband when his little plane landed. I wondered if it would be the next one to crash. "See to it he gets to the water taxi, Sigburt," she trilled. "He's getting forgetful." Then she laughed like a schoolgirl. "It's wonderful to be back."

Eileen and I got in a land taxi, ancient and rusty. The Bahamian driver was so friendly, I started feeling something I hadn't felt in a long long time. What was it? I'd have to wait until the second day to find out.

He drove us to a shaky landing where we were helped into a water taxi. The boat was in the same shape as the land taxi. We putt–putted across a wide harbor and pulled up to a large square cement dock. A waiting decrepit van delivered us to my friend's house on our little island in the sun. I sensed numerous characters hiding behind bushes, waiting for me to settle in and come out to play.

By the way, those blood–curdling flights cured me of my phobia. Isn't that weird? I've been able to fly ever since. Or maybe my sheep–standing has risen, making me a less stupid and fearful sheep?

I doubt it. God deemed it time I learned to get back on a plane.

Aunty Em and I basked in characters, saw and ate things we'd never seen or eaten. Became one with conch. Certain things are undeniable proof that our creator is sexy. You can't not have had sex on the mind while inventing conch shells with an alluring rosy opening. Or make hibiscus flowers with long, long stamens that hang from the core looking pleased with themselves. Get a conch shell and a hibiscus flower too close and you've set the stage for a tropical tryst.

Please don't get upset with me, I'm just making merry.

On our second day, I identified what I hadn't felt in a long long time. The Dream. My 3 x 1/2 mile sized island had no television, no telephones and one scratchy radio station which I listened to at Mister Willie's shack.

Out of this world, my new friend Mister Willie (pronounced Villie 'cause Bahamians switch Vs and Ws around) reminded me of a Bahamian Anson, and I saw myself sitting at the old man's feet for years to come. I can still hear him saying one of his oft–used expressions, "Oh my goodie." Then he'd grin the pale gum–grin of the toothless while shaking his head from side to side.

We often sat propped in rickety chairs listening to scratchy radio stations. Only two chairs fit in Villie's kitchen. I'll never forget his favorite soap opera, She Gave it All Up For Love.

Back then, the islanders walked in innocence, so friendly, loving, and sincere...Haight–Ashbury revisited.

The beach, a stone's throw from our house, stretched the length of the island, blanketed with silky pink sand.

I started planning how to get Pollyanna there as fast as possible. Most of all Pollyanna needed to meet the people, feel the vibe, meet Mister Villie and listen to the radio with him. She had to know pink sand between her toes and wade in that color of water. She needed to see under the water, too, where neon polka-dotted fishies swam in between reefs decorated with purple sea fans waving like mermaid's hair. I knew that, like The Dream, this sheltered place would become pitifully corrupted. It was doomed, so I had to hurry, get my daughter there soon, the sooner the better.

And my mom. I couldn't help myself. Still trying after all these years to share what had been important about The Dream, I wanted to bring her to this place where it could be compared. I longed for her to catch a whiff of that impossible Love, that crazy Love I'd startled her with when I'd first tried to explain in 1965.

After Daddy died she traveled the world and replaced the busyness of teaching school with the busyness of traveling. My mother was brave. She chose to overcome the hand she'd been dealt by holding her head high and winning the battle over self pity. Mom lived a generous, decent life and in doing so left me with the model. The handbook. In the end, she understood The Dream, thereby recognizing the Lord who'd fulfilled it. Trumped it.

GUNKY HURT

EILEEN AND I spent ten days on the island and returned spiritually pumped. We'd been affected and changed. In a super exciting way.

Deposited back in Miami, The Olive went west and my train returned to the north country. The boyish angel girl picked me up at the station in LaCrosse. More than a temptation, she was my best friend. It weirded me out and felt awful like an animal or a bird would feel if you pushed their fur or feathers backwards. A tough time gained on us. I prayed.

I'd been back from the island a couple of months. One day, for the 2,007th time, I begged the Lord to take away my feelings for my friend who had to be born a girl. So far he hadn't. That day though, I felt so screwed up, missing the peace that had become life-giving to me, I maybe meant it more because something was different this time. I collapsed on the floor in front of my kitchen sink in tears. "Please, Lord, take this feeling from me, I give it up to you."

I'd pleaded the same words before, believe me, but I'd reached the end of my rope, or my own efforts, or the proverbial any-words-you-want-to-use. I lifted my head off the floor. God rested his hand on me. A slight pressure touched my arm. Then he helped me stand up and the secret feelings I'd carried were gone. Nothing left, not a glimmer.

God let me know right then, the day would roll around, maybe after years of rolling, when the girl and I would be reunited as sisters. Christian sisters. In the decades to come I'd need to bring those words back to mind and cling to them like the old rugged cross. Gunky heartache and devastation had their way with my friend and she nose–dived, crashing into all kinds of internal problems, mental and physical. I hurt her.

On my end there'd been deliverance. I'd heard the word, but now it'd happened to me.

What he helped me realize was that I'd withdrawn from the airspace of his peace. I walked away from him, not the other way around, to do my own thing, cradle feelings he suggested were not best for Suzee Carson. When I turned to fling myself into his arms, I found he hadn't moved a millimeter.

PINK SAND FOR POLLY

I DID BRING Pollyanna to the island and she began her relationship with it and its inhabitants. In April she'd turned seven. I sold a steer to get the money for our trip, a steer meant for our freezer. I felt an urgency to take her there before the innocence got messed up. To me, it was more important than the steaks that wouldn't make it to our freezer.

On our first visit, June 1979, I read The Chronicles of Narnia by C.S. Lewis out loud to Pollyanna during the hottest part of the day. Just me and my girl. A Bahamian friend taught us how to drink the liquid out of jelly coconuts on the beach. Pollyanna and I bonded deeper than ever.

Until I insisted she go to the island school, the one white child there. She might have finally forgiven me that in the last year or so. I repeat, might.

Twenty-five years later, after more than a dozen years of adventuring there, she met and married the husband she has today. My granddaughter spent her first three years of life on the island.

Heap big magic in The Bermuda Triangle. Pow!

GOD STORY. WOOO WOOOO!

REMEMBER WHEN I talked about becoming a freelance Christian? How God connected me to like-minded believers from around the world? It began at a summer camp in Mendocino, California. Invited to a free camp in the Redwoods where there'd be a teacher from Australia, all I had to do was get there. My spirit started pacing, how could I do this? It stirred my spirit this way since God knew I needed to hear what would be taught. Grace. God's gratifying, charming, fresh grace.

The cheapest way to get there cost more than I had. I don't recollect the exact numbers, but let's say the round-trip train ticket was $289.35. I had vacation days built up at work and Mom could babysit Pollyanna. It'd be summer, no school. Still 1979. The Toddler was off on a construction job. It's just that I couldn't figure out the money part.

I prayed. Others prayed. The time for camp drew closer. One day I went to the mailbox and found a letter from Aunt Dorothy. Along with it, she'd sent me a savings bond she'd bought the year I'd been born. What? No one ever told me. It had matured and the value happened to be $285.00. I danced.

Then I laughed and cried. Next I joked with Jesus. Lord, you're $4.35 short for my train ticket. Good show, though. Not too shabby. And I heaped thanks on him.

The following day I went to get the mail and waiting for me was an unexpected insurance refund check. For $4.34.

I am addicted to God stories. Because it is the highest high when I can see his hand at work on this side.

Call it what you will, but I call it a God story. That's my take.

The Wagon Train

Ten months later I bought Pollyanna a starter horse, akin to a bike with training wheels, a lazy gelding named Spring. He had not one ounce of spring in his step. Bomb-proof. When the time came, she'd go with Delay and me on the annual wagon train ride. I wanted us to keep bonding, building in learning experiences while I still had the chance. The event lasted a week and covered roughly seventy miles between Richland Center and Baraboo, Wisconsin.

In the summer of that year, 1980, we loaded up and met at the fairgrounds. Riding along on horseback with the wagon train, we were called 'outriders'.

During that trip Delay crossed his chosen line of strict independence. We'd ridden a long way, more miles than most days. After a few beers and supper, Pollyanna and I joined other tired outriders and picked our place to roost. People mumbled their goodnights. I heard clanking and clattering as they put away their gear. Crickets and settling horses made the other leftover night noises. Smells of fresh mowed alfalfa rose out of the fields.

We tethered our horses to a wagon and I tucked Pollyanna into her sleeping bag. Before crawling in my bag next to Delay, he lay down next to it. Near me. This would happen just one more time during the coming twenty-two years. That night by the wagon he seemed to realize what he'd disclosed lying down by me. It meant he'd let go of his valued independence. He stood up abruptly and gave a vigorous shake as if to rid himself of his moment of weakness.

After we hauled our horses home in a friend's trailer, we traded Spring, Pollyanna's horse, for Rosie the pony who had more spring in her step. And, befitting your standard pony personality, pretty much did things her way. Her favorite move was to put on the brakes at a dead run. Pollyanna learned Rosie's foxy ways, but still flew over her head many a time. The bloody noses came and went.

To enlarge upon Rosie, I'll use a story about Pollyanna's nemesis who lived across the road. A grade school boy that reminded me of the Godfather in training. He pushed Pollyanna around like she was his hired henchman. Like he was practicing how he'd bark orders at one of his hit-guys after signing up with the mob. Cocky as they come. He wanted to ride Rosie, dominate her, show off. Pollyanna gave him permission with glee. When the young Mafia wanna-nabe shot into the air over Rosie's head, my daughter tasted sweet revenge.

Delay and Rosie got on well, but he couldn't help her overcome the naughty-pony problem.

Race Time At The County Fair

THE NEXT APRIL, 1981, I began training Delay for the big race at the county fair in September. At first we worked out on country roads. After four months I moved him to a barn at the fairgrounds where we practiced first thing in mornings and again at dusk. He tore around that track. He grew sleek and toned from consistent exercise. My horse became the talk of the town, again.

In stunning shape by fair time, Delay made running a half mile look easy.

Race day! All entries rode with saddles except us. We couldn't feel each other through a saddle.

We leapt off the starting line, Delay into winning with his whole heart. Making the first turn, he crouched next to the rail, covering ground like a lean, sleek cheetah. We were out in front, but I sensed another horse almost lined up with Delay's hindquarters. I glanced back. The rider inched over, too close to my horse, trying to crowd Delay towards the rail to gain some ground. I knew that to keep us out of danger, I needed to ask Delay to slow up, even if it meant losing the lead. I pulled him back and away from the rail. The other rider slammed his heels into his horse's sides and streaked past us. Delay didn't need kicking or whipping.

Pulling him back lost us the race. I'd felt Delay begging me to trust him, to let him go...let him win. I couldn't risk it. We took second place. I jumped off and walked him up and down between the barns to cool him off. Pissed, he whipped his tail back and forth with gale-like force, making his rump bump from side to side like some wild and woolly rumba dancer.

He hated my decision. It had cramped his style. Bargaining, I mentioned the word 'paybacks', reminding him of the times I gave in to his will.

Walking on narrow ledge mountain trails for example. Okay, any trail. When I got off to lead him. Delay, a fast walker, took the middle of a nice trail while, next to him, I stumbled through ruts along the edge. If on a steep mountain trail, unable to keep up, I'd find myself sliding off the slope, slamming into his side. He listened, pushed his nose up making that weird face horses make when it looks like they smell a skunk. All teeth and lips pulled back.

If he'd wanted, having never been trained or taught manners, he could've bucked me off, bitten and kicked. He showed forgiveness by being gentle in his dealings with me.

After the race it took longer, but in a while he forgave me as usual.

MAGNETISM AND MAGIC

MOM CAME OFTEN and sometimes brought a best friend or two. Relatives followed suit, as did cronies from my childhood, along with characters I'd collected from the places I'd lived. By the autumn of 1982 the farm acted like a magnet, its welcoming atmosphere informal and plain as a Jane. We opened the door and the magnet did the rest. Innumerable guests and dogs crossed our threshold.

I decided the kitchen sent out invitations behind my back. Picture an over-sized room with oak cabinets lining the walls. Its flooring looked like cobblestone due to the 'rug' I picked out. Old timers from those hills and hollows called their linoleum floors 'rugs'. The cupboards and drawers were turn of the century vintage. Opening one of the bottom cupboards, out came a tin bin for holding flour. The grey, heavily-chromed cookstove helped my bread rise in its upper warming ovens. Homemade bread makes a kitchen smell just like it should.

Writing this, I can smell and hear bacon frying in the cast iron skillet on the stove top. Call me crazy, but the sizzling noise reminds me of a hillbilly singing for his breakfast.

A long wide table made of old gray wood planks filled the middle of the kitchen. More often than not, anywhere from six to sixteen people assumed their individual postures of relaxation around it.

The only way I could figure out how to 'serve the Lord' (too religious sounding for me) was simply to feed people. That is what you do when you serve dinner. Come and get it!

I liked paraphrasing scripture. Adapting words to fit the times, sneaking spiritual principles in to avoid the turn of the skeptical nose. Main goal? Avoid force feeding. Seeing is believing. It's the thing that enhanced my attraction in the love affair I shared with the Shepherd Prince of my soul, my Mr. Right.

Never once did he tire of picking out endless prickle burrs snared in that catch-all fleece of my human nature.

I'd made more forever-friends with families who lived around our farm. In the autumn I'd kept up bow-hunting. Thanks to a brother from the infamous Steele family, the one named Larry, I also hunted with a 30-30 rifle that had a peep sight, no scope. This was hunting Wisconsin-style. He showed me how to clean the animal I shot so the meat would taste its best. I filled the freezer with white tail deer well-fed on field corn and alfalfa.

Pollyanna took pride in me being a successful hunter. Instead of freaking out, she'd get the camera to take a picture of me and the slain deer. Made me feel better. I didn't enjoy shooting an animal but boy that wild game tasted great with a glass of red wine.

The Toddler left once and for all. Loneliness for a man's arms to hold me was undeniable, but I knew I'd be single for a long time, maybe always.

On an overcast evening ride up the hill that fall, I met a memorable neighbor friend of mine on his horse and we rode far across fields into woods. The leaden sky had turned dark faster than we'd expected and then serious thunder started. Taking shelter in a two-story red barn, we sat high up the stack of bales in chill air that had a charged feel to it for more reasons than one.

Rain pounded the roof so hard Delay pinned his ears and thunder shook the world outside. We watched steam rise off our horses. Did you wonder about my description of this friend as being memorable? Forever unforgettable is the innocent sweetness of our kisses. His eyes closed, laying long black lashes on his cheeks. The lightning showed me when I peeked.

The smell of horse sweat and ozone was the perfect compliment to clean smelling hay. When the storm let up, we took off. It'd been a safe reprieve from human yearning. Waving, I hollered goodbye and galloped home to the hollow that held my farm (and me) in its arms.

THE PINK PALACE

A YEAR AND a month brings us to another Christmas time on the farm in 1983. Christmases run together when I look back. Mom, cookie parties, prime rib roasts with Yorkshire pudding, lots of snow, Pollyanna hanging her stocking with care. One Christmas Mom and I, feeling we'd stepped right out of a Charles Dickens book, tackled plucking a fresh goose.

Time passed steady-like with memories as fine as fine china. Delicate but with vintage strength. More training in what matters most for my girl-child. Like I'd had.

Living, lined out, was easy to follow. Tradition.

I hired another notorious Steele brother, the one named Don, to paint the farmhouse pink. A friend showed me how to use a jigsaw and I cut out swirly shapes from plywood for decorating the gables, creating that gingerbread Victorian look. Fabulous to behold, it became known around the neighborhood as The Pink Palace.

Once, at Christmas, some resourceful young gentlemen went to the trouble of tying a red razzle-dazzle garland around the whole house. It went from the bottom up to the roof and crossed from one side to the other. They'd taken the pains to create and place a red bow to scale right in the middle between the picture window and the upstairs windows. I drove down Hill Road one snowy day after work and saw the farm looking like a very large Christmas present. Which in essence, it was.

Another dilly of a surprise happened one Christmas day when a farmer drove into the driveway pulling a horse trailer. He delivered an Amish driving horse with a harness and wooden shafts included. I already had the most idyllic black sleigh, a cutter, with velvet interior and little doors on each side that latched. The handles and runners were made of black wrought iron. The runners curved into a circle at the top in front.

The farmer said my husband, who lived far away by then, had asked these gifts be delivered to me. "Yip, wanted to make sure you had a horse to pull that sleigh of yours," said Delbert the farmer. The Toddler gave from his heart that time.

Pollyanna and I named our new horse Jingle. He was a professional! We delivered Christmas cookies all around the hills and hollows in the sleigh.

Now I ask you: Does it get any better than that?

Ambushed, Island Style

POLLYANNA, DELAY AND me. I'd never been content to the degree I'd reached living on the farm. I wanted to live right there the rest of my life.

The Toddler had moved to Florida. I hadn't seen him for about two years. No divorce, hadn't gotten around to it. I didn't think about him much.

The Wynken dog turned fourteen years old and had an episode, a stroke I think, and went to wait at The Rainbow Bridge, and there is no way in the world I can handle writing one more word about that.

During my island years, meaning I managed to get there for three weeks annually, certain friends caught the bug like the flu and were also forced to go through the tests of traveling to get there since they had to get there to get well. The island made an antibiotic from flowers, pink sand, raw conch, and ocean bio–luminescence. We had to take the cure, and it worked best to do it together.

A ritual got started, a Bible study that lasted a couple hours a day. We'd read a book and use the accompanying study guide. We read Classic Christianity by Bob George. HOT! Another year we read The Ragamuffin Gospel by Brennan Manning. These books are about grace. Grace is every-thing. Grace is The Dream as you know by now since I've harped on it. I just love bringing it up 'cause every time I get to get off on grace all over again. When I ride my horse and she neighs, the nei–i–i–igh now sounds a lot like gra-a-a-ace. Wouldn't leave home without it. That sugar grace.

During a visit in April 1984 to the pink sand place, God ambushed me. Mister Villie, after listening to his scratchy radio preacher, asked me, "You still married?"

"Yeah, sort of," I said.

One thing led to another and he said, "You ever forgive him for cheatin'?"

"Sure," I said. "It wasn't that hard 'cause after awhile my wounds grew calluses. He did it plenty."

My friend made the 'Hmmm' noise. "Hmmm what?" I asked.

"You forgivin' him seventy times seven?"

"No," I said, "I didn't need to. Why?"

"Your husband, he vant you back? I just vonderin'."

"Why do you wonder that?"

"Just thinkin' about Jesus."

"Like what about Jesus, exactly?"

"If your husband, he vant you back, you gone gotta do eet." He always said the word it in the way it rhymed with eat. And left the word in the air tipped up, yet not quite a question.

He has passed now, but I can hear his inflections plainly as I quote him. I'll see Mr. Villie again, and this fact continues to egg me on toward Whack.

Something thrummed like a grouse beating its wings in my chest. The sleep walker I'd become stood up and plodded, zombie–like, along a pot-holed track. Bumping into one of the few phones that were now on the island, I came to and called the Toddler collect. I knew the name of the town in Florida where he lived and information gave me his number. This procedure took almost an hour. Making a phone call from the island in those days took awhile. Waiting provided enough minutes to further snap me out of my revelation trance. Staring at the dial on the black pay phone as I shifted from one foot to the other, sweating away, I thought it through. Considering what Mister Villie had said, I knew God had used those words so I'd need to examine my actions of the past two years. I hadn't filed for a divorce. Why not? I used the excuse that I never thought about it. Why not? I dug far in with my ethereal fingernails. Did I, could I, was there anyway some deep–seated hope held on inside? Hope that I wasn't in touch with? What the heck? Had I dilly dallied because I still cared? Dilly dally. Hold back. Was the message of Delay's name still relevant? Was there more than one life lesson to be gleaned?

The operator's voice jolted me out of my reverie. When asked if he'd accept a collect call from me I heard the Toddler choke-cough and heard a loud thunk. It was his butt falling hard onto a chair.

Cut to the chase I advised myself. "Hi, do you want me back?"

"Is this a joke, Suzette?" He used to call me Suzette.

"No way," I listened as those words pushed through my vocal chords. I felt like a voyeur on a party line. Who said that? Oh no, it was me for sure.

"I never stopped loving you," said the Toddler.

"Wow, well then I'll rent out the farm and we'll move to your house. Do you have a house?" What was I doing? And why? How come it felt so right? God or the devil? I knew better. I knew it was God.

"I do have a house," the Toddler said, "with roommates, but I'll kick 'em out 'cause my parents gave me this house when they moved to live at the beach."

Sounds insane, but that's how it happened.

THE FLORIDA PLACE

WE DID IT. By that June we'd found a family to rent our farm indefinitely. Delay hung out with a trusty neighbor and Pollyanna stayed to spend her usual summer weeks with Grammy. I went to Florida to view the Toddler himself along with his living situation. I held such hope. If things worked out, Delay and I would be swimming in the ocean and beach-riding. A happily ever after ending might still be eked out?

Situated inland wasn't a fun place to be so we found a great house near the beach in Stuart, Florida to lease for a year. My benefactor friend who'd gifted me with my excursion into a different kind of life, i.e. the little island in the sun, had left Wisconsin and moved to Jensen Beach, a few minutes away. I loved this man with all my heart. He loved me back and doted on Pollyanna from the day he met her. He nicknamed her Rama of The West. Why? Don't ask me, I have no clue.

Pollyanna flew down in time to start seventh grade and I started working at four separate nursing registries. I also began a full time theatre life. The local community theatre attracted my kind of characters. Gee, actors qualify as sort of legal characters. Double whammys. I fell in love with them and chose to become involved one hundred and one percent. In a certain way, I look at June 1984 to June 1985 as one of the best years of my life.

In putting together a long-lost marriage, at first hope launched itself like a rocket. The Toddler felt better about himself, found steady work and came to my plays. He took Pollyanna fishing. I had some fun doing a variety of nurse jobs and loved being able to say no. It didn't bother the agencies and they called often. I compared it to being a substitute teacher.

I had my transcripts sent to Palm Beach College where I planned to get a degree in theatre. What was it with me and college?

Little by little, the Toddler and I realized we weren't going to make it work. Alcoholism is a foul disease. I wanted to stay if he'd think about A.A. He bared his soul, telling me that to dig deep enough to know why he drank meant he'd find demons that were too frightening for him to face. I promised I'd be right there. He said he couldn't, fear paralyzed him. One year from when we'd arrived, he helped pack a U-Haul. The Toddler and I bawled like babies. Pollyanna and I left.

I had done all I could. If I hadn't tried one more time Jesus knew I wouldn't have been cleared in my conscience. He used Mister Villie to guide me to freedom.

We drove to the beach, I pulled off my wedding band and heaved it as far as I could into the ocean. I cried my way through every state between Florida and Illinois.

Pollyanna begged me not to move us back to the farm. She'd discovered city life. I bargained with my girl who'd just become a teenager. I told her I'd continue to rent out the farm and search out a town not more than 30,000 population where I could find a job. Her side of our negotiation required one bargaining chip. Looking at me with narrowed eyes (also known as 'the stink eye') she stated, "The town has to have a mall."

HOME SAFE

WE WENT TO Grammy's, of course. I longed for that carpet. Pollyanna found comfort too, since spending weeks of summer every year at Grammy's felt normal.

I left her with Mom, went to Wisconsin and put my resumé in the hands of clinics and doctors offices in Lacrosse. The city of Madison didn't fit my population criteria, too big.

Afterwards, I hung out with friends near my still-rented-farm. Plenty of time to find stillness and think about what had come down.

One morning I found a clump of daisies on the hill above my farm. The next step, divorcing the Toddler, required a last thumbs up from God. A few deep breaths calmed and quieted me. I asked. Delicious peace, palpable, lay on the crown of my head, then spread to cover the rest of me.

Basted in peace, I'd been given my final clearance.

A farmer friend said he'd pay me to help put up hay. This sort of a time out I could use. Then, news of auditions for the musical, Godspell reached my ears. The show would be in Spring Green, Wisconsin, forty miles away. My brain went into overdrive. If ever a show existed that spoke to the center of my desire, it was Godspell. I'd seen it once, enough for it to grab the numero uno place on my wish list.

I auditioned. I got a part. I walked on air. My brain went into make-it-happen-no-matter-what-mode. I was off and running. Okay, I'll put my tent up on the farm where I can work bucking bales and at night go to rehearsals.

My dream will come true. I'll be notified for a job in Lacrosse before Pollyanna has to start school and we'll find a house, live there. It has a mall!

Little by little, doubt began a dialogue. You might be pushing things. Isn't getting settled the first priority? Doubt started sounding like God. I hate it when that happens. Bent on arguing when I thought my own doubts were messing me up, I was forced to consider the wisdom in regard to the priority thing.

I high-tailed it to the clump of daisies. God, talk to me, come on, you know what a big deal Godspell is to me. You know how bad I want to play in that show. How can you take it away from me after you gave it to me on a silver platter? I knew he understood.

I waited to hear him say, "Dear me, I forgot. It seldom happens, but I had to have been thinking about the kids who don't eat their dinners when all those children are starving in Africa or something. Sorry, ignore what I said about priorities. Honey, of course you must be in that show."

Here is what he did say as I sat calm and quiet. "This will be a heavy blow and you'll find it tough to believe 'cept you know better. I promise you'll get to do Godspell, but not now. Trust me."

Well, okay. I can't imagine how this'll work. You're watching me get older by the second and know the cast traditionally is made up of teenagers or people in their twenties. But, yeah, I believe you, I do.

The daisies barely moved as I stood up among them. My heart had moved, though, and changing my plan turned out to be easier than I'd expected.

Expanding my search, I traveled by Amtrak and Greyhound to Montana, handing off resumés and supplications. No no, I meant applications.

Jaunts across borders into Utah and Idaho allowed me to scout out designated-sized towns. And, of course, check to make certain of a mall. My daughter had clout.

I returned to Moline, sat in my mom's basement in the dark and prayed. We waited, and waited, and waited. School started in a couple of weeks. What was God doing? Sleeping on the job?

Patience may not be my strong suit.

Bozeman, Montana

In August, 1985, the West played tug-of-war with the Midwest and won. Next stop? Montana, where it turns out Delay, Pollyanna and I'd feel at home. Here's how it came to pass.

An eleventh hour call came from Bozeman. A doctor in an office where I'd applied needed an RN. The Hanneman family, Sonja, Rusty, Reagan and Erin, came over and we packed another U-Haul. We took all we needed as far as clothes and towels and bathroom stuff, plus, by hook or by crook I set my mind like cement to take Pollyanna's bedroom set. I wanted her to have some sort of continuity. I couldn't mash in any other beds or furniture since it would be a stretch for our car to pull a small U-Haul.

Teenage-hood tittered behind my back. How would I help her fit in, feel secure? In South Dakota the red engine light started coming on as it climbed those long uphill sections of I-90. I prayed. We needed to stop often until the light went off before we continued. With almost 300 miles to go, and the engine light on again for at least the fifteenth time, doubt tried to put me in a full-nelson, tried to sucker punch me. "Please God," I said. "Give us a sign we are meant to be moving to Bozeman, Montana." Had I been out of my mind to base moving on the criteria of a bargain with a thirteen year old?

We started on up the long hill and at the top, the engine light went off and a full rainbow lit the land!

I knew God was at the helm. Silent, no need for words, we smiled broad smiles and drove on to Bozeman trouble free.

313

One day Polly would enter into her own Love affair with God and I believe my praying out loud in times of doubt and need, even when she was rebellious, made it impossible in the long run for her to ignore the results. Answered prayers were like home runs scored in another dimension. It's how she learned about his invisible reality and power. Wanting so bad to deny authority and play it cool as a teenager, she couldn't. Let me tell you, it wasn't easy saying desperate prayers in the company of a little girl starting to grow opinions faster than tadpoles turn into frogs.

We checked in at The Rainbow Motel. (Really.) I bought a paper and let the doc I'd be working for know I'd come to town. He wished me luck finding a house to rent since Montana State University students had also just come to town to get settled before college started. I have to admit the college word stimulated some part of me. I sent it packing.

Go away, I don't do that anymore!

I bet my transcripts felt abandoned back in Florida. I'd been accepted, but Palm Beach College had seen the last of me.

The rental section listed available houses and I called on them. They'd been rented. Except for one and nobody answered when I called.

First stop, the mall, which passed Pollyanna's inspection. Whew! We ate dinner there in a restaurant named The Livery Stable, decorated with a cowboy/western motif.

In the morning I bought the next day's paper. No new listings, but when I tried the number from the day before, this time a woman answered. She said she'd gotten tons of calls, but asked me if I'd come over. She knew I was a nurse and had a daughter. I think she preferred the idea of us over college students.

The house couldn't have been more perfect. Wood floors, a back deck, tiny garden, lilac bushes, two bedrooms, darling. She asked if I'd be agreeable if she left her furniture there. Duh, yeah, I didn't have any. Then she apologized that one bedroom wasn't furnished, the single room in her house that wasn't. I stared at her. "You're not going to believe this. The only furniture I've brought is my daughter's bedroom set."

"Really," she said.

Me and Pollyanna rented the house that day. She even decided since we'd be okay with keeping her furniture and the 'rightness' she felt about the situation, to drop the price she'd put in the paper.

"One more thing," said this beautiful woman in her forties, "do you plan on leaving anytime during winter?"

"Nope, except we'll leave every spring on vacation for as long as we live in your house, why?"

"Pipes freeze in the coldest part of winter. Spring isn't an issue. Do you mind me asking where you go at springtime?"

"Oh, I've fallen in love with this little island in The Bahamas," I said.

She tilted her chin. "What's it called?

"You wouldn't have heard of it 'cause it's so small."

"Tell me, my father is an artist who lives on an island down there."

I said the name and she said, "You've got to be kidding. I practically grew up there. We have a house in the village by the vegetable stand. It's like a second home to me."

Then, as do all people who've been there, we spent the next hour prattling on about the islanders, telling stories and bonding.

What are the chances of renting a house furnished except for the one room I had furniture for, getting it for a lowered rent and meeting a person who'd been intimate with the same remote island that'd touched me to the point of being a potent motivation in my life?

See? Isn't my Lovey Dovey the best.

I Find A Job And Delay Finds A Home

THE DOCTOR I went to work for turned out to be a different one than who'd hired me. The one who hired me found it might take longer than expected for his partner to get moved to Bozeman from California. That's when I'd be needed. "I know you need to work and I will understand if you take another job," he'd said.

I looked in the paper the next day and an opening in a busy clinic had been posted. I trotted seven blocks to the medical building and applied. I met the doc. He hired me then and there.

By October, my boss and I'd become best friends. We were a team. We found bowling shirts at the Salvation Army and I sewed our names on them in sequins. We fantasized about dancing in to patients rooms as a doc and nurse vaudeville act to tend to their health needs.

The first extracurricular thing on my to-do list involved locating Bozeman's 'theatre people'. Every town has theatre people. Asking around, it didn't take long to find Todd and Jay. They were happy to meet at The Bacchus Pub, have a burger and talk about putting on plays in Bozeman. That was the beginning of my new nickname, 'Godspell Suzee'. I began my campaign over those burgers. God had promised me. I didn't mention that part.

During the third week at my new job I met two friend's-till-the-end at the office. The woman, Chris, came to see the Dr. I worked for, her skin white-ish/

gray set off by powder blue...lips. Thought I was going to say eyes, didn't ya. She had hepatitis and, man, she looked appalling. A strange person, Bobby's Girl, a real fine character, brought her to the doctor.

The next day I got to give Chris's husband, Danny, a big dose of gamma globulin the nice old fashioned way: in the rear. I connected well with these guys and they invited Delay to live in their pasture.

I'd been praying about getting my horse to Montana. He'd stayed in Wisconsin until I had a place to bring him.

Danny and Chris knew a couple who were coming west with an empty horse trailer. They picked up Delay and delivered him to his new home outside Bozeman. It disturbed me when they described loading him into the trailer as an experience of a lifetime. In fact, so traumatizing that they never let him out during the thirty hour drive to his new home. He had a bad attitude about horse trailers.

I'll elaborate. I've yet to bring up Delay's one considerable problem. He flat-out refused to be loaded into horse trailers. Oh, sooner or later he'd condescend to step into a trailer or the back of a pickup, but it took hours. At first, blowing and snorting, he'd pretend he had never seen a trailer before. He behaved like a wretched horse from an underdeveloped country that didn't have a trailer to its name. Next, he'd dance around the thing, leaping all kind of sideways, bouncing backwards, losing his balance. Or he'd plant four feet like they were as deep-rooted as an ancient oak tree. What an actor.

I dreaded these times and more than once it crossed my mind that perhaps my darling Delay didn't hate horse trailers one whit. Perhaps he enjoyed being a reluctant loader and even looked forward to it. I wouldn't put it past him.

I'll tell you a little story to illustrate the intensity of the stand Delay took. A well-known horse trainer needed the worst possible loading horse in southwestern Montana to use in a demonstration at a clinic for Problem Loaders. Friends volunteered Delay without even asking me. "Fine," I said when they fessed up, trying my best to not sound snotty or offended. Within fifteen minutes the trainer, Buck Brannaman had Delay loading like a Ringling Brother's circus horse. From then on Delay loaded like it was his new favorite pastime.

THE COUSINS

THE WEEKS FOLLOWING brought winter with them and the characters just kept on coming. For instance, The Cousins. Six boy cousins adopted me. I can't tell you how horrible they were. When I was growing up, a company manufactured a line of knick-knacks that came singularly in a small plastic box. They were called Little Horribles. Now I understood. The inventor had had cousins like these.

On the day I met them, stealing food from my plate became one of their very favorite things to do. This wouldn't go away. The friends they had were also impudent and eccentric. They teased me, watched over me, took me on adventures, tutored Pollyanna in math, showed me Montana and made me feel special.

I loved my job and my Cousins who protected and tortured me at the same time. Pollyanna enjoyed the mall. Bozeman, Montana had panned out.

After Christmas my boss asked, "When do you want to take a vacation? Let's take two weeks off."

"How about like March or April?" I said.

"Great!" he said. "Let's do end of March."

Pollyanna had spring break in March of 1986, so we invited our tested and tried friends from around the country, flying through triple rainbows to meet them on the island.

I Make A List For God and Hand It Over

By summ1er, I craved time alone in the mountains with my horse. Pollyanna went to Grammy's to visit as usual, presenting me with the ideal time for my retreat. Larry, a friend of Chris and Danny's, dropped me, Delay, and our gear off by a trailhead. I had reasons to hang out alone with my Lord. I had a list!

We rode for hours to reach the tippy-top of the mountain. I didn't have a tent, but I had a couple of tarps. Stars came out and we slept.

The next day I brought out my list. Below Godspell, I'd lined up my wishes for a husband. Lord, I don't want to be alone the rest of my life. I've made these funky choices when it comes to husbands. I want to try again and I'd like you to send me this model of a man:

2. An authentic believer

3. Adventurous

4. Outdoorsy

5. Into being strong and fit

6. Six feet tall

7. Blue eyes

8. Comes with a job

9. Three years older than me

10. Funny

11. Honest

12. Sexy

You'll note I listed sexy last on the list. Fooled by lust, mistaking it for love was my MO.

I left out being knowledgeable about The Dream since being a believer covered it. The Dream = Love = my friends, 'Team Trinity'. I laid the list out on my tarp so God could get a complete look at it. I crossed my legs and sat. I waited to hear his small still voice. I waited all day.

Late afternoon the next day I heard from him. Good grief, why'd he have to take so long? I figured it was part of that 'God's timing' program. "Hi Lord, thank you for paying attention to me. Here I am. Well, you already know that. Is the list too big?"

"No, Mine," (we sometimes call each other 'Mine') a small voice from within answered and then he asked me, "Is there anything else?" I told him "No." He said, "You got it, Babycakes."

We stayed another night and rode out in the morning. The guy who dropped us off had made a time to pick us up.

We got to the meeting place ahead of schedule. I took off his saddle, tied Delay to a post, and kicked back in the swale with my head against the saddle. It felt like I'd gone through the car wash of peace, top to bottom, full service. I leaned back laughing at how absurd so many people would view what I'd done.

I saw a red pickup truck coming up the canyon in my direction. It slowed way down, swerved toward where I relaxed in the ditch and a cowboy on the passenger side rolled down his window. He tossed a cold can of beer to me and I caught it. He never said a word, just tipped his hat and the truck continued up the canyon.

A DIVINE APPOINTMENT

I WENT FOR a little jaunt on a plane in October 1986, meeting Nan in Salt Lake City, flying on to San Diego to play with old playmates from kindergarten in Moline. A Cousin babysat Pollyanna.

We had a grand time at our reunion. When we went to the airport, our flight home had left. Maybe we were a tad late. Maybe we'd been up all night the last two nights? I don't know. We took the next flight to Salt Lake City, with a stop in Phoenix. I almost missed that one, but ran on board just in time. Nan sat by the window and I had to crawl over this guy on the aisle to my assigned middle seat. Nan started using her eyes to point my eyes to look at the guy. Nan obviously thought he qualified as a hottie.

The airtime to Phoenix took about forty-five minutes. During that time, the guy told me later, he'd known me to be his soul mate. I had an inkling of this due to the way he looked right through my eyes. It made me nervous. He knew something I didn't and it rattled me. Meanwhile every time I moved closer to Nan, there were her eyes and now her eyebrows were going up and down.

Gawd, Nan, stop that, I thought.

If, by chance, you're wondering what he looked like, look back at my list. It is a detailed description of the man. Which brings up an issue I have with God. My list should've included one more requirement...dark brown hair to go with the blue eyes. Now, God being God knew that, without me having to put it on the list. You know what? The model number he presented used to have dark brown hair to set off the blue eyes. The current state of the hair happened to be so silver white it stopped people on the street. He had shining hair that you could almost read by. What did God mean? What did he want me to take from this? Be specific? Would you like the hair to be dark brown now, and if so, make sure you qualify this, 'cause otherwise I, The Almighty, might get creative with the hair.

Go, God! You're kind of funny and clever and stunning in your dealings with mortals.

The guy'd been to San Diego the day I met him on the plane to sign papers on a sailboat which he intended to single hand around the world.

I would have a heck of a time allowing myself to fall for a clean-cut, honorable and decent man. Having grown up with every girl's dream of a daddy, I've never understood how this could be, how I found the wonderful men of the world repulsive, and the bad boys attractive. I do understand it's a common predicament with females, but it shouldn't have been that way for me. I thought men fell in love with women who had similarities to their moms and girls the same in regard to their dads.

My gentle man courted me for five months. He flew me to Arizona twice to meet his friends and family. After the second visit, he took me to the airport and told me "Look, I won't bother you anymore. I want to marry you and I'll be the happiest guy in the world if you say yes. I know you may never love me as much as I love you and this isn't a problem as far as I'm concerned. If you're interested, call me. If you aren't, I don't want you to stress out having to explain yourself. Just don't call. I think we've been given an incredible shot at a rare and fantastic relationship. I think it'll be a shame to not go for it. But the ball's in your court."

He kissed me, turned and walked away. Out of my life? His honesty distressed me. I wasn't prepared for the exquisite loneliness or this severe pang of ache. Running after him, I searched the crowded concourse, trying to pick out his yellow shirt. He was gone. Emptiness. I was fond of this man who at least drew affection, if not love, out of me.

Had my expression been captured, it would've been the first and last time I looked that way. My face bones and skin reacted like they were all caved in or something. I cried.

It was a shocker. I'd met a man as noble as, yet less resistant to my affection than, my horse, Delay. Back home in Bozeman I sat on the edge of my bed, knowing if I didn't call him within the next few minutes that I would watch the window slam down on the opportunity. I wasn't attracted to him in the usual way governed by lust. Something new worked inside me. I called my mom and her friends vacationing in the desert. In unison they yelled at the phone, "Say yes!"

I hung up and stared as the window of my opportunity to make a healthy choice closed to within inches. When there remained a second before it'd shut tight, I dialed Steve Branch's number as fast as my fingers would go and the second he said hello, I shouted, "YES!!"

Goin' To The Chapel...

I MARRIED HIM pronto. Before I changed my mind. Actually it was five months later when I became Mrs. Stephen Branch. Suzee Branch–like–on–a–tree, my new Indian name. You must say it as one word emphasizing the 'on'. I love it.

We were married in Phoenix, Arizona, having found a small chapel and a bubble machine to rent. We asked around for a marrying man and were led to a person named Elvis Priest. I'm not kidding. Now, Elvis Priest was a bona fide grace–filled preacher as solid in the faith as they come. God brought us to Elvis. After we sat for a thorough interview he pronounced our divinely–appointed status and said he'd be delighted to marry us.

To put it mildly, Pollyanna was not keen on the arrangement, but my mother resided in seventh heaven due to the fact I'd said yes to a fine fellow. My fine fellow and I laughed like hyenas picturing her face when we told her we'd be married by Elvis Priest. We imagined her slight case of disappointment and perhaps a furrowed forehead since the minister didn't have a conventional name. Then we found out the church provided a pianist named Mitch Miller. We laughed until we produced copious amounts of laugh–mucous, from which I got me a case of aspiration pneumonia. Thanks to antibiotics it disappeared by our wedding day.

At our wedding Rusty and Mindi sang, In My Life, written by John Lennon. We became husband and wife beneath the inscription, "That in all things, He might have the pre–eminence," (not John Lennon, God).

In a few months Steve Branch would be buying a horse. That was over twenty– six years ago.

AT THE CABIN IN PRESCOTT

STEVE BRANCH BOUGHT Him's Elf a horse named Mac. Besides being suicidal, Mac is the onliest horse I've ever seen topple over, legs out, after falling asleep. Horses tend to sleep standing up, they know how to do that. The first time Delay saw Mac crumple onto the ground, he stared down with contempt at this member of his own race. Then he looked at me. One ear back and one forward showed my horse had a question. "Why has the new person in our lives chosen a retarded equine for his partner? In doing so, he's landed me with a goofball for company." I didn't know what to say.

I called Mac suicidal. Maybe that is too strong. He just found ways to hurt himself most horses couldn't come up with if they tried real hard their whole life long.

We, including new puppy named Glitter, spent a year living up a mountain in a cozy log cabin outside Prescott, Arizona. My husband and Mac (when he was upright) rode miles and miles of trail through foreign terrain with me, Delay and Glitter from June 1986–June 1987. I didn't like that type of land at first, but there came a time when it liberally shared its hidden beauty. Like photographs, we stuck those explorations into our memory picture books.

By the way, the community theatre in Prescott did not have Godspell on the roster. Tick tock.

My husband's main reason for spending seven years of his life in Phoenix was to be near his father. Ever since his dad died, Steve jonesed for the Rockies. Born and bred in Colorado, he'd fallen in love with Montana mountains and wanted to move there. Almost as easy as he fell in love with me. A gallant man, he'd attempted to woo Pollyanna the fourteen year old, but she'd have none of it. She "hated his guts." Yeah, that pretty much sums it up. He was the intruder into our closer than normal mom/daughter relationship. Oh well, that would work itself out in time. Difficult, but it would.

Speaking of difficult, I went through some of that in regard to being married. What had I done? I'd made a healthy choice, but I didn't feel in love with my husband. I had asked everyone I trusted if I should marry the man. He even agreed to flying around the country to meet these trustees. As I've explained, I couldn't trust myself. They unanimously answered yes. I was confused between lust and love, remember, and since I didn't feel the lust part, I didn't think I loved him. I married him trusting that the love would come later. God had given him to me, after all.

One day I walked into the forest and found a big rock, big enough to sit on. I needed to 'get down' with my Lord. I complained and sniveled. This went on for at least two hours until I shut up, ready to listen. Sometimes God answers verbally in my head, so I'm sure I squeezed my eyes tight, thinking he'd notice how ready I was. It might influence a quick answer.

I heard him, but he was jivin' me! The voice he picked was that of Louis Armstrong. Before I tell you what he said, I need to remind you of my horse's problem concerning trailer loading. Okay?

So this is what God said in Louie's voice: "Dolly, I'm goin' to load you into the horse trailer of Love!"

This, as you can imagine, stunned me for a number of reasons. The important thing is that from then on, I let go of my worries. I waited to be loaded. Stubborn, like Delay I suppose, it took ten years, but indeedy-do, I fell in love with Steve. Just like when I responded to God's love, him loving me first, I also responded to this man's love. Another revelation in regard to Delay's name? The ten year delay for me to finally fall in love?

On our way to Montana we detoured east so I could show my husband the farm. The renters had moved out. We drove a Ford truck that pulled our two horses in a trailer. Every time we were positive that truck was done for, time to sell it for parts, it would roll out of the garage (tomb), ready to add more miles on the speedometer. We named it Lazarus. Tall mounds of our

belongings filled the topper–less rear. Also heaped back there was the brooding fourteen year old who'd rather brave the wind and weather than sit inside,
breathing the same air as the step–father.

My Farm In The Hollow

I took Stephen to my farm. He loved it. Delay remembered those pastures with ease. Mac didn't hurt himself. We even considered living there instead of Bozeman. Pollyanna had a life and security in Bozeman that I didn't care to tamper with. I suggested we keep the farm rented until she graduated from high school.

After spending the summer of 1988 there, we lucked out by renting to a man who'd treat it like his own. Then we hit the road again, loaded to the gills as before, and drove to Montana.

In the end, like the boat, it became too hard to manage investments from far away. We sold the sailboat and the farm.

There came an autumn we flew to Moline and Mom took us to Dubuque where we rented a U-Haul truck. Then we traveled to the hollow where my farm snuggled against the high hills. Driving away from it that grey hazy autumn day killed a small part of my heart, like a tiny heart attack might do.

Bozeman Town

WE LEASED A house at the end of a lane to start Montana life as a family. We spent a year there. The teenager stayed in her room and wore all black, including spiked collars like you'd see on a pit bull. Dyed her hair black, too. Gadzooks, who was the girl? Where'd Pollyanna gone anyway? Oh, this WAS her. Eeek.

During this phase, I found her sitting in her closet, door shut. I'd followed the noise of her crying her eyes out, and there she was in the dark, covered with her long black leather coat. Oh, and her sunglasses, plus the most special accoutrement that fitted snugly around her little neck, the black dog-collar with chrome spikes.

"What in the world is wrong, are you okay?"

"No, she choked," (was the collar too tight?).

"Tell me, then."

"It's not fair, it's just not fair," she sobbed.

"What's not fair, honey?" I had trouble with her frustration since I couldn't understand a thing about this anger.

"I CAN'T HATE YOU. I want more than anything else to hate you. And I can't and it's not FAIR."

I backed away, shutting the door as I told this stranger, "I love you."

Of course she never picked up her clothes which lay strewn around the house. We nagged her all the time. There was a particular lone shoe that lay forlorn in the middle of the living room for maybe two weeks. One day while she may have been at school (at least I hadn't gotten the call, "Where is your daughter?"), Stephen Branch put dirt in the shoe followed by a short leafy plant. The child walked around it for a few more days before the stepfather couldn't stand it anymore. He walked her over and pointed her head down at the shoe. Pollyanna did not laugh, but I saw her face. She was keeping score.

Delay and Mac had five acres. We inherited a horse named Scamp who joined them and became our packhorse.

We lived up the hill from Danny and Chris. One winter night, having been asked to supper, we trudged through nine inches of snow to their house.

Thinking back, that night we'd turned into those people they make bad jokes about. Yes, we met the requirements for being counted as two persons who were not the sharpest knives in the drawer. Why? Because the temperature happened to be fifty degrees below zero and with the wind chill, for that date, it became a record-breaking ninety-some degrees below zero. The ends of both our noses had frostbite. But dinner was great.

MEADOWLARK DRIVE

WE FOUND A house at the end of another road, on Meadowlark Drive, which we bought and moved into August 1 1990.

I reunited with my theatre friends, who by now greeted me saying, "Hi and nope, no Godspell yet."

Delay continued to take care of me, putting up with certain novel plans which included him.

Once I braided his long, flowing mane with hundreds of sweet pea flowers so I could show him off in a festival parade down Main Street. He overacted, more studly than ever. Old time ranchers claimed he was 'cut proud'. He had to do something to compensate for those flowers hanging all over him. He danced up a storm and pranced so high the spectators ooo'd and aaah'd. Delay tuned right into them. Plainly, he milked the crowd.

Over the next nine years we'd roam a thousand miles through Montana's high country. Delay retained his star status as we racked up countless Rocky Mountain adventures. Being a daredevil myself, I asked Delay to do some reckless things over the years because I knew he could handle them. He had no problem carrying me up hunks of icy snow fields. When going back down these treacherous small glaciers most riders dismounted, but not me. Delay knew his stuff and loved it whenever I gave him the chance to use his talents.

Horses don't forget because their lives depend on remembering. In wild herds the leader will skirt a certain cave where a cougar once hid and ambushed them. Because of this ability I've given my horse free rein when I got lost, knowing he'd remember the way back.

I trusted him much more in dicey situations than I trusted myself. Delay had a job...me. I knew he deserved far more than I could ever give back. I figured the best gift I could give him was to honor his act, his air of independence, pride and nonchalance. I pretended I didn't know he was pretending.

My horse the actor.

GODSPELL

SPEAKING OF ACTORS, more than five years after returning to Montana from Arizona rumor had it a theatre company would be holding auditions for Godspell. I knew these guys and they knew me, they couldn't get out of knowing me!

I'd done shows in Bozeman at various times, joking with my theatre friends about doing a geriatric version of Godspell. The thought of this muddled my spirit, but I would not give up. God had promised me.

The rumor proved to be true and the performance dates would coincide with Easter of 1995.

I auditioned and made it to the next step: callbacks. Even though I remembered God's promise I became a complete shambles. In agony, I waited.

When the morning came to check the posted cast list, I made my eyes travel as slow as possible. Name by name. There! Me! At my 'advanced age', I worried about my heart.

Before our first read through of the script, the company, director and choreographer sat in a circle. Each actor told who they were, why they auditioned, what they liked about the show, and some personal background.

In my altered state of joy, I remember it hard to find words to express much of anything. I said Godspell was a dream come true and decided to tell these people that years ago God had promised me the day would come when I'd be in Godspell.

Now I'd done it, admitted to hearing voices. Didn't mean to begin by giving my new theatre clan reason to think I might be schizophrenic, but I couldn't help myself. Everyone said something like "wow" or "are you serious" or stared at me.

I looked around at the faces in the circle. I couldn't help but notice the director make quick eye contact with his wife who had a part in the show. She looked pale. I wondered about it.

Well into rehearsals, the director's wife decided to share a story with me in private. Spending so much of our time together, the cast developed strong bonds.

"I don't want to hurt your feelings, but Suzee B. (there were two Suzys in the cast, Suzy V. and myself, Suzee B.) this is an amazing story."

"Tell me, tell me," I couldn't wait, what could hurt my feelings? I was in Godspell.

"On the night my husband went to post the list, well, he'd had a real battle trying to make a decision between casting you or someone else. The struggle ended by him choosing the other person."

"Really." I said.

"Keep listening. After putting the list out around midnight, he came home and we went to bed. He couldn't sleep. Neither could I with all the tossing and turning going on next to me. Somewhere near 3:00 in the morning, he sat straight up and told me he had to make a change in the cast right away."

"What? Why?" My eyes started swimming, like I was losing my balance.

"Because he knew you were supposed to be in the show." She looked me in the eyes. "You okay?"

I planted my feet. "Yeah, what comes next?"

"He got out of bed and posted a different list."

"Wow," I said, marveling.

"Think about the night we sat in the circle and everyone told about themselves. You blurted out God promised you a long time ago that he'd make your dream come true. You'd be in Godspell. My husband and I freaked. After everyone left we stared at each other perplexed and silent. He stood up, walked around in the room for a few minutes and looked at me some more before he said, "God promised her. No wonder I couldn't sleep. That's why I had to change the list. What if I'd ignored that unease? God promised her!"

"See what I mean about it being an amazing story?" she said.

Can't imagine what I must've looked like right then. "You have no idea. I am blown away. And my feelings aren't hurt, either."

Godspell sold out night after night and was held over. Even with me, Suzee B., by far the oldest cast member singing, dancing and cavorting around the stage. My dream came true as promised.

TILLY THE FILLY

MAC WENT TO a different home which prolonged his life since he became an arena type of horse. We missed him, but were happy for the guy, too. He no longer had to face the rigors of the rugged outdoors. Or sleep in it. Or tip over.

Steve rode Scamp while a new horse just for him grew inside a borrowed mare's belly. We kept the mare until the foal was born and weaned.

One June night in 1995 Steve went to our barn to make a routine check. The mare could give birth anytime so we checked every couple of hours. It's not like they can't do it alone, but we wanted to see. Plus, we planned to do the imprinting thing which meant Steve needed to start the second the foal came out into the world. It takes weeks of performing daily duties with the colt and the mom to build a lasting bond with baby.

An urgent whisper, coming through the open window woke me. In a loud raspy whisper Steve said, "Suzee! It's here! It's here!" I'll never forget how much his voice reminded me of a child on Christmas morning saying, "He came! Come see, Santa came!" The birth had happened in the dark barn, so Steve didn't know if he had a colt or a filly yet.

A few minutes later, Pollyanna came home. Late, but at least she now wore baseball caps and flannel shirts. My black–witch–daughter had bit the dust, and Polly had reappeared, thank you very much. She actually talked to the step–father nowadays. In fact, she walked into the barn and within moments named Steve's horse Chantilly Lace. In the famous words of the Big Bopper: "With a pretty face, and a pony tail hangin' down."

Delay sniffed all around the closed barn door, not pleased at being shut out of the action. My super hero ears could tell from the timbre of his sniff.

Tilly had arrived.

TINKERBELL

CHRIS, WHO'D DISPLAYED the beautiful powder blue lips in the doctors office, loaned me her black Quarter Horse mare. It takes a special friend to allow you to use her horse to be bred so you can get a foal of your own without having to buy a mare to do it.

I paid a stud fee to breed the black mare to the same foxy Arabian stallion who'd become Tilly's father.

Eleven months later my friend's mare birthed a dark bay filly, on May Day 1998. I'd prayed and prayed for a baby boy I'd geld to make another horse like Delay, the best horse in the world. Delay was fit and raring to go, but I knew one day he'd retire and I hoped he'd teach my baby horse, one half Arabian and one half Quarter Horse just like him, how to take care of me.

Just listen to this and see what you think. When my horse was a foal, a woman priest who lived in our neighborhood walked from her house over to our corral. "Would you like me to bless your horse?" she offered. How did she know?

After jumping up and down, clapping my hands like a five year old, I reached to hug this lady I hadn't met, refraining from lifting her off her feet. She responded well. She didn't titter or turn to snigger in secret. Her spiritual savvy kicked in, alerting her that here was a floundering person.

This horse and I had already lived (key!) through plenty of, uh, little altercations. The woman reached into her shoulder bag, pulling out a small bottle. Holy water. I wondered if on-duty priests and ministers carried it

345

like policemen pack guns? She dipped her finger in the holy water and made a cross over a white splotch made of two cowlicks in the center of my filly's forehead. One whorls to the right and the other whorls in the opposite direction. Come to find out that's supposed to indicate a certain disposition in a horse. Their horse–anality.

You've heard the term, a hand full?

Now would be a fitting time to introduce Tinkerbell. Starting at birth, I used the same imprinting method with her that Steve used with Tilly. I led her with a rope (called ponying), when I rode Delay. She learned to follow along, depending on him to let her know what was what. We walked through water, crossed ditches, met other horses over fence lines, those kinds of things. I realized this girl horse was a born social butterfly.

Tink and me would give almost anything to have known about natural horsemanship back then. About the relationship. How horses never, because they cannot, lie. How they are so misunderstood. For instance, standing tall and looking like they weigh a ton, people think it takes a heavy hand to get their attention. But watch a fly, a flippin' fly, land on a horse and see the horse's skin twitch to get rid of the fly.

To show you this kind of relationship and the ways it transfers to marriage, business, raising children, knowing God, etc. would, once again, entail writing another book.

I call her a number of nicknames. Tink, Tinker, Stinkerbell, and Tinker Toy. I sing to her to the tune of Mccartney's Michelle: "Tinker, my Bell, those are words that go together well, my Tinkerbell." Like that.

Bottom line? My horse has been anointed, and I take this to mean I should trust she'll be 'on the right lead'. I am trying. She feels the same about trusting me. That I will lead her in the right way. She is trying.

Steve rode Tilly by now. When she'd turned two, he broke her himself. Later we'd decide we liked calling it 'starting' a horse rather than 'breaking' it. As horse people, we didn't know what we were doing, but we did our best and took advice. It wasn't until we found Parelli Natural Horsemanship in 2004 that we began learning the truth about horses. Humbled, we've never stopped being astonished, addicted devotees of Parelli. Our horses are even more grateful to Pat and Linda Parelli than we are.

Seven months after Tinkerbell was born we went Christmas caroling for the last time with the horse people in our neighborhood. Tink stayed home. This Christmas Delay blew his cover. Instead of arguing, stretching his head giraffe–high to avoid the traditional set of sleigh bells I made him wear, with composure he acquiesced. A first. He bowed his tall head down to make it easier for me to put the sleigh bells over his ears and around his neck.

That's when I knew he'd secretly liked those bells all along.

WISCONSIN

OMG, NEARING THE last chapter. Sometimes I haven't known how to say what I wanted to say. Like all rides by horseback, like all blazed trails, I had to ride through the rough patches, the bogs, the slippery fearsome places. You see, I've written this for you and so I simply say thank you for reading.

A king-size desire cropped up again and again even after Steve Branch and I believed, each time, God had closed the doors on it forever. We'd enjoy the peace that comes from accepting God's plan and carry on with Montana life. Until the urge would become bigger than both of us, forcing our choices to backtrack in the direction of the king-sized desire. We invariably wondered if God had maybe changed his mind.

We wanted to move to those rolling hills in southwest Wisconsin. We wanted to buy another farm, grow sweet corn and tomatoes, raise chickens, the whole nine yards. The way to know if that lifestyle defined our true selves required we sell our house in Montana and go for it. But our house wouldn't sell.

We kept testing the waters.

Another spring bloomed. God switched the red lights to green ones. Our house sold. Stephen Branch and I moved back to the Midwest in June 1999.

I reminded Delay of the grass in Wisconsin and straightaway I felt awful. In my enthusiasm, I'd forgotten most of his teeth were now gone. Grass fell out of his mouth in wads when he grazed, but I could see he enjoyed chewing. Still tasty. We discovered a brand of senior horse feed, miraculous for older horses. Delay loved the stuff and although he'd turn twenty–nine in a month, showed no signs of slowing down.

We packed up. By now we were old pros at that.

It took two trips to move because we owned three horses. Tinker was still apprenticed to Delay.

Delay.

You should've seen him when we took a break from driving across South Dakota. On a long haul it's important to unload horses regularly. They need to stretch and be offered water. We found a rest stop high on top of a hill, looking out at a panorama which included the Missouri River far below. It shone silver. My horse shone red against the green grassy grounds surrounding the rest rooms. His presence still stopped people. Even at his age his coat and body looked magnificent. And, oh my, his spirit.

Kids and adults approached to watch him strut his stuff, wanting to touch him. But he acted like a wild stallion that day. Then the wind picked up and blew hard. Delay stood stock still, looking far into the distance, blowing powerful snorts from his wide open nostrils. He smelled the river, the sky, the vastness, everything, and felt like a young horse again, I could see it. Raising his head high in the air he screamed and whinnied, acknowledging the wild. Looking dangerous, he enjoyed every second of commanding his area. The children and others sensed to keep their distance. In all our years together I'd never seen him like this.

Exultant is the word.

Proud, so proud of my horse, I believed he would live for a very long time. My horse's desire surged, not just out of his blazing eyes, a thrill in them that made the white parts show, but in his carriage.

I am Delay. I am alive and I am still running through the world with Suzee on my bare back. And I am not finished yet!

Delay. You were something. How I miss you.

THAT'S THE THING

STEPHEN, ME, OUR two dogs, Glitter and Ruckus landed in Grammy's basement for starters and put the horses in the country outside of the–by–now–familiar Moline place. Then we made trips to Richland Center through August until we found and rented a house on eighty acres near that Wisconsin farm we'd sold. Time to start our life over.

Me and Delay again roared around on paths through groves of maples and oaks, leaping across high green hills under lilac skies unique to the Midwest at twilight time.

Our trail gets rutty now.

I've told you love stories, one of them about my horse. Now I'm stuck with the telling of how he died.

One day I drove forty miles to the feed store that sold Delay's special food for older horses, but the sign read "closed." His food almost gone, I opted for a similar mix sold at a different store, consoling myself with the fact it contained all the same basic ingredients. I could tell Delay didn't like it as well. Away on business, Stephen couldn't be reached. I felt uneasy. Before leaving, he'd been adamant about not feeding Delay another brand of senior feed. I told myself it wouldn't happen again and I'd make sure to get the right stuff next time.

The following day I fed Delay and told him I'd be gone for awhile to take a walk in the autumn woods. I didn't try to pet him, of course. We'd sealed that deal twenty–seven years before.

When I tramped out of the woods a couple of hours later Delay looked sick, but didn't act like it might be colic. He pooped when I started walking him, and horses with colic normally can't poop. He drooled cups of saliva and had to feel awful. I called the vet and kept talking to Delay as we walked nonstop. The vet arrived and gave him a shot for pain. He administered a treatment, hoping it might help, but he didn't have a diagnosis. What ailed my horse was a mystery.

Leaving me with another shot to use for pain if needed, the vet said by morning Delay would either be better or not. Delay had a chance. He had a chance. A chance.

In semi-shock, and unable to talk to my husband, I felt helpless. It started to drizzle as late afternoon turned to dusk. I watched Delay lie down and stand up over and over.

Finally enough time passed making it safe to give him the other shot. It relieved me to give him relief. I didn't notice when darkness came. He'd stopped trying to stand up. I moved closer so I could sit next to his head. Remembering our pact, I knew I took a risk, but Delay laid his head in my lap. Rain fell softly. I was thankful for warm night air. My tears fell onto his hair as I begged him to forgive me for not getting the right food. Afraid it'd been all my fault, I told him again and again and again how sorry I was. He picked up his big horse head and looked straight into my eyes, groaning a low groan. Delay turned away from me. Time for me to leave. He meant it. I'd been given the order because he was busy. He had work to do.

I stood up and told him I loved him, that I understood. I prayed his work would make him better. He would somehow fix himself. But he was busy dying. I turned and walked away. I did not look back.

I found him at first light in a nest of long grass where he'd painstakingly chosen to die. I could trace tracks, showing where he'd circled and searched until he'd found the right place. I screamed and wailed and cried for a long, long time. Afterward, with utmost care, I swaddled my mind with layers of impenetrable wrapping to protect myself until I'd be able to tell his story. Write it down.

When I told Pollyanna of my guilt, she said, "Oh Mom, maybe he didn't die from the food being a different kind, and even if that was the reason, Delay has already forgiven you." I recollected his big-hearted willingness and unselfishness and in that moment I knew my child spoke the pure, hallowed truth: the truth that would set me free.

Because, of course, he forgave me. He always forgave me.

That's the thing.

MORE OF ME BEING A PERFECTLY UN-PERFECT CHRISTIAN

AFTER THAT, STARTING in October of 1999, my life in Wisconsin fell into a tail spin, resulting in a dire nose dive.

I'd been a fool, inventing a whole three-act play in my mind.

Act 1. Mom would drive up often. We'd make pumpkin pies for Thanksgiving and cookies at Christmas. She'd help me decorate for Easter and Aunt Dorothy would come over from Minnesota in the summer. In general we'd be having ourselves a cheery time just like before.

Act 2. My buddies of long ago still living in the area would be dropping by also just like before. I'd cook large numbers of meals on my wood cook stove (brand name: Banquet Darling), for friends who frequented the big farm kitchen.

Act 3. Pollyanna: I'd be as excited for Santa to arrive as I would be to watch Pollyanna open presents Christmas morning. Then we'd go outside to make snow angels and play Duck Duck Goose.

The play in my mind was made of memories. It's hazardous counting on past memories to show up in identical form to shape the present.

The truth for Act 1. Now, Aunt Dorothy had died seven years ago. Where was my head? My mom had grown old, wouldn't be hopping in her car to drive 150 miles alone to visit us. So again, where was my head? When I visited her in Moline, I'd gone downstairs and found a small box she'd wrapped as a present. The scotch-tape she'd used had been placed in the wrong places and pretty paper hung off the box here and there. Going, going, soon to be gone. Yes, that destroyed me. Too close.

The truth for Act 2. My local friends, the ones who never planned to have children, changed their minds after age forty and were involved with kids. Full time.

The truth for Act 3. It hadn't occurred to me in full, the fact that Pollyanna was no longer present to perform her part. She was grown up and married, working as a florist in Montana. Florists don't get much time off at Christmas, definitely not enough to travel. I met with ghost images of Pollyanna around every corner. Her grade school. Where she'd played. Where we'd picked blackberries. The church where she went to Sunday School. Where she'd ridden her pony, Rosie, next to Delay and me on the county roads, through the fields and woods. This truth for Act 3 shattered me.

Add to this Polly, back in Montana, was having the roughest of times in her marriage while I lived a thousand miles away, unable to hold her tight to my chest.

A thing overtook me, something I thought God had vaccinated me for. Something that could never, ever happen to me.

Depression.

Ashamed, I found it hard to admit to myself or my husband that I now knew moving to Wisconsin had been a mistake. I'd wanted to relive the times on my farm. You can never go home again. I'd tuned out that wise and well-known adage. Who, me?

Loneliness, sadness, loss of my horse. The life I'd imagined? A mirage.

Topped off by an affliction called frozen shoulder, moving my arm even a teense unleashed a yowl as pain dropped me to my knees.

I developed chest heaviness that scared me straight to the E.R.

The doctor told me chest pain was a classic symptom of depression. I felt hopeless enough to try a slew of antidepressants, but couldn't tolerate the side effects.

Last but not least, menopause came out of the shadows to heckle me.

I even became despondent about The Dream. Depression stole my sensibilities. I knew full well what The Dream had been about, who it'd led me to.

But try telling that to my morose mind. It flipped me the bird.

HELP ME

I took my old leather bag from its special place, sat on the floor and emptied the treasures out on top of a short-legged coffee table. My three green sea-glass I Ching stones. A silver fairy charm. A soapstone pipe big enough to hold a pinch of pot. An acorn with its hat on. A bead ring. A bear claw. A eucalyptus nut. I dug my fingernail into the nut and held it to my nose. A powerful smell unlocked a door and I somersaulted backwards in time to find myself standing in San Francisco's Golden Gate Park. I wept like a child for the past.

Depression, like a car that'd run a red light, t-boned the vehicle of my life. Broken in two, and in critical condition, I needed an airlift rescue from the hinterlands. Lost outside of Whack somewhere. I wanted back in!

I don't know for sure how I got out of Whack. Or when my feet stepped across its border. Must have been tricked. I didn't see it coming, and once out of Whack, how soon I forgot the power at my finger tips. Besides mislaying my armor, I forgot most of my battle tactics.

I'm not saying depression wouldn't have taken me down, since this garden ain't what it used to be. I'd need time in God's intensive care unit to recover. Add to that...righteous rehab. Meaning Lovey Dovey, in charge of the rehabilitation unit, would prompt me to remember my lines, i.e right thinking.

Are you hip to a Wendy House? It's in the book, Peter Pan. One of the Lost Boys, Tootles to be exact, influenced by that jealous naughty fairy, Tinkerbell, shot Wendy with an arrow. Peter Pan had taught Wendy how to fly, but wounded, she fell out of the air and crashed on the ground. She was in a bad way, unconscious. Peter and the boys built a little house around her. A protected place for her to get well. A Wendy House.

I can relate to this safe kind of healing. Dr. L. Dovey, whose patience and bedside manner rock by the way, treated my depression after making the small secure place for me to be still. Dr. Dovey built Wendy House walls of peace around my mind and prescribed a hefty dose of trust along with a tincture of acceptance. The medicine tasted sour, bitter. I wanted to spit it on the floor. But Doc D. encouraged me to ride out the side effects.

Yes, the treatment would be prolonged, but in the end it would restore my courage and strength. I'd be able to not only face the days to come, but anticipate them as I once had, watching with expectation for God's hope and Love to show up all over the place.

Dr. Dovey told me I'd been felled by an arrow much more venomous than the one in the Peter Pan story. An arrow designed by someone much more evil than some mischievous fairy. No, I'd been picked off by my mortal enemy, a lethal pro determined to extinguish my light. Put it out for good. Serious business.

Then Dr. Dovey promised that enough passage of time would help achieve the mending. Time, like a border collie, would incessantly shoo me along, herding me into the flock.

The final ingredient in my medicinal concoction: TIME. Back inside my Shepherd's fold, we'd reconnect, and secure in his presence again, I'd continue to heal, be transformed.

The sadness slipped away. Twelve years later I was me again. Not the same me, but a better version of who I'd been, through no doing of my own. And I knew that the project (not home improvement, but Suzee improvement) would go on until my final breath.

Officer Dovey, playing traffic cop, blew his whistle and signaled me toward the grandeur of one implausible truth...in his sight I am as right on as Jesus, as righteous. There is nothing I can do to screw it up and lose his ridiculously undeserved affection. He Loves me so much he'd die for me...oh wait...he already did that. Blush blush.

Back in Whack, God helped me forgive myself for what I saw through my lying depression eyes as unforgivable sin. I'd accused me with might and main for my shame–filled mistake of moving to Wisconsin where I'd thought I'd recapture days long gone by. Recapture youth?

Instead, I'd fingered paper on a poorly wrapped box representing the reality of my mommy's preparation for her initial descent.

Instead, I'd killed my horse. Even if not on purpose, I still felt responsible.

Delay, a living visual aid of God's grace for this earthbound, unperfected, slow learner helped save me. Because...

No matter what, he always forgave me. That's the thing.

The thing that, in a delayed amount of time, allowed me to forgive myself.

EPILOGUE

MOM DIED IN 2005 cradled in Steve's big arms.

Steve and I made a pact in 2000 to stay put in Wisconsin until her life on earth was finished. If we'd gone back to Montana and Mom needed me I'd be too far away, too many plane trips for all those reasons of responsibilities at home, inconvenience and cost. At least from Wisconsin I could drive to her house in three hours.

She'd stood firm on one point her whole life. She did not believe in parents following their children. We'd invited her many times to come live near us or with us. "NO!" That'd been the ongoing response.

One day, during my weekly visit to Moline, she called from the kitchen where she was doing the dishes. "Suzee, can you come here a minute, please?" (Okay, writing about this was NOT in my plan and to make matters worse, a slow song off the soundtrack from Mama Mia is playing on my iTunes. The one about the mom seeing her little girl off to school, so excuse me while I turn THAT off as fast as possible...).

"You know, I've been thinking, if the offer to move to Montana and live with you is still good, I believe I'd like that." See, she knew her hands were shaking when she held her cards playing bridge with her friends and that just wasn't going to cut it. She wanted to get out while the gettin' was good.

I called my husband within minutes and he was on a plane the next day to find the perfect house with an apartment for my mom. He missed Montana and the mountains like crazy.

In five days he found a house twenty minutes outside Bozeman in the village called Manhattan, population 1,300. Mommy could drive to the post office, the Senior Center, and get her hair done, keeping her independence intact. Let's see, she was coming up on ninety years old and as I've told you, she was (the worst of 'F' words: failing) which was kicking my ass hard.

We moved back to Montana, Mom in tow.

In the final chapter, I know what I did. Cutting to the chase, I say, "The sadness slipped away. Twelve years later I was me again." Leave you hanging? Make you look up and think, huh?

It reminds me of a person picking up flat stones to skip across a lake. You throw one just right and it goes in quick step-like motion skimming across the surface. Blip, blip, blip...until the momentum ceases and it goes under. I turned those years into blips across the lake of my life.

I'll fill in some of that. In case you are curious. I have to think about you and your needs, not just my own. Personally, I just wanted outta there. Knew the conclusion and wanted it over, not feeling like facing anymore closure owies about Delay or anyone else.

Plus a book has to stop somewhere. Mick Silva, my Portland editor, told me I'd know I was finished when I was so sick of it, I couldn't stand looking at one more word one more time. Or when my book felt to me like a teenager you just want to kick out of the house.

Now, with a Montana driver's license, my mom accepted her fate, and made the most of it. She was the last of ten Iowa children (how she missed her brothers and sisters) and had left her Moline home of over fifty years.

There was some time left to share a few secrets, tie up loose ends and have a few good laughs. She took pains in choosing what to wear to wow them at the Senior Center. We watched movies and she had 'just a touch' more in her wine glass each evening.

Mom had an actual revelation that I will treasure until we are together again. It was only forty-two years in the making. She tried all those years to rearrange me, especially my wardrobe after I grew my own mind about clothing choices. I walked into her living room in her new Montana downstairs apartment and she became transfixed by my pin of the day. I love sparkly glittery gaudy pins. These, along with the rest of my apparel (and my hair) had upset her forever. But on this day I watched her eyes open wide and she spoke in way that surprised us both. "OH! You're wearing your pin. Now I see," (she was 'getting me' at long last in a way she could understand).

"What do you mean, Mom?"

With true wonder in her voice like she'd discovered plutonium she said, "That's your STYLE!"

Meanwhile, Pollyanna, living on our island married to Andy, came home every year so that was good. She spent time with her Grammy who still managed to make Polly's favorite cinnamon rolls, the ones Polly loved when she was a child. The kind in a Pillsbury can that you rap sharply against the edge of a counter and it pops open to reveal the dough carved neatly out into cinnamon roll shapes. The white icing sat in a round tin at one end. Opening those unnerved me, something about that pop always made me jump even though I knew it was coming.

Then Mom missed a step down, breaking her hip on a concrete floor at a Shakespeare In The Parks play. Not good. She spent much time in bed when not struggling with a walker. My stoic mother was not touchy–feely so I liked to corner her and give her lots of kisses. It's true that whenever Polly was home, together we trapped the woman since she couldn't escape fast enough by walker, but we knew she loved the love. She'd protest weakly, giggling all the while as we covered both sides of her face with kisses. And Mom wasn't a giggler by nature.

One day I knelt on all fours above her face as she lay on her back in bed. I knew I was pushing it, being so in her space, but she stared up at me and asked, "Suzee, is life a good or a bad thing?"

"Good," I replied without hesitation.

"Are you sure?"

Again without hesitation, "Yes."

Then she said, brown eyes drilling into mine, "Why?"

Now she had me. I didn't know exactly how to answer that one. I prayed and it came. "Because God made it." Success on my part. Until her next question.

"Who's Bob?"

Also turns out Mom had some Parkinson's going on that eventually ripped off her ability to speak her thoughts or remember to chew her food. At other times she was right there. We tried all the drugs, but she couldn't tolerate them.

I need to bring Joanne into this. We hired her to help me take care of my mom. She called her Grammy from day one. Joanne could do what I could not handle. The hardest parts were dressing Mom and watching her eyes scan the clothes and shoes in her closet that she'd never wear again. My mom loved clothes and looked like the Queen of England most of the time. Her bearing and fashion taste, her ladyship qualities and graciousness marked her as the real thing.

This stately woman should've been granted a sweet boy like golden-haired Oliver, but instead ended up with a female version of the Artful Dodger. All I could do was cry when we stood looking in the closet as she chose what to wear. I'd have to leave the room, compose myself (sure), and then help her into one of the only two dresses that fit her now and that didn't hurt her sore aged body putting them on.

But Joanne was born to love taking care of Grammy. To her, my mom was Elder Barbie. Joanne dressed her with some gifted touch that allowed Grammy to wear a few of her other clothes.

Let me showcase Joanne's heart for you. She'd come flying upstairs, yelling for walnuts as she took the steps two or three at a time. "Grammy wants a Waldorf Salad and I really want to make one for her. Hurry!", she'd pant.

Many nights I would come down at bedtime, groggy with emotional fatigue, to tell Mom I loved her and kiss her goodnight. There I'd find Joanne, having washed and set Grammy's hair after nine o'clock P.M. mind you. Grammy sat in her wheelchair with her eyes closed, a small smile on her face soaking up the attention and knowing she would look beautiful as usual when Joanne was finished. Joanne would be spraying away, styling it even though Mom was going to directly to bed where all that work would be smashed as soon as her head hit the pillow. I'd run away again in tears.

A certain evening I was so exasperated, socked in by depression while watching this slow decline of my mommy, that I gave her one of my anti-anxiety pills, the only one without bothersome side effects. Actually I gave her a half. Which turned out to be a very wise choice.

Steve and I drove her up a mountain side to a good view and as the drug kicked in, she became a 'homey', like remember home boys calling each other, "Hey Holmes," all limp and crossing their arms to point down with two fingers at the floor wearing mohair sweaters and being dramatically cool. This was now my mother, she'd morphed into Holmes. She kept laughing and laughing as she listed to port. And then starboard and back to port again. Pretty soon all three of us were laughing and it wasn't fair 'cause she was the only one wearing Depends. We could hardly get her out of the car when we got back to the house.

At the start I said my mom gave me a gift, the love of theatre. Now I am at the finish and in the end she left me with a last unexpected and profound gift. In her dying she taught me by example how to get it done the right way. When it's my turn I'll be able to die well also, just exactly the way she showed me. Without panic, or any unfinished business. She decided which bus she wanted to catch and did it.

Polly had been busy making a baby inside herself and they decided to come to Montana, she and Andy, for the birth. By now, Grammy was basically immobile and in a wheelchair. She waited for the baby to arrive, checked to make sure she was perfect, all fingers and toes accounted for. She held little baby Bowie, peered at her with interest for eleven days and then boarded that bus at age ninety-four.

Hospice came for an initial visit, checked her out and made arrangements to bring in a hospital bed the next day. They assured me, having experience with end of life signs, she had at least seventy-two or more hours of life remaining. I didn't particularly look forward to that since she was doing the awful labored breathing thing.

I'd been asked to work for two weeks as a nurse for a few hours a day. The morning of the day she chose to die, after reading the 23rd Psalm at her request and singing some songs I remembered from the Methodist Church she attended for over fifty years, I asked her if I should go to work. I told her I'd be back in four hours. "Yes," she answered and it was a strong "Yes." You can imagine, after all that college, she was thrilled it was paying off.

Well, Hospice brought the bed right after I took off. Steve picked her up to move her into it and she died in his arms on the way.

First off, Mom wanted nothing to do with leaving her own bed which we'd brought from her house in Moline to be put into that other bed.

Second, my mother didn't want me present. Clearly not, as she knew full well the pain that would come for me if I was there. She circumvented a final good-bye.

So, I honored her and did not even go downstairs for one last look. I hid when the people came with the body bag. She liked that.

I stayed depressed but got better in increments, especially since Dr. Dovey had me in tow and also because Delay had taught me how to forgive myself which spread into all areas of my life. I began getting serious with this book in 2008. That is when Polly, Andy and Bowie left the Bahamas and moved to Montana. Does this make me happy? If I were a dog, I'd be wagging my tail so hard I'd knock my back legs clean out from under my dog-self.

THE END

Useless Information

Homespun words are scattered throughout this book. For instance, 'swamped-ed'. I like making up words.

THE T.A.M.I. SHOW — T.A.M.I. stood for Teen Age Music International.

THE DIGGERS were one of the legendary groups in San Francisco's Haight-Ashbury, one of the world wide epicenters of the 60s counterculture which fundamentally changed American and world culture. Shrouded in a mystique of anonymity, the Diggers took their name from the original English Diggers (1649–50) who had a vision of society free from all forms of buying and selling. The San Francisco Diggers thrived in the SF Bay Area in the mid 1960s. They were the bohemian/underground art/ theatre scene, combining street theatre and art happenings in their social agenda of creating a Free City. Their most famous activities revolved around distributing Free Food every day in the Park, and distributing 'surplus' energy at a series of Free Stores where everything was free for the taking. The Diggers coined various slogans that worked their way into the counterculture and even into the larger society. "Do your own thing" and "Today is the first day of the rest of your life" being the most recognizable. The Diggers, at the nexus of the emerging underground, were the progenitors of many newly discovered ideas such as baking whole wheat bread baked in one and two-pound coffee cans at the Free Bakery; the first Free Medical Clinic; tie dyed clothing; and, communal celebrations of natural planetary event, such as the Solstices and Equinoxes.

SPADES were what we called our Afro American brothers and sisters.

SPARE CHANGE or spare-changing was basically panhandling. We'd sit on Haight Street with hands held out while saying "Spare change?" to passing tourists.

HIPPY HILL was near the entrance to Golden Gate Park off of Stanyon Street and a very popular place to hang out. We'd sit, smoke pot or not, smile a lot, dance, play or listen to others play music of all sorts and sometimes drink wine and visit.

BAD actually meant good or great.

AXE meant an acoustic or electric guitar. For example, Jimi Hendrix was famous for playing a really bad axe.

JUICER was a word for a good little drinker. Or I could say a person who drank notoriously hard.

PLASTIC PEOPLE were just that. Not real, or those who acted phony and valued the physical/material life over the soulful/spiritual side. Plastic people were more robotic than human.

BLUTO was Popeye's blackguard nemesis always vying for Olive Oil. I referred to Norman who lived up in Ward, Colorado as "the whole Norman" (not just his arm that hefted the gallon of Wild Turkey Whiskey) being as big as Bluto who was hugely oversized compared to Popeye. These are cartoon characters that were perhaps before your time.

CARTER'S LITTLE LIVER PILLS were formulated as a patent medicine by Samuel J. Carter of Erie, Pennsylvania in 1868. It was a very popular and heavily advertised medicine up until the 1960s, spawning a common saying (with variants) in the first half of the 20th Century: "He or she has more _____ than Carter has pills."

SUZEE CREAMCHEESE is a fictional character of an innovative band, The Mothers of Invention. On one of their album cuts they talk as if they are on an acid trip. "Suzee, Suzee Creamcheese (spelled Suzy). This is the voice of your conscience speaking." And Suzee Creamcheese responds with a hearty shout, "FORGET IT!" Some of my mail arrives addressed "Suzee C. Cheese" to this day.

SARAH, one of the big time players from my band of brothers and sisters, as I explained in the story, went MIA. I went on to say many 'children' of the day either died, overdosed or got lost. At the time of the writing Sarah hadn't been found although we tried for 40 years. I just want to tell you that in the most mystically ordained of crazy cosmic methods, she has been found at long last. And in the end it didn't have much to do with our efforts. Best of all, she is alive and well! With stories to tell.

DUCK CLUB MEMBERS — Huey, Daddy, Ruby Duck, Dreamcheese, The Duckling, Fryer, Brando McDuck, Strawberry Duck Forever, Sir Francis, Duc Watson, Dirty, Downer, Louie, Dewey, Daisy, Donald, Mother Ducker Duck, Little John, Admiral, Undecided, Delicate, The Silver Duck, Deluxe, Count Duckula, Sir Duck, Pro Duck, Red Headquarters Duck, Giant Duck, Anastasia Duck, Delver, The Invisible Duck, Rhett Duck, Mick Duck, Queen Guinevere Duck, Chuck Pisces Duck, Charlie Dog Duck, Drummer Duck and Fuzzy.

THE BUCKSNORTER'S HASH AND INCENSE CLUB MEMBERS — Porky Porksnort (keeper of the hash), Catrina Caterpillar (recruiter), Catfish McGill (spy), Semolina Ostrich (spender of the tear), Possibly Paul The Porpoise But Perhaps Peter The Porpoise (the mighty igniter), Crazy Christopher (the official christian crawler), Hugo The Happy Hash Hacker (happily hacks the hash for Porky), Poncho The Neater Zebra (P.R. man), The Moose Minister of the Temple of Mescalito (baptizer), Tujunga Bad–Ass (bouncer), Seaman the Sailor (the big flipper), Cheerful Charlie (crowd pleaser), Goodness!! Gwenn (galactic granola giver...Goodness Gwenn has got it to give), Mississippi Foghorn (the golden silver honk).

Author's Acknowledgments

I FIRST EXPERIENCED the power of unconditional love and forgiveness from my parents. Later my child Pollyanna, my husband Steve, certain dogs and a horse would continue to teach me. They all get an A plus. The people in the groups named below know who you are.

My very large family of relatives who've faithfully accepted me just the way I am. Abby and Jam who stand out because they are cousins who write and have shared writing and those obscure thoughts about writing!

Campers from the Peter Wade camps around the globe plus all my brothers and sisters who hail from the Kingdom of Whack.

The Blues Sisters, one and all. And a rare Blues Brother or two, including Harrison my Godson who brings tears to my eyes (laughter!) and calls me Goddess Mother.

Annita, Gwenn, Eileen, Teresa (who has been such a nag about me writing, geeesh. Happy now, T.?), Jan and Bill, Regi and John, Joan Chinal, Dennis, Sonja, David and Kathy J. for keeping up with this project and offering never-ending encouragement.

My writers group, especially Susan, Wynne, Jenny, Lisa and Lynn. Lynn – had we not met for that cup of coffee this book would never have happened.

My Moline collection who have been by my side since kindergarten, junior high, high school (especially the Class of 1965) and others from there who came along throughout the years, turning this into our shared journey.

371

There are teachers and then there are the teachers you will never ever forget. Mrs. VanArsedale (grade school), Mr. Ringquist (jr. high), Mr. Sinclair along with Mr. Coder (high school) and later, Stephanie in theatre at MSU, Dorothy Darby Smith from Gonzaga U. and Spokane Civic Theatre and Stan DeHart from U. Florida for impacting me like a magician in regard to the art of theatre. Also 'Mother' Jean Birkett from U. of Wisconsin who skillfully infected me with the drama bug.

Andy (the P.S.I.L.) for reading and editing for free as long as I put the 'Perfect Son In Law' thingie in here.

David Pickering for reading since draft number one AND editing AND formatting this book for both ebook and paperback versions. I am amazed he has any hair left on his head.

Mindi for editing plus lightening my heart with joy and for spurring me on, giving me words now and then to help the story.

Mick Silva for believing my story is needful and compelling and for his substantive and line edits.

One more thanks to Annita (Ruby Duck) who worked the final and grueling out loud read-through. Exhausting! I raise my glass to her.

Cover design by Flathead Media.

ABOUT THE AUTHOR

SUZEE CARSON BRANCH lives west of Bozeman, Montana in the small Western town of Manhattan. She spends her time writing, walking her dogs in the mountains, playing with her horse, riding the high country, reading books out loud to her husband for fun, watching movies and auditioning for community theatre. Suzee has published articles for Equus Magazine and an international walking magazine. She's self-published Two of Us Upon The Cotswold Way about walking 120 miles on ancient footpaths through the heart of England. She's also written and performed a musical farce in Montana and Florida and staged a play in The Bahamas. You can email her at suzee.branch@gmail.com or find her online at www.suzeebranch.com.

Made in the USA
San Bernardino, CA
23 October 2013